DATE DUE

DISCARD

The Eye of the Storm

ALSO BY ROBERT SLATER

Jack Welch and the GE Way
Soros: The Life, Times and Trading Secrets of the
  World's Greatest Investor

The Eye
of the
Storm

How John Chambers Steered Cisco
Through the Technology Collapse

**ROBERT
SLATER**

HarperBusiness
An Division of HarperCollins*Publishers*

HarperCollins books may be purchased for educational, business, or sales promotional use. For information please write to: Special Markets Department, HarperCollins Publishers Inc., 10 East 53rd Street, New York, New York 10022.

Designed by Debbie Glasserman

Library of Congress Cataloging-in-Publication Data

Slater, Robert, 1943–
    The eye of the storm : how John Chambers steered Cisco through the technology collapse / Robert Slater.
        p.   cm.
    Includes bibliographical references and index.
    ISBN 0-06-018887-1 (alk. paper)
    1. Cisco Systems, Inc.—Management.   2. Chambers, John, 1949–
3. Corporate turnarounds—United States—Case studies.   4. Computer industry—United States—Management—Case studies.   5. Data transmission equipment industry—United States—Management—Case studies.   6. Computer industry—United States—History.   7. Data transmission equipment industry—United States—History.   8. Internet industry—United States—History.   I. Title.
    HD9696.2.U64 C5767   2003
    338.7'6213981'092—dc21

                                                        2002027565

03   04   05   06   07   **QW/F** 10   9   8   7   6   5   4   3   2   1

Contents

Preface

Over the course of a year, people usually do not change much. The same could be said for American corporations. However, during my yearlong research into John Chambers and his company, both Chambers and Cisco Systems went through sudden, shocking change, and accordingly, I had to make major adjustments in the manuscript to reflect the change.

I began researching this book in the spring of 2000, when Chambers and Cisco were at their height and seemingly bound for endless success. By the time I finished my writing, the man and the company were in the throes of an unprecedented setback. The business community had trouble understanding how the seemingly unshakable Cisco could have been stopped in its tracks. Forced to take a whole new look at Chambers and Cisco, I knew that my task had become infinitely more challenging.

During that spring of 2000, as I set out to describe the company and its CEO, my task was clear and relatively straightforward. I planned to explain why Chambers and Cisco had grown to such dizzying levels faster than any other major American corporation. I intended to argue that the company's culture and strategies were the basic cause of the Cisco success story. Only 16 years old, a mere pup compared to more venerable American businesses, Cisco was, for one day that spring, the number one market-cap company in the United States. I sensed there was a great tale to tell.

In the right market at the right time, with the right kind of leadership, Cisco seemed to be unstoppable. Tornado-like revenue growth, the doubling of its payroll every 18 months, and the likelihood that things could only get better gave Cisco Systems an aura of invincibility. The high-tech industry was the main driver of the American economy, and the high-flying Cisco Systems was the poster child of that high-tech world. Ergo, Cisco was one of America's most important corporations. I had no reason to doubt that Cisco would stay at the top of its game. It never occurred to me to ask: Was the company taking into account the prospect that its growth engine might suddenly grind to a halt? Had it taken steps to protect itself against an unforeseen and sharp downturn in the economy? Was it growing too fast? Was John Chambers capable of navigating Cisco not only in the good times, but in the bad? Those questions only became apparent to me much later in my research.

Here and there some Cisco experts speculated whether John Chambers and Cisco could weather a sudden economic storm, but in the face of such spectacular company growth, I did not take their cautionary comments seriously. After all, as I put the finishing touches on the manuscript in the spring of 2001, Cisco remained one of the most successful business enterprises on the American scene. To be sure, it had by then begun to feel the effects of the same sudden economic downturn that had affected many other American businesses. And John Chambers undoubtedly faced the toughest challenge of his career. But I, like many other Cisco watchers at the time, was convinced that just as Chambers had weathered and overcome a number of other storms at Cisco, some of them unpublicized until the publication of this book, he would in due time resume the company's march forward. I put the book to bed believing that Cisco's bout with the suddenly turbulent American economy early in 2001 was a mere blip on the radar screen, nothing serious.

As it turned out, I was mistaken. As I spell out in much detail in Chapter 3, the Cisco growth machine lost its once-vaunted momentum during that grim winter of 2000–2001, and as its vision was going awry, I knew that I had to reexamine many of the assumptions I had made about John Chambers and Cisco. No longer could I simply delineate the nature of Cisco's success. Now I had to take a hard look at what had caused the company to rise so spectacularly—and what had led the company to plummet so precipitously.

Just as I had believed that there was a great story to tell in explaining the causes of Cisco's rise, I felt that the story was, if anything, more fascinating by virtue of the shocking new swing in Cisco's fortunes. To my great surprise, John Chambers expressed the same view to me in our interview on May 30, 2002, that is, that my book had a better story to tell as a result of Cisco's setback and the early stages of its recovery, which were occurring at the time of the interview.

Bear in mind, as noted earlier, that no major American company had risen as fast as Cisco; nor had any company, having reached such heights, plunged so sharply. For one brief moment in the spring of 2000, its market capitalization was the largest in the world, at $531 billion, its value twice that of the entire public market of Spain. A year later, its market cap hovered around $135 billion. The ride to the top was without parallel, but so was the fall.

In what turned out to be the first version of the book, I had analyzed in some detail the company's culture and the strategies that had worked so well for John Chambers on the way up. In this revised effort I have gone beyond that, showing which strategies contained serious flaws and thus contributed to Cisco's troubles. In short, whereas the first draft of this book spoke only about John Chambers's vision, this revised effort describes in addition a vision that went awry during that gruesome period in the winter of 2000–2001.

What gives this book a unique perspective is the unparalleled access that I enjoyed—both before, during, and after Cisco's startling setback—to John Chambers and to his senior colleagues. That access gave me the opportunity to examine Cisco—before and after—with the cooperation of the very people who were experiencing the triumphs and trials. I benefited from this incomparable access at a time when Cisco was shunning all other authors who sought its cooperation on books and when John Chambers spoke very infrequently to the media about the internal workings of Cisco. I had frequent and continuing access not only to Chambers but to his senior executives as well. Between the start and finish of my research, Cisco went through major transformations internally, and I was able to get first-hand impressions from the front, as it were, on an exclusive basis.

What made my research so compelling to me was knowing how many others were watching Cisco and wondering what was happening within the inner sanctum that I had been able to penetrate. From the moment in March 2000 when Cisco Systems became the number one market-cap company, all eyes shone brightly on it. The media stepped up their coverage of Cisco, and people like myself began seriously to consider writing books that would probe its magic formula. Quite a number of authors sought Cisco Systems' cooperation for such book projects, but the 50-year-old John Chambers, president and CEO for only five and a half years, believed firmly that it was too early for Cisco to cooperate in such a project.

By the time I approached Cisco in the spring of 2000, contract in hand to do this book, Chambers and his public relations team were in full lockdown mode, reciting to me all the reasons why they didn't want to take part in it. I began a series of interviews with some ex–Cisco hands, and some of these people voluntarily pressed John Chambers to cooperate. Soon thereafter, he changed his mind.

He phoned me in mid-August 2000 to pass on his decision. He had one condition: that I write about Cisco Systems, and not about him personally. I assured him that I planned to devote a good deal of attention to the company, especially the period before his leadership, but I also noted that he was hardly a minor player in the story, and I wanted very much to keep him a focus of the book. Under any circumstances, I found it difficult to distinguish between the activities of the company and the man at the helm. We found sufficient common ground for me to begin a series of in-depth interviews with Chambers and many of his senior colleagues.

I interviewed John Chambers eight times between early September 2000 and May 2002. I also interviewed many of Cisco's senior executives, sometimes more than once. Chambers made sure that I attended a number of his appearances before company employees, which were normally quite private affairs. Between our interviews and those appearances, I was able to learn a great deal about the way his mind works and about the way he orchestrates Cisco's culture and its strategies.

For Chambers, cooperating with an author was a new experience, and, as he does in so many different aspects of his life, he went at it with great enthusiasm and optimism. He told me repeatedly that he hoped this would be the greatest business book ever written. He also hoped that it would prove of sufficient depth to keep others from writing books on Cisco Systems. In response to such comments, I said that I hoped, more modestly, to write a fair and accurate account of the company.

As I went about my interviews, talking to people at Cisco, former Cisco executives, and Cisco competitors, I found an unusual degree of candor, considering how tight-lipped business executives often are. I asked myself why these people were speaking so openly about their colleagues and about the company. Perhaps it was because Cisco retains the feel of a small business enterprise, or perhaps it was due to the relative youth of the company.

Whatever the reason, the surprising candor gave me the opportunity to take an approach to the company, its culture, and its strategies that has more of a personal side than normally seen in books of this nature. Cisco veterans were especially frank about the company's early days and the problems it experienced as personalities clashed, personal feelings and ambitions seemed to rule the day, and mini–palace coups popped up here and there. Accordingly, I devote some space to this early history of the company, because it casts an interesting light on the roots of such modern-day issues as relationships with customers, frugality, management style, and, most important, the hypergrowth the company eventually experienced.

Nearly everyone I approached agreed to be interviewed for the book. But despite many efforts, I could not secure interviews with Len Bosack or Sandy Lerner, the two cofounders of Cisco. They have briefly told their story elsewhere, and I have relied on those accounts.

Because this book is the first with which Cisco Systems has cooperated, I frequently heard the question *What kind of book will you write?* It came especially from those within Cisco. Those within Cisco hoped the book would celebrate Cisco; those without were more objective. When Cisco's troubles arose in 2001, its spokespeople expressed the hope that I would treat the setback as a blip, not as a major incident in the company's history. As I explained to them at the time, because I am writing about the company at this juncture — and not 10 or 20 years hence — the setback inevitably has to take on a larger portion of the story than it might had the book been written years later.

I ignored all of the urgings from various quarters on how to write the book, adhering to the policy that I have followed during my lengthy book-writing career: Tell a good story, be fair, be accurate — and don't take sides. Considering the various audiences interested in how this book reads, I doubt I will fully satisfy each and every one of them. What I do hope is that readers find this as compelling a business story as I have.

I wish to give special thanks to a number of people who played a particularly large role in the book.

First, I extend my gratitude to John Chambers for opening the doors of Cisco to me. Once he decided to cooperate, he chose to spend a great deal of time with me to make sure I understood all that he was trying to do and had done at Cisco. I am grateful to him for our frequent and lengthy conversations. I am especially appreciative that he chose to continue talking with me even after the company's troubles began and he knew that the book would include substantial narrative and analysis of Cisco's difficulties encountered in 2000 and 2001.

Next, to Abby Mates Smith, Cisco's corporate public relations manager, I offer my thanks, for arranging interviews and tracking down numerous facts about Cisco and its people, and for always being there when the need arose. She proved a valuable source of knowledge about Cisco's strategies and culture, and I am grateful for our many conversations and e-mails.

To Terry Eger, I owe a great debt for shedding so much light on the early years of Cisco, helping me understand the company's technologies and business strategies, giving me so much of his time. Terry was the ideal companion during my journey, as he managed to explain just about every single policy, strategy, and event in Cisco's history. I thank him for our meetings and our e-mail dialogues, which helped to shape this book in so many ways.

To Amir Hartman, a former Cisco executive who is now running his own consulting business, I express my thanks for offering some fascinating ways to look at Cisco Systems and at corporations in general. At crucial times during my research, Amir gave me a whole series of insights that have found their way into this book.

Finally, my thanks to all those Wall Street analysts who helped clarify so many points about the company's relationship to the Street, but especially to George Kelly.

I also wish to thank all the others I interviewed: Sam Albert, Douglas C. Allred, Christin Armacost, Barbara Beck, Ray Bell, Lissa Bogaty, Brad Boston, Craig Benson, Lydia Blankenship, John Bolger, Susan L. Bostrom, Claudia Ceniceros, Howard S. Charney, Larry R. Carter, Michael E. Ching, Gary J. Daichendt, Kate DCamp, Mark Dickey, John Doerr, Randi Paikoff Feigin, Carly Fiorina, James R. Forster, Charles H. Giancarlo, Mimi Gigoux, Kathryn Gould, Ammar Hanafi, Paul Johnson, Richard J. Justice, Edward R. Kozel, Scott Kriens, Randall Kruep, Kirk Lougheed, Mario Mazzola, John P. Morgridge, Michael Neiberg, William R. Nuti, Jim Oelschlager, Robert Peters, Randy Pond, Martin Pyykkonen, Carl Redfield, Ron Ricci, James Richardson, John Russell, Greg Satz, Daniel Scheinman, Peter Solvik, Christopher T. Stix, Robert Sweifach, Donald T. Valentine, Mike Volpi, and Jack Welch. I interviewed a number of these people several times. I thank them all for their contributions and their patience.

Working with my editor, Dave Conti, at HarperCollins has been a pleasure for me. He has been there throughout the project, offering guidance and a professional touch that is most appreciated. He has helped especially to shape the structure of the book, a tremendously important part of the overall project. I thank you, Dave. I also thank Edwin Tan, associate editor at HarperCollins, for making significant improvements to the manuscript.

I turn to my immediate family; I thank especially my wife, Elinor, who read through early drafts of this book, and who always made me feel that I was doing something incredibly important in putting all these sentences together. And I thank my children—Miriam, Shimi, Adam, and Rachel—for their constant support and interest in the book, and for enriching my life is so many ways. I am grateful too for the joys that my grandchildren, Edo and Maya, gave to me throughout the writing of this book.

Finally, I dedicate this book to the memory of a close friend and colleague, Michael Elkins. One of the great journalists of our era, he taught me much. I have always been proud to count him as one of my cherished acquaintances.

Introduction

It was early March 2001.

What a year it had been for Cisco Systems and its president and CEO, John Chambers—a roller coaster of a year indeed.

Just a year earlier—in March 2000—Cisco was at the top of its game. In fact, it was the number one market-cap company in the world. And John Chambers was routinely called "King of the Internet." His company was the most important manufacturer of Internet infrastructure, and Chambers was the chief spokesman for the Internet, especially Internet business.

That was a year ago.

Now John Chambers was wrestling with the toughest decision of his business career. His remarkable success as the CEO of Cisco Systems had convinced him that he would never have to face this decision.

It seemed beyond anyone's imagination that Chambers would ever have to announce layoffs.

Since becoming president and CEO in January 1995, Chambers had gone on a hiring spree. From 1998 to 2000, Cisco's headiest period of hypergrowth, employee rolls had more than doubled, from 20,000 to 43,000.

No other major company in America had grown so dramatically fast as the Silicon Valley wunderkind. To the adoring media, John Chambers might well have produced the greatest record of any CEO in his first five years, and Cisco Systems was bound for nothing but glory.

Forget about the pink slips. Cisco was printing money.

Then, toward the end of the year 2000, with a suddenness that shocked everyone, the American economy fell apart. CEOs of Cisco's client corporations simply stopped all new orders. So stunned was Chambers that he looked to nature and the Bible for an apt metaphor. It was, he suggested, as if a "100-year flood" had descended upon American business.

At first, Chambers had hoped that the flood would subside in a month or two and that Cisco could meantime find a safe harbor. He promised Cisco employees that he would not tamper with their jobs.

But the flood burst through America's dikes and spread to Europe and Asia.

Cisco no longer had a safe harbor.

A difficult, troubling image leaped into John Chambers's mind: the pink slips he had been forced to hand out to employees at Wang Laboratories, seemingly an aeon ago.

He hated doing that.

He had committed himself to never again getting into a position that required layoffs. Throughout the 1990s, as he climbed the executive ladder at Cisco and then took over the company, dismissals seemed impossible.

And yet he now faced the unimaginable.

He could have quit and in that way avoided taking the painful decision. But for Chambers, walking away in bad times was not an option. He genuinely believed that it was during these bad times that he was needed most to work his company out of this jam.

Was there still a way to avoid the layoffs? Chambers certainly hoped so. But as he inched toward what he knew would be the most wrenching decision of his career, he sensed the door closing on him.

Even into early March, Chambers was hoping for a miracle. He repeatedly told employees that there would no dismissals.

Thursday, March 8: Chambers visited a number of customers.

They gave him dismal news. They could not order any more Cisco equipment. Chambers was concerned. Hopes for a miracle had all but vanished. He now felt he had no choice but to prepare his senior colleagues for possible layoffs, not immediately, but soon.

He would tell them, "Here is where our business is, and this is what our customers are telling us. Here are my thoughts. What are your thoughts?"

A member of his communications team called him at his Los Altos home late that evening to tell him that Reuters was going to release a story saying that Cisco planned to lay off 5 percent of its workforce. She urged him to approve a statement denying the story. To leave the Reuters piece unanswered would send a chilling signal to Wall Street and to Cisco's employees.

Cisco's stock would plummet.

"The 5 percent rumor is absolutely wrong," Chambers told the colleague. "That's our 5 percent forced attrition."

The colleague breathed a sigh of relief. Chambers would now certainly permit a Cisco statement of denial.

Chambers knew that his colleague was right, that the lack of a denial would rock Wall Street. Chambers also knew that issuing a denial would be misleading, for he had virtually made up his mind to do the layoffs.

The Cisco CEO was wide awake. Unable to sleep, he had been running on his treadmill—he had always found it to be the best way to relieve stress and to think clearly.

By 4 A.M., he had made up his mind. Chambers phoned his communications manager and several of his senior executives. His voice suddenly turned somber. "I have decided to do a layoff. I don't think there's any way around it, given how fast our business is dropping. We have to go with an announcement today."

In a few hours he was scheduled to face several hundred Cisco employees who would be gathering for a monthly breakfast with Chambers, giving those with birthdays that month the chance to grill the CEO up front and personally. They were bound to ask him if he planned to do layoffs.

At 6:30 A.M., Chambers summoned his senior staff to the office. He ordered them to begin working on the sorrowful news release.

Two hours later, showing up for the breakfast meeting with employees, he broke the shocking news: Cisco would be cutting 5,400 employees and it would lay off another 2,500 temporary employees.

The official announcement of the layoffs came at noon, after the board had been notified. The layoffs—the first in the company's 17-year history—constituted the saddest day of John Chambers's business career.

Only a year earlier, Cisco had been the most valuable company in the world. Cisco's growth engine seemed to be shooting for the moon and beyond.

Now the engine was in serious need of repairs.

What had happened?

PART ONE

The Vision and the Flood

1 The Vision

I t is September 11, 2000, a Monday morning in Silicon Valley.

John Chambers bounces through the door of the auditorium in one of the 40 buildings at Cisco Systems' San Jose, California, headquarters campus. He dashes to the podium to deafening applause from the 125 sales recruits.

The applause gets louder.

Smiling ear to ear, the president and CEO of the premium networking company of the Internet age gives a high five to the previous speaker. The Cisco recruits are about to launch careers with the most successful high-tech business of the era. And though they need little pumping up, Chambers wants to make sure they enter the fray totally motivated, totally steeped in Cisco's culture. To Chambers, corporate culture is all-important; he has come to believe that great companies require great cultures. In time, he will modify that maxim by suggesting that great companies need to suffer a setback before they can become great; but that is far in the future.

It is no accident that the atmosphere resembles a college football game much more than a business lecture hall. For Chambers views himself as both coach and cheerleader, inspiring his "players," imploring them to make even greater demands upon themselves. Stretching is a crucial element of the company's culture.

A smile fastened to his face, reddish blond hair slipping over part of his forehead, Chambers is so optimistic about his company's future, so self-assured. He genuinely believes that he has put all the right people and all the right systems in place to guarantee that Cisco will keep growing indefinitely.

To be sure, he mouths all the necessary caveats about how it is always possible that Cisco Systems could suffer a setback if the employees took their collective eyes off the ball. No one is more paranoid than John Chambers, he insists. He's personally experienced what happens to companies who grow stodgy and arrogant and forget to execute. He will never let that happen to Cisco Systems, he assures.

Few in the audience believe for a minute that John Chambers would ever let the company get into trouble. He insists that he worries that Cisco might get too far from its customers, from its employees, too far from its partners. But the company's financial record suggests otherwise. So many times in the past he has been buoyant about the company's prospects, even when the business environment posed difficulties for Cisco, and so many times the company has delivered on John Chambers's promises. Go ahead, John, be paranoid if you like, the audience seems to be saying, but don't expect us to buy into such talk.

WE WILL CHANGE THE WORLD

Over the next 90 minutes, John Chambers takes the recruits through Cisco's strategies, its culture, and its vision. Today marks the final skull session before they are sent onto the field. Chambers barely pauses for breath. He appears to love to be center stage, to relish being in front of an audience, to delight in telling the Cisco story. Why should he not? At this phase of the game, in the fall of 2000, it's a success story beyond anyone's wildest dreams, his included.

Chambers believes with all of his heart that Cisco Systems is well on its way to becoming the most powerful and most influential company in history. "We will change the world," he promises. Though he sounds matter-of-fact, though he knows full well that he is articulating the boldest assertion a business leader can make, he mouths the words without hesitation or concern that the assertion will be challenged, without worrying that he will seem presumptuous. To others, the five-word phrase is bombastic. To John Chambers, it is a vision that he is fully expects to implement.

In promising that Cisco will change the world, he is placing the ultimate stretch goal before his 40,000 employees. He is comfortable setting forth a far-reaching vision for his company, because he is convinced that history, specifically business history, is on his side.

In earlier American history, the Industrial Revolution with its factories and smokestacks and huge bureaucracies set the tone for American business. But that is all in the past. A Second Industrial Revolution, launching the new digital age, symbolized first by the computer, then by the Internet, has set the tone for our era. John Chambers likes to say that Cisco is doing to the Internet revolution what mechanical technology did to the Industrial Revolution.

Chambers's message is: Those who join the new networking age, who take advantage of the Internet, who adjust to the age swiftly and unconditionally, will become the winners in today's business world. It hardly needs to be said—and so Chambers does not shout the point—that the more that people embrace the Internet, the more they will need Cisco's products.

Cisco's original product in 1986 was the multi-protocol router, a specialized computer that provided the "plumbing" for the Internet, sorting data packets and sending the packets on their way. In time, the unique and unprecedented Cisco product would fuel the burgeoning demand for computer networking. Routers are complicated items, as are all of Cisco's networking products, so you won't find much comment about their inner workings in this book. Installing routers and switches in the Internet, Cisco operates behind the scenes as the invisible builder and developer—a plumber, if you will—whose products seem too obscure and complex to dwell on in public. Even John Chambers doesn't wax poetic in his public appearances about the way routers and other networking devices work.

But some history of networking is worth reviewing. While the 1980s were the personal computer's birth years, computer communications also became popular, especially in the latter part of that decade. At first, there were local area networks, or LANs—work groups brought together by wire to share files and expensive peripheral computer devices, for example, laser printers. But it was the advent of e-mail and the creation of the World Wide Web that drove the demand for interconnecting computers into all kinds of networks, large and small. And so the 1990s became a decade of networking, as LANs expanded into wide area networks (WANs) and into the greatest WAN of all, the Internet.

To make all this possible, vendors had to build the "plumbing," the networking hardware that served as the infrastructure for these increasingly larger networks. As we will explain in more detail in Chapter 4, Cisco got its start when two romantically inclined employees, both working on the same university campus, could not send e-mail to each other because of disparate computer networks installed by their respective departments. To permit these two computer networks to interoperate, the two young computer professionals came up with a device called a network router.

A router forwards data packets from one LAN or WAN to another. Based on routing tables and protocols, routers read the network address in each transmitted frame and decide how to send it based on the most expedient route (traffic load, line costs, speed, bad lines, etc.). Routers are used to segment LANs in order to balance traffic within work groups, and to filter traffic for security purposes and policy management. They are also used at the edge of a network to connect remote offices. A multi-protocol router—Cisco's original product—supports several protocols, such as IP, IPX, AppleTalk, and DECnet.

Most routers are specialized computers that are optimized for communications; however, router functions can also be implemented by adding routing software to a file server. Routers often serve as an Internet backbone, interconnecting all networks in the enterprise. This architecture strings several routers together via a high-speed LAN such as Fast Ethernet or gigabit Ethernet.

Often described as resembling a small microwave oven, the Cisco router came in a white box and had a few wires dangling from it.

The phenomenon of networking arose because of the trend toward distributed processing and the remarkable growth of personal computers and workstations, first in universities, then in corporations and governments.

Just as important, without the Cisco routers, there would not have been a World Wide Web. By the year 2000, over 75 percent of all Internet traffic traveled over Cisco products, and the future looked just as rosy: 275 million people were using the Internet, and the number was expected to mushroom to 1 billion by 2005—three and a half times more traffic, three and a half times more Cisco product to sell over this five-year period.

The networking market had reached $49.3 billion in 2000, and Cisco was hoping to get the lion's share of it.

In his talk to the sales recruits, Chambers barely mentions the company's products, the routers and switches that have made Cisco supreme within the Internet infrastructure industry. It seems a conscious decision on his part. Switches came along after routers to help ease the problem of limited network bandwidth.

With products so far removed from the average person's awareness, it would be surprising if an Internet user *did* know what products the "plumber" manufactured. In its early days, Cisco was almost entirely (90 percent) based on the router. By the mid-1990s, Cisco correctly anticipated that switches would become a major product within networking.

Another networking device that complemented routers—the intelligent hub—did not increase bandwidth. Network routers could increase bandwidth by segmenting traffic into separate sections or work groups, but routers were expensive, were not very fast, and were difficult to manage in large numbers.

Networks required a new device that had the simplicity of the intelligent hub and some of the intelligence of the router. In late

1992 and early 1993, vendors began producing LAN switches. Now network managers could relieve some of the congestion. At the beginning, the switching and hub markets coexisted, but over time LAN switches replaced intelligent hubs.

Routers and switches are the "traffic cops" of the Internet, the equipment that makes the entire network function smoothly and efficiently. Because they steer the data to the right destination, they are essential. As John Chambers describes his products: "We are the intersection of everything from interstate highways to the stop sign at the edge of the access road. We direct how to get there and take complete responsibility for the information getting there. So, simply put, we make the intelligent intersections."

No one, not even Cisco Systems, owns the Internet, nor does Cisco own the technology that keeps the Internet functioning productively and efficiently. What then has given the company such primacy over the Internet? Cisco's early triumph in making IP (Internet Protocol) the standard protocol is largely responsible. IP provides a unique identifier for each client connected to the Internet, permitting different clients to locate and communicate with one another. In effect, the protocol governs the flow of traffic. Gaining first-mover advantage, Cisco created its Internet Operating System (IOS), which used IP, and in time, IOS became the most popular software of its kind. Cisco developed the most comprehensive set of protocols that supported IP. Significantly, the IP standard was open, allowing anyone who wished to use the Internet, thus paving the way for rapid growth. Cisco was in the right place at the right time to gain a dominant position in the router and, later, switch markets.

The Second Industrial Revolution has moved through two distinct phases. During the first—throughout the 1980s and early 1990s—Microsoft ruled, as the personal computer became the dominant office and household appliance, and Bill Gates's software became the basic tool for using that appliance. By the mid-1990s, as the personal computer took a backseat to networking, the revolution hit its second phase; and as the primary manufacturer of the gear that ran the Internet, Cisco became the primary force, replacing Microsoft as the major business enterprise of the digital age.

How did that happen?

Part of the answer has to do with Cisco's having the right products at the right time. But just as important was the creation of a distinct Cisco culture, an amalgam of strategies and values that have played a crucial role in the company's operations.

Some of those strategies and values predated the era of John Chambers at Cisco Systems. He has been president and chief executive officer since January 1995. Some important seeds of the Cisco culture were planted by the founders of Cisco Systems, Len Bosack and Sandy Lerner, and by John Morgridge, who was president and CEO from 1988 until 1995.

But it was John Chambers who orchestrated the strategies and nurtured the values that fueled the company's enormous success in the second half of the nineties. And it is for this reason that, although we spend some time on the company's early years, we focus on the John Chambers era at Cisco.

Cisco's main product, the network router, had its own unique "brew" and could not easily be replicated by competitors, creating an overwhelming entry barrier for main rival Wellfleet. Because Cisco had moved into the switching market, it *could* compete with another company, SynOptics; since SynOptics was predominantly a hub maker, it did not compete in the router market.

At the start of the five-year period from 1992 to 1997, Cisco accounted for 15 percent of the networking hardware industry's profits; by the end, it accounted for nearly 50 percent.

Rather than dwell on the virtues of Cisco products, Chambers prefers to focus on the company's business strategies and culture. He learned the hard way not to become inextricably linked to one particular piece of technology or another. Earlier, while at IBM, he watched with growing dismay as senior executives allowed their love affair with mainframes to blind them to the arrival of the personal computer; then, while at Wang Laboratories, he was equally discomforted when the company's leadership clung to minicomputers while the personal computer was quickly taking their place. Not making a religion out of one particular technology has proven a deft business strategy for John Chambers.

BEING OPEN

The one feature of Cisco's culture that John Chambers has promoted more than any other is its fundamental interest in being open—to customers, to change of all kinds, and perhaps most important, to changes in the market. Chambers, and before him John Morgridge, credited the company's success largely to their catching market transitions at very early stages.

Armed with their early-warning system foretelling customer wants and needs, Chambers and his colleagues picked up on the single most important market transition of the 1990s: the decision to fall in love with the Internet. Using that valuable piece of intelligence, Chambers set out a vision earlier than anyone else of the Internet as the crucial tool for American business.

Chambers turned Cisco into a switching company, offering a product that had distinct advantages over routers; he then broadened Cisco into an end-to-end enterprise that provided the gamut of network products; and more recently, he has been seeking to take advantage of the convergence of audio, video, and data in networking. Helping the process of reinvention has been Chambers's novel strategy of business acquisitions: rather than rely upon Cisco's research and development facilities, he systematically acquired small start-ups, eager to absorb their executive and engineering talent and, if possible, their products, into Cisco's embrace. By May 2002, the number of acquisitions stood at 75.

On this September morning in 2000, John Chambers is a happy man. He's had a terrific week as one business leader after another sought him out for his take on the supercharged world of high tech and the Internet. Political leaders rearranged their schedules for a sit-down with him. Corporations cheerfully sent their entire boards and senior executive echelons to an audience with the man the media call the "King of the Internet." They want to sit at Chambers's feet because no one explains how to capitalize on the Internet, the hot new business tool of the nineties, better than the Cisco CEO.

Chambers came to the fore at the right time, a time when the business world was slowly learning about the wonders of the Internet, yet many executives had little idea how to use the new business tool for financial gain. It was only in the late 1990s that many American business executives woke up to the potential of the Internet. But before they would invest large sums in the infrastructure, CEOs and political leaders alike required someone who could clearly explain all of these complicated notions.

HE GOT IT

Word spread that Cisco Systems had acquired a special expertise in mastering the Internet for business purposes. The fact that Cisco was the dominant player in the Internet infrastructure market—first routers, then switches—was, ironically, not its main attraction to these executives. It was, rather, that John Chambers got it. Not only did he seem able to understand and explain the new high-tech world, but he headed a company that had become a model for how to live and flourish in that world.

As he promoted the Internet, Chambers found that his message and his vision resonated in all the right places. As business and political leaders sought him out, he rose to the occasion. He seemed smarter than most, more charming, remarkably persuasive. Whether one-on-one or in front of large audiences, he appeared ideally cast as spokesperson for this new high-tech world.

He had a vision that he constantly spelled out: High tech had become the key driver of the American and world economies, sparked by the Internet, a phenomenally exciting business tool that was only in its infancy and would only grow in significance as time went on. Gradually, the Internet would change all aspects of our lives, the way we worked, played, learned—everything! He sought to convince everyone that Cisco could transform the way we communicate and could help machines communicate with a high degree of sophistication.

Businesses and countries only had to invest in the Chambers vision and then reap the benefits: higher productivity, greater efficiencies. Chambers loved being industry spokesperson, loved the coincidence of timing and good fortune that had given Cisco's products such allure. He bubbled over with enthusiasm at all that seemed to lay in Cisco's grip: "The Internet will change our lives in ways that people are just beginning to grasp," he suggested to me in the fall of 2000. "We are at the heart of that. If we do it right, we can help change the direction of companies and countries. We will change the world. And we're going to do it in ways that other people have never thought. We are reinventing so many business principles . . . at a speed that is breathtaking."

No one articulated a vision for Internet-driven life better than John Chambers; no one appeared to have such a grasp of our future. But the vision did not come for free. Chambers had a not-so-secret agenda: He knew that selling the Internet was an ideal way to sell Cisco products. Explaining to CEOs and political leaders what the benefits of the Internet were constituted so many sales pitches to potential customers: Chambers adroitly exploited their curiosity about the Internet to bring them into the Cisco fold.

Back then in the fall of 2000, John Chambers was speeding through another nonstop week. He was always in motion, racing into a lecture hall, grabbing a plane, speaking to audiences that sometimes include the president of the United States, hurrying off to a private dinner with the prime minister of Belgium. He was on the road half the time, joking about how he had to jog over the weekends to take off the weight he had accumulated during his travels.

And so the sales recruits on that September morning learned that John Chambers had had another whirlwind day on the previous Friday, placing a phone call to a CEO in Silicon Valley, then flying at 7 A.M. from San Jose to Santa Fe, New Mexico, to meet with 160 dot-com CEOs hosted by Benchmark, the venture-capitalist firm. Chambers talked to them about how they could use the emerging Internet technology, how they could share best practices, and how they could become E-companies. He made the key point that without this technology their companies would not survive. He told them that within five years all businesses would have to become E-companies. And, of course, he explained to them why he believed they would benefit from partnering with Cisco Systems.

I'LL COME TO SAN JOSE

Then it was on to Phoenix, Arizona, where he lectured 60 Emerson Electric executives. He had presided over similar meetings the week before with senior executives from the Ford Motor Company and Applied Materials, he told the sales recruits. Chambers was particularly impressed that the Ford executives spent two days at Cisco when the Firestone tire recall issue was swirling. (Talking with me that evening, Chambers affirmed that these meetings were in large measure about getting Cisco more business. He had talked to the boards on how they could E-enable their businesses. "In exchange, we knew that many would commit to Cisco's end-to-end network.")

Finally, on that Friday, September 8, Chambers flew back to San Jose for dinner with Guy Verhofstadt, the prime minister of Belgium. The prime minister's visit offered a glimpse of the respect that key figures have had for John Chambers and Cisco Systems. The prime minister had originally asked Chambers to meet in Brussels; then, when Chambers said that he could not make the trip, the Belgian leader suggested they meet in New York, where he would be attending United Nations sessions. But the Cisco leader said he would be unable to get to New York at that time. And so—as Chambers excitedly explained to the sales recruits—the Belgian prime minister came to San Jose for dinner.

Let's not gloss over this episode too quickly.

To get a sense of Chambers's and Cisco's importance, let's recall what happened here. A government leader, whose calendar seemed more flexible than John Chambers's, finally decided that he would journey to San Jose, California, rather than miss the chance to meet with the Cisco president and CEO!

At their dinner, Chambers explained to the Belgian prime minister what the Internet could mean to his country's economy, and what Belgium's government must do in order to prepare the way for building a networking infrastructure. Chambers had been spelling out that message relentlessly ("If you're not ready, you'll be in trouble"), but it was only now, five years later, the Cisco leader told the sales recruits, that government leaders were beginning to understand.

Why did CEO after CEO, political leader after political leader, rush to hear John Chambers's message? Plain and simple, backing up his insights and his forecasts was the Cisco Systems record. It was a record of such consistently high growth that the name Cisco itself had became synonymous with American and worldwide prosperity.

Just five months earlier (on March 27, 2000), Cisco Systems became the nation's most valuable company, with $531 billion in market capitalization. The stock peaked at $80.06 that day.

It hardly mattered that Cisco remained at the top of the heap for only one day. It was a spectacular achievement. A year earlier, it had the tenth highest market cap in the United States. When Chambers took over as president and CEO in 1995, the company's market cap had been only $9 billion. That led *Fortune* magazine to give Chambers a giant pat on the back: "That has to be the greatest first five years any CEO has ever had." Cisco had reached a $100 billion market value in 1998—only eight and a half years after going public—making the company the fastest in history to reach that mark. The previous record holder had been Microsoft, but it had taken Bill Gates's company almost 11 years.

Among the beneficiaries of Cisco's skyrocketing stock were Cisco employees, several thousand of whom became millionaires by virtue of the stock's climbing 8,000 percent after it went public early in 1990 at $18 a share, or 6¼¢ on a split-adjusted basis.

In 1999, Cisco's stock had risen 162 percent, trading at $72 a share. It rose to a high of 80 a share in the spring of 2000. All the time it was rising, the stock reflected Cisco's spectacular revenue growth. In 1995, Chambers's first year at the helm, the company had $2.2 billion in revenue. In the ensuing decade, its net revenues grew steadily, reaching $6.4 billion in 1997, $8.4 billion in 1998, $12.1 billion in 1999, and $18.9 billion in 2000. Net income rose just as steadily: from $1.04 billion in 1997, to $1.3 billion in 1998, to $2.02 billion in 1999, to $2.6 billion in 2000.

RIDING A ROCKET

Propelled by such unprecedented growth, Chambers was on the rocket ride of his life, and he did not want to get off. He seemed to revel in the momentum of the Cisco growth engine. He delighted at the forecasts that spoke of the Internet surging ahead dramatically in the next few years. And he was a happy man. Even as he was suggesting to these recruits that the better part of wisdom was to be a little paranoid, he appeared to believe that the rocket he was riding was unstoppable.

It became easy for him to predict that Cisco would become a $50 billion company within the next four or five years. In the fall of 2000 he told audiences that he was confident that Cisco would beat that prediction. It seemed no great stretch of the imagination for him to assert that Cisco would become the first corporation to possess $1 trillion in market value. ("Better than a fifty-fifty chance," he told Cisco employees at a company meeting on September 14, 2000.)

To exploit the rocket ride, Chambers had no trouble deciding on a push toward hypergrowth: hiring 1,000 new employees a month; building new office parks; acquiring start-up after start-up, 21 alone in 2000; and planning to more than double Cisco's workforce from 40,000 to 100,000 employees over the next few years.

As Cisco headed for another record-breaking revenue figure for fiscal 2001, the media noted that if Cisco kept growing at a mind-boggling 40 percent a year, it would become a $110 billion company by 2005, almost as large as General Electric was in 2001. More astounding, it had taken GE more than 100 years to get that large; John Chambers would get there in only 21!

Not surprisingly, the business media lavished praise upon John Chambers for taking Cisco to such heights. Network and business magazines routinely ranked him at or near the top of the list of digital world titans. *Worth* magazine named Chambers the number two CEO in America in April 1999. For the second time in three years, *Business Week* named him one of the top 25 executives worldwide. *Chief Executive* magazine named Chambers CEO of the Year for 2000. Cisco came in for honors as well. In 1998, *Forbes ASAP* designated Cisco the country's most dynamic company, and *Fortune* called Cisco one of the 25 best companies to work for in the United States. In 2000, Cisco was ranked number one and described as the "most intelligently Net-savvy company going" by *Business 2.0*.

During Cisco's early days, the company remained largely an engineering enterprise, an inward-looking organization that managed to sell an awful lot of routers despite a group of employees who didn't like one another very much. The culture at the time focused on frugality and customer involvement, but there seemed more chaos than order, and nearly everyone credited the company's success to just plain good luck—simply having a great product.

Then, in 1991, John Chambers joined the company as senior vice president. For four years he learned the business, gradually taking on most of the management chores. In 1995, the business was his, and he began to change the face of the company. By dint of his strong personality (someone once joked that he always seemed to be making a sales call), Chambers instilled in Cisco a higher purpose. As a means to enable Cisco to penetrate even larger markets, Chambers elevated Cisco's profile, giving the once obscure "plumber" of the Internet a new, spruced-up public persona.

Radiating a rare degree of self-confidence, even audacity, John Chambers began to preach that Cisco could change the global community forever by interconnecting everything on the planet.

Bold words. Risky statements. But Chambers radiated so much self-assuredness that he did not sound at all radical. Whatever he says, he says with such conviction that his ideas seem plausible, his predictions sensible. It's hard to find fault with someone who, when speaking on a public stage, seems so much in control, so easy on his feet. It seems difficult to imagine, but a time existed when Chambers was so nervous that he literally became ill prior to making a presentation. As he noted in an interview with me: "I used to get so scared of speaking my knees would shake and I would throw up before I presented. You should have seen my tapes from the IBM training. I was memorizing everything I said. I was not as effective." Eventually he overcame the problem, and today he says, rather self-evidently, "I have no fear of speaking now."

LIKE MISTER ROGERS ON SPEED

Talking to the recruits on that September morning he is the consummate public speaker, uttering sentence after sentence in rapid-fire sequence, moving all the time, to the left, then the right, finally straight down the middle aisle, always making eye contact with a member of the audience. He fires off a question to no one in particular, then rivets his eyes on someone at random and asks for the answer.

His voice goes through the modulations of an actor onstage. At times, he whispers; at times, he shouts.

"You have a chance to make customers grow and maybe survive." This, he shouts. "We have the chance to become the most powerful company in history." This, he shouts, as well.

The effect is dramatic.

His mind is racing. One sentence follows the next in machine-gun style.

(He once said, only half-jokingly, "I can type 15 words a minute . . . and I can talk 200 words a minute." Less kindly, a *Fortune* magazine writer once quipped that Chambers "tends to talk like Mister Rogers on speed.")

The sheer explosiveness of his delivery gives the impression of a man racing, racing, racing, never willing to slow down. And he never does.

He is an actor. He is a preacher. He is a coach. He is the head of the company. He is all those put together.

"You are the best there is in the world, and you're going to play fair," he tells the recruits.

Even if he were a dull speaker, the sales recruits would feel compelled to listen respectfully to their new boss. But this man sweeping through the audience is not dull. He is passionate and electrifying.

This is a very personal meeting for John Chambers. He looks around the audience and feels an immediate empathy with the audience. He has been in their shoes. Indeed, he is still in their shoes. He began his career in sales, first at IBM, then at Wang Laboratories. He was in charge of sales when he began at Cisco in 1991. Four years later, when he became president and CEO, he began spending more time with customers than with anyone else.

Because talking with customers is important to him, because he probably has more contact with Cisco's major customers than anyone else in the company, he sounds ever so uncomfortable about giving any customers over to the sales force entirely. He wants to share in the experience. "You are in temporary possession of my customers," he tells the audience. He's not joking. He means it.

He is convinced that Cisco scaled the heights because its executives listened to their customers and adjusted their product line accordingly. He wants these sales recruits, above all else, to listen as well.

. . .

The meeting with the sales recruits ends. They are fired up. As Chambers walks out, again the applause is deafening.

Twice more that week, Chambers will stand in front of Cisco employees, seeking to spread the company's culture, answering questions from the audience. No matter what the audience, he will rarely change his tone or the themes of his talk. On Thursday afternoon, September 14, he appears before 6,500 employees who congregate under a huge tent down the road from Cisco's headquarters. For the other 33,500 employees, many of them spread around the world, the session is televised live through their computers via IPTV (Internet Protocol TV). A day later, 400 employees who celebrate September birthdays come together for a birthday breakfast question-and-answer session with their CEO.

During all the time that Cisco was ascendant, this was a fairly routine week for John Chambers. He was always moving about, always getting up in front of audiences, always explaining what Cisco was about. He tried to reach out to every employee within shouting distance, or at least within IPTV distance. He understood that it was easier to create a business culture than to spread it to thousands of employees, many in far-flung places. He firmly believed that getting the company's strategies and values across to the Cisco family would help the organization absorb all the changes it had to go through: new product lines to be marketed and sold, numerous acquisitions to be integrated, thousands of new employees to be absorbed. It was no wonder that John Chambers tried to develop eye contact with all 40,000 Cisco employees.

That was September 2000. It was a golden time for John Chambers and Cisco Systems, a time when Chambers was indeed King of the Internet, its chief promoter, the go-to person for anyone—prime ministers, finance ministers, CEOs, CIOs—who wanted to know where the Internet was heading.

Indeed, Chambers's Cisco Systems had risen to the pinnacle of the high-tech world. Not only had it been, albeit for a brief period, the number one market value company in America, it was also the premium model of a company that "got" the Internet: Its products, routers, and such provided the infrastructure for the Internet; its processes and functions exploited the Internet better than any other American firm; by manufacturing a product and actually making a profit, Cisco Systems seemed the ideal meld of old and new economies.

And by virtue of its huge annual growth rates, Cisco was from 1999 to 2001 Wall Street's darling, the Street's most heavily traded stock (almost 15 percent higher than its closest rival, Oracle). With its value soaring, it had made millionaires of countless people. The only question that seemed relevant was how high could Cisco go?

Cisco's prospects for continuing hypergrowth seemed endless. That heady atmosphere led John Chambers to adopt a management style that, in his view, was attuned to a supercharged growth environment. The boom times allowed him, so he thought, to be more cheerleader and preacher than chief executive officer. With so much opportunity, with so much market demand, Chambers concluded that he was better off assuming the role of Internet business spokesperson than handling the day-to-day affairs of the company. He was better off spending a good deal of his time on the road visiting customers than keeping close tabs on his colleagues back at headquarters.

Chambers took a close look at the great business leaders of our age and concluded that they were able to build companies to last by creating strong cultures and being highly disciplined. He decided that he would do the same at Cisco. He was exceedingly proud when others (especially former GE chairman and CEO Jack Welch) called Cisco a very disciplined company. He took that as a great compliment. Chambers was convinced that without the discipline, Cisco would not have been able to grow at such speed.

Yet, Chambers did not possess the tools to create a tightly run, micromanaged company. Though he had studied electrical engineering for two years and was good at math, he was no technical whiz. He possessed great skills, but they were the skills of a salesman.

He was charming, persuasive, and aggressive. John Doerr, a partner at the Silicon Valley venture-capitalist firm Kleiner Perkins Caufield & Byers, called Chambers "a man who . . . listens well and becomes the natural leader in a meeting." He was indeed a natural leader, but when he came to Silicon Valley he had to decide whether he would lead or follow.

Being an outsider (he came from West Virginia) had its advantages. He adopted some of Silicon Valley's conventions—its entrepreneurial spirit, its informality, its insistence on frugality. But he felt no need to adhere to the conventions of his own engineers: he had no time for their "NIH" (not-invented-here) mentality; instead, he broke with the Valley's tradition of avoiding acquisitions, making Silicon Valley and beyond his personal R&D lab.

From his favorite business mentor, Jack Welch, he adopted the "number one, number two" strategy, which required having only those products or businesses that were first or second in their markets. He also adopted the Welch strategy of establishing stretch goals (with the one difference that Welch tolerated employees who did not attain stretch goals; Chambers would not). Significantly, Chambers picked the strategies that would make Cisco grow, not those that would assure a focus on business fundamentals, that is on being disciplined.

To be sure, Chambers believed that he was imposing a sufficient degree of discipline on Cisco. But he defined discipline differently than some business theoreticians did. To Chambers, being disciplined meant creating incentives that would align employees with the culture. He was especially keen on their improving customer satisfaction, and part of a bonus was based on such improvement. Being disciplined also meant asserting in every speech to employees that he was paranoid, worrying that if Cisco did not execute well, it would suffer a catastrophe. Chambers wanted to avoid complacency. He encouraged employees to listen to others, especially customers, to keep ahead of competitors. "How are we doing?" he liked to ask just about anyone he met, always seeming eager to take the company's temperature, fighting that enemy, complacency. Chambers seemed humble. He seemed modest. The effect was appealing. "It's the only company," says former Morgan Stanley analyst Chris Stix, "where we've seen that kind of behavior, that they want to learn from you."

To John Chambers, discipline also meant building a culture and making sure that all Cisco employees adhered to it.

The theoreticians would argue that cheerleading was no substitute for discipline, that assertions of paranoia were no substitute for closely monitoring a company, and that a reliance on hypergrowth made the company forget to do the basics. "Basics" normally means putting a focus on earnings, working capital, and operating margins; setting expectations and meeting them; having consistency and rigor, and holding people accountable. Cisco was far removed from this world; it was focusing on revenue and gross margins.

In other words, John Chambers—visionary, coach, cheerleader, preacher—was perfectly attuned to the high-growth atmosphere in which the company found itself. His skills were those of a growth king, not of a business disciplinarian. That would be fine as long as the hypergrowth continued.

Autonomy and empowerment were critical watchwords in the Chambers management style. Ironically, Chambers, the business leader who seems to be in every place at every turn, understands the value of decentralizing decision making. He wants to avoid having to make all the decisions. He believes that he can get more discipline out of the organization and create a more effective company by turning decision making over to his junior colleagues. Hence, Chambers told *New York Times* columnist and author Tom Friedman: "I can only make so many decisions, and gather so much information, at the pace of today's economy. I want to make the big strategic decisions, but after that, if I have disseminated the decision-making process down to the people who are closest to the action, and if I have disseminated to them the same information I have, then I have a thousand decision-makers working for me and there is a better chance that we won't miss the market."

Being away so much of the time, believing that his managers were closer to the sales environment than he was, he encouraged them to take on major responsibilities. For that he needed the best people. He was always juggling, promoting, demoting, in the hope of getting the ablest senior executives to carry that extra burden. Though the company is only 18 years old, most managers have had at least two predecessors, sometimes as many as five. What others would describe as a shaky, unsettling management environment is, to John Chambers, one of Cisco's hidden competitive advantages: "We've evolved our leadership team in a decade while it would normally take place over decades. So we've probably been the smoothest company in the world about management transitions. Within that, we do it without creating customer disruption, and even when the transitions were for negative reasons, the outside world didn't see it as negative."

That is because Chambers works hard at avoiding confrontation and controversy. When he joined Cisco in 1991 he became terribly conscious of how fractious a crowd Cisco's employees were. He vowed that he would neither tolerate any infighting nor allow it to infect business performance.

On those occasions when an executive complained to Chambers directly about the behavior of a colleague, the CEO made it clear that he preferred not to deal with such issues frontally, hoping the problem would just go away or at least not lead to a public issue. And Chambers is adept at keeping the public from learning the true reason for certain executive changes. Once, a major business magazine was doing a cover story on Cisco Systems, and when the story appeared, Chambers learned that two senior executives had used it to promote the personal ambitions of one of those executives. The two executives left the company soon afterward. The actual reason for their departures was not made public at the time. In a second incident, one executive privately voiced concern to Chambers that he had a problem with the CEO. The executive, once very close to Chambers personally, felt strongly enough to leave the company. The public learned only that the man had left Cisco to spend more time with his family.

Though he empowered senior executives to act independently, Chambers sought to cultivate the impression that he was a very hands-on CEO: He let it be known that he was constantly monitoring the complaints of major clients, that he gave out his home telephone number to customers and sometimes got phone calls at 2 A.M., that he checked the company's numbers daily. He liked to point out that he used employees and customers as a barometer, encouraging them to contact him directly (one of every three e-mails he gets are from customers). Some 500 e-mails arrived in his mailbox every day; another 120 voice mail messages were left as well: "The neat thing is, and here's where you learn from your mistakes of the past, your employees and customers will see the issues way ahead of time." Above all, he seemed to feel that getting in front of as many employees as possible would help his labor force come to understand and then execute Cisco's culture.

There is very little formalism within the inner sanctums of Cisco, a formalism normally associated with structure and discipline. Chambers feels strongly that he wants to bridge the gap as much as possible between himself and his junior employees. As a result, he has a relatively small, modest-looking office. An equally small conference room adjoins his office to the rear. Some junior staff on the same floor face windows; the senior executives' offices do not. Some vice presidents and directors share conference rooms! Chambers's office has a homey look. On one wall is a sign saying "Gone Fishing." A glass dispenser of gumballs is near the front door. Near Chambers's desk is a photo of him with President George W. Bush and another photo of the 1998–1999 Duke University basketball team with the players' autographs. On one shelf is a model of Chambers's plane, a Falcon 2000. (Though he owns his own plane, Chambers still flies commercial at times, and when he does, he follows company policy of flying coach.) He has surprisingly little privacy for a company head. Someone sitting in the large lobby near the executive wing can easily glance at Chambers on the phone or huddled with another Cisco executive.

Much of the discipline that Chambers thought he was imposing on Cisco had to do with making sure that the company always knew where it stood financially. Chambers always boasted that it was Cisco's clever use of its technology that gave it a competitive advantage over its rivals. This was a company that performed spectacularly quarter after quarter, but if orders began to slow down, the Cisco technology would serve as an early-warning system well enough in advance for the company to make the necessary adjustments. The key point was that the technology provided a fail-safe mechanism — and there would always be plenty of time to adjust to any economic downturn. When senior executives of other companies flocked to Chambers and his CFO, Larry Carter, to learn how the fail-safe technology worked, it was easy for John Chambers to convince himself that he had imposed enough discipline on the company to avoid any unpleasant surprises.

Orchestrating Cisco into the model E-company, a vital part of company culture, John Chambers, not surprisingly, is an avid Internet user, though he is the first to admit that he has never especially liked technology for technology's sake. "I love how it changes the way you work or the way you play." He spends several hours each night on the Internet, looking at customer and employee e-mails, reading business periodicals on-line (especially the *Wall Street Journal*), watching for rivals' announcements, looking at the Cisco Web site, poring over certain stocks. He listens to his voice mail via the computer as well. ("Which is why it's so obvious to me that the two — voice and data — will come together on the computer.") He also prepares for fishing vacations by surfing for the temperatures in the region he will visit, and for a sense of how well other fishermen have done in that region recently.

He and his family have been playing a modern-day player piano at home over the Internet for three years. He connected a piano to the computer, downloaded music from the Internet, and began to have some fun: "When I first started, I would tell my friends that I was working on something and I would play on the piano. They couldn't see my hands. I had no musical talent whatsoever. They would be in shock that I could do this; then I would wave to them and the piano kept going."

. . .

Much of John Chambers's notions about discipline were "soft": it was listening, reading e-mails, hearing voice mails, standing in front of audiences, conveying messages. It had less to do with running an organization, more to do with cheerleading and coaching. It was the perfect recipe for a company that was in full throttle, on the receiving end of a market with a voracious, and seemingly endless, appetite. In that go-go environment, discipline—the careful monitoring of each and every business operation—has far less value attached to it than what appear to be the key drivers of that environment: speed and motion.

In an environment that turns hypergrowth into a sacred mission, a CEO can be forgiven for believing that nothing counts as much as doing things fast. Speed becomes the key strategy, the approach to things that keeps the cash flowing. It seems significant that John Chambers made so much of speed as a way of life. For him, it was the ultimate weapon to use in creating what he believed was a culture of discipline. If one characteristic summed up John Chambers's management style, it was that he seemed in constant motion. "I sensed that the man's adrenaline was pumping away minute after minute," said one former Cisco executive whose office was near Chambers's when they worked together in the early 1990s. "He never seemed fatigued." Indeed, Chambers appeared always to be either addressing a meeting, running to a meeting, or planning a meeting. His movements were always fleet, as if walking were a waste of precious time. Never did he simply wander out of his office. He bolted out of it.

He seemed always to be racing, not running, not walking, and all for a purpose. In nearly every phase of Cisco's business, speed became essential. The entire high-tech industry prided itself on working at Internet time. No one took greater pride in this than John Chambers. Though Chambers did not include it as part of Cisco's cultural values, speed was certainly something that he valued. Moreover, Chambers believed that when he made mistakes, they tended to be because he had gone too slowly. "Even though we're a company that is used to moving at light speed compared to everyone else, almost every mistake has been when we've moved too slowly."

When specifically did he move too slowly? I asked him.

"In almost every area. [He laughs.] We moved slower in optical than I would like to. Now having said that, once we moved, we moved very efficiently, and the market's responded very, very well. We moved even slower than I could have with hindsight with our acquisition strategy, even though compared to anyone else we wrote the book on acquisition strategy. Most of our competitors who have done acquisitions have failed. Most of the acquisitions that we've done have worked. We've moved into markets in hindsight a little bit slower—in the small-to-medium business for the consumer. Each move we've made I would have moved faster, even though we've been tremendously successful."

Always in motion, always running at top speed, Chambers put himself in front of large groups, whether employees or customers, as often as possible. Indeed, few CEOs made as many appearances before employees as he did. He had a very clear message to sell to employees: Cisco was on a roll, growth was fun, exhilarating, but it took hard work, focus, and, of course, discipline. Discipline meant many things, but above all it meant speed. The image that I retain of John Chambers after watching him appear before meeting after meeting of employees is of a man on the run. He ran up to a stage. He ran out of his office. He ran across a room to greet you. He always seemed to have just stopped jogging.

His oratorical skills were honed to a fine degree. At times, he shouted. At other times, he whispered. He rarely seemed to pause to take a breath. He spoke in machine-gun style. He has learned, like a good actor, never to stand in one place too long, so on stage he darted to the left, to the right; leaving the stage, he moved up and down the aisles, gaining direct eye contact with people in the audience. He not only moved fast, but he also spoke fast (one aide tape-recorded her early meetings with Chambers to make sure she caught every word). Chambers liked to joke about the speed of his delivery—his wife, a speech therapist, called him her only failure—but he would not slow down.

In the fall of 2000, when I started attending employee meetings, some 15,000 of Cisco's 40,000 employees were working at the San

Jose, California, headquarters spread over a campus of 40 buildings. So it was easy for Chambers to get before hundreds of employees without causing anyone to lose too much work time.

All of the strengths and skills that Chambers possesses come together when he gets onstage. All of his career he has been a salesman, and in nearly every conversation or public appearance he adopts the role of a salesman. And he is very good at it. He knows how to take a room, to command an audience, to get everyone's attention in the blink of an eye. Public speaking has become second nature to him. "This might be one of my best strengths—my communications skills. Not just to communicate a message, but also to communicate it in a way that an intellectual person could understand it or the average person could. I am able to put it in terms that we understand. I can articulate a problem in five minutes whereas before I struggled with it for hours. In ways that the average politician, or parent, or child can understand."

In front of an audience, Chambers falls back at times on the salesman's patter: We will change the world. We want to become the most powerful, most influential company in history. Hyperbole? Not to John Chambers. More like the tools of the trade. "We like to say," observes Michael Ching, a first vice president in Global Securities Research and Economics at Merrill Lynch, "that John Chambers is Cisco's best salesperson. He speaks with a passion and an enthusiasm that rivals the best salespeople out there; but he also does it in such a sincere fashion. He gets you to believe in a story. He convinces you he has the best solution. He has a great balance of being aggressive in terms of closing the deal but not being obnoxious about it."

Even when no sale seems in the offing, he goes into salesman mode, talking passionately about Cisco, about information technology, about networking, about the Internet. When talking one-on-one with some, he has his salesman hat on: What would constitute a win for you? he asks. What do you want to achieve from our conversation? Robert Peters, the founding vice president of marketing at Cisco, saw Chambers the salesman up close: "Brutal may be not the right choice of words. I would say: pervasive, all-encompassing. He takes no chances.

He gets it scripted. He manages the situation at all levels. He knows exactly what's going on. He is very, very effective at sales management."

Indeed, John Chambers is always selling. One classic story has him 20 minutes late for his first board meeting as CEO; he was late because he had been on the phone with a distraught user. At first, the rest of the board grimaced at his tardiness, but when he explained why he was late, they told him he could use that excuse anytime. On another occasion, during an interview with a reporter from *Fortune* magazine, he left a Cisco conference room to make a telephone call that had been previously scheduled—to Microsoft's Bill Gates. A Cisco partner had given Chambers a strong sales lead that the Cisco president wanted to pass on to Gates. Again, Chambers was "selling"—hoping that Gates would one day reciprocate.

Chambers was considered Cisco's top salesman. Cisco executives were always eager to invite him to a customer meeting, and often he made the difference in closing a deal. Competitors wished he would be less aggressive. Carly Fiorina did not meet John Chambers until after she became the CEO at Hewlett-Packard in the summer of 1999. But she had certainly known of him. When she was president of Lucent Technologies' Global Service Provider Business, Cisco Systems, in the person of John Chambers, was her most serious competitor. Lucent and Cisco competed for the business from telecommunication service providers, who wanted to build up their networks. "John," Fiorina began, "was this almost mythic character I competed against. I always knew where he was and he knew where I was because we literally followed each other into customer meetings. It seemed to me he was almost everywhere. I knew him by competing against him. I knew that he was a relentless competitor, charming, persistent, and that the combination could be very disarming and he was really tough to beat." Fiorina could tell whether Chambers had already been to a customer: "The customer's behavior changed after John Chambers had been to visit. We suddenly had a harder fight. The competitive landscape had changed. You could feel it. You could see it every time he went in." As for the results, Fiorina says: "I won some, I lost some."

For Chambers, the frenetic motion and pace seemed designed to send a message to colleagues. Tireless himself, he expected others to be equally or almost as tireless: "It's a work-hard culture. Don't come here unless you want to work hard and you enjoy it because that's not going to change." Chambers made no secret of presiding over a pressure-cooker environment, where the high-performing executives stayed and the laggards left. There was pressure to nail customers, to finalize deals, to detect market trends and transitions, to acquire, partner, or invest in the right businesses—not just to put in a long day, but to make sure that Cisco's numbers were always on the rise. That meant vendor financing; that meant getting every possible chunk of revenue on the eve of a quarter's closing; that meant never considering a customer's no as final.

With all that pressure, why didn't Cisco executives run out the door to less demanding jobs elsewhere in Silicon Valley? One way Chambers kept executives around was by offering them a good deal of valuable Cisco stock options, and then insisting that they not leave. On promoting them, he made it a condition that they stick around at Cisco for at least two years: "If you put someone in a position and they leave in the first six to 12 months, the damage you do to the company is huge." To Chambers, the worst thing an executive can do is to go over to a competitor and then seek to hurt Cisco: "I think it's wrong. I would never hurt my family. Most of my senior management team would never work for a competitor."

Empowering, decentralizing, cheerleading, relying on the technology as a fail-safe mechanism, John Chambers genuinely believed that he had built a disciplined organization. At least, he wanted to believe it. It was an organization, he believed firmly, that was flourishing and was well within its tolerances for making a safe landing should the economy begin to weaken.

He loved being tested. He couldn't wait for the next challenge. He was supremely confident that he and Cisco Systems would weather it.

2 The 100-Year Flood

Year after year, John Chambers rode the Cisco growth engine to glory. No one delivered better news to Wall Street; Cisco's revenues were soaring. When Cisco surpassed General Electric and Microsoft to become the most valuable company in the world in March 2000, *Fortune* magazine asked about Chambers: "Is he the best CEO in the world?"

Year after year, Cisco continued to sell more fancy equipment for the Internet. The demand appeared insatiable. For 43 quarters in a row the company met or beat Wall Street's expectations for higher earnings. The media swooned over John Chambers, as illustrated by this comment from *Business Week* on August 28, 2000: "An unabashed evangelist for radical changes in management, he has made his company a living laboratory for the 21st century corporation. When observers speak about a new, progressive business model for a new era, they inevitably put Cisco at or near the top of their lists."

John Chambers wanted to build the greatest business growth machine in history. He spoke calmly about Cisco reaching $50 billion in revenues in a few years; he unabashedly forecast that the company would become the first with a trillion-dollar market value. These statements came in the fall of 2000. He repeated them frequently. It was beyond his imagination that anything could derail the chugging locomotive.

Since it had gone public on February 16, 1990, Cisco Systems had been growing by more than 40 percent each year save for 1998, when it grew by a "mere" 31 percent.

For much of 2000, all had seemed right on the course for another marvelous year at Cisco. Its revenues and profits soared. Revenues rose impressively each quarter of that year: $3.9 billion for the first quarter, $4.4 billion for the second, $4.9 billion for the third.

On August 8, 2000, Cisco reported a 61 percent rise in sales, to $5.72 billion, for its fourth quarter. The stock closed at $65.50 that day. Chambers was, as usual, decidedly upbeat: "We predicted five years ago that we were in the midst of a Second Industrial Revolution that would determine the prosperity of companies, countries, and individuals. Today, the Internet continues to drive the strongest U.S. economy in history. We see no indications in the marketplace that the radical Internet business transformation in practices like customer service, supply-chain management, employee training, empowerment, and E-commerce that is taking place around the world today is slowing—in fact, we believe it is accelerating globally." Annual revenue for 2000 reached $18.9 billion.

Nothing that happened over most of the August through November quarter dispelled Chambers's wildly optimistic forecasts. Cisco's revenue soared 66 percent to $6.5 billion, and profits raced 67 percent upward to $1.4 billion over the same period a year earlier. On November 6, Cisco beat analysts' earnings estimates by a penny a share for the 13th consecutive quarter. The stock closed at $55.13 that day as Cisco urged analysts to raise their revenue and profit estimates.

In November, Cisco was predicting that its fiscal 2001 revenues would grow 50 to 60 percent over fiscal 2000 revenues. Through much of November, Cisco's equipment orders appeared normally brisk. Revenue growth rates year over year hit 70 percent. Though certain segments of the American economy displayed weakness,

Chambers saw no worrying signs for Cisco. "If each time that had occurred," said Chambers, "we had put on the brakes and watched for a couple of quarters, we would not be where we are." The service-provider sector was softening because phone companies had clearly overbought, benefiting Cisco and others. Cisco vice chairman Don Valentine observed that "what we never understood in the first quarter or even the second quarter of 2001 was how significantly the phone companies had overbought."

For Cisco, all seemed smooth sailing. Its revenues for the second quarter of 2001 reached $6.7 billion, and the company appeared headed for a possible $30 billion revenue year. Cisco board members, representing such major American corporations as Hewlett-Packard, Applied Materials, and Airtouch, reported to Chambers that things were maybe a bit slower, but no one sensed any imminent danger.

By his own admission, John Chambers never imagined that Cisco might face a disastrous, sudden setback. Worst-case scenario: no more than a 5 to 15 percent downtick in Cisco's mind-boggling revenue and earnings growth from quarter to quarter. CFO Larry Carter simply assumed that any economic downturn would be gradual and that Cisco would enjoy plenty of advance warning, as much as a quarter or two.

In the 10 years since Chambers had joined Cisco, the slowest revenue growth he had suffered was 3.5 percent, in the second quarter of 2001 and the third quarter of 1997. Cisco had never experienced negative growth.

TOO LITTLE GRUMBLING

In late November, though his own business was enjoying a 70 percent revenue increase that month, Chambers began to hear uneasy noises from Cisco customers that their businesses were drying up; they were being forced to defer capital investments. Chambers was not unduly fazed: he simply urged his staff to shift gears by searching for revenues more aggressively abroad.

Then came the week of December 4. Equipment orders showed the first indications of weakness. Rumors spread that Cisco would be forced to scale back on its yearly estimates. The stock fell 3 points. Chambers was troubled by Cisco's excessive lead times in product delivery: The normal one to three weeks had stretched out ominously to six to 15 weeks. Even more troubling to Chambers was the lack of customer grumbling about those lengthy lead times. The absence of such grumbling meant only one thing: demand for Cisco product was evaporating; customers were shopping elsewhere or not at all.

On December 4, Chambers appeared in front of 500 analysts at a Cisco-sponsored conference in a San Jose hotel. Cisco orders had dipped 10 percent that day. But Cisco often encountered order swings of 30 to 50 percent in a day, so Chambers saw little cause for alarm. He confidently told the audience that Cisco was not changing estimates: "The key is how you take advantage of that, rather than how you play defense. We do better in the tough transitions. During economic downturns, we gain market share."

Buoyed by those November sales figures, Chambers predicted that Cisco would have 24 product groups each generating more than $1 billion in annual sales in 18 to 24 months—an increase over the 12 product lines that currently produced that much revenue. Still, ominous storm clouds were gathering. For the next five days—through December 8—Cisco's orders were off 10 percent on a daily average. While this was only slightly below normal, Chambers began to take notice of a fearful trend: "I wasn't concerned," Chambers told me, "but it had happened five days in a row." Over the next week, Chambers called fellow CEOs. What they had to say was "surprising, almost startling. Seventy percent of the CEOs used the same words. 'My business hit a wall. It went off a cliff.' It was like somebody turned off the light switch." More distressing than any of this to Chambers was the failure of Fed chairman Alan Greenspan to cut interest rates sharply.

A wrenching truth was beginning to surface. That truth was linked to the storm clouds over the American economy, the CEOs pulling back on capital investment, and Cisco's orders displaying continuing weakness.

John Chambers sensed that the time had come to put the brakes on the Cisco growth machine.

December 15. Calling his senior management team, Chambers gloomily forecast that Cisco revenues could be off in the next quarter by perhaps $1 billion to $1.5 billion. Chambers decided to impose an immediate "soft freeze" on matters such as hiring, discretionary spending, and inventory. Leaders of each segment of the business were given until January 2 to come up with a plan for slowing hiring dramatically and removing discretionary spending. Through the end of December, orders remained "pretty good," in Chambers's phrase. He was still hoping that those five days in December were a mere aberration. Chambers instructed his colleagues to keep a close watch on events for the next 45 to 60 days.

In early January 2001, John Chambers grew defensive. He had a hard time figuring out why the company's sales had simply dried up. When the stock was at its highest point ($80 a share) ever in March 2000, he had asked analysts what Cisco should do to alter its strategies, if anything.

Don't change a thing, they told him.

He listened.

Projecting that Cisco would grow at a 33 percent clip, the analysts fell way short: for the first quarter of 2001, announced in November 2000, the company doubled that forecast, coming in with a 66 percent revenue increase.

That's what made Chambers so defensive early in 2001.

Told not to alter his strategies, he went along, doubling growth estimates only to find that the roof was falling in.

Cisco Systems had weathered troubled times before: in the early 1990s senior executives worried that the company might be devoured by its competitors. But what happened to Cisco Systems early in 2001, the sudden, pernicious effects of a full-blown American recession, was different from past bumps in the road, for it occurred in the full glare of public light, magnifying the company's troubles into a shocking, wrenching, and worst of all, enduring crisis.

Every John Chambers utterance regarding the quickening economic collapse produced a headline, as did every step taken by Cisco in response to the dramatic downturn. Whereas once Cisco had been the bellwether of good times for the high-tech world, now it became a symbol of high-tech wreckage. Yet no one trotted out doomsday scenarios for the company. It was far too resilient, much too safely ensconced as Internet king for such scenarios to make sense. No one trotted out doomsday scenarios for John Chambers either. The Cisco board stood solidly behind him and supported his recovery efforts. Rather than needle Chambers about the setback, board members like Don Valentine and John Morgridge sought to comfort him and to offer friendly advice on how to speed the company's recovery.

Given the sagging economy, any public utterance from John Chambers was listened to attentively. Chambers was watching product orders in early January and still holding out hope that Cisco would weather the growing storm. But by the second week of that month, Cisco was directly in the storm's eye.

On January 10, appearing before Morgan Stanley's Internet, Software, and Networking Conference in Scottsdale, he gave the impression that he was trying to avoid Wall Street's concluding that Cisco had "missed" its quarter. He still felt comfortable with the quarter.

A LITTLE BIT MORE CHALLENGING

The company's second quarter of 2001, closing in on January 27, appeared, in Chambers's words, "a little bit more challenging" than expected. Disclosing that Cisco had begun to slow its hiring pace, he warned, "Our visibility isn't as good as it normally is." That proved an understatement. Chambers had always told his senior executives that the one thing he didn't want in business was to be surprised. This time he was surprised, and most unpleasantly. For the last two weeks of January, "our orders hit the wall," in Chambers's words. It was exactly as his customers had described. Cisco was in the eye of the storm.

When disaster struck in the form of a sharp, sudden economic downturn in the United States, John Chambers believed that Cisco Systems would be immune to the tailspin. When he began to understand that even the mighty Cisco could not escape the effects of the downturn, he compared what had happened to the U.S. economy to a "100-year flood." To make it clear how sudden and unusual and cataclysmic was this event, he turned to nature and the Bible for an apt metaphor.

On Saturday, January 27, shortly before midnight, Cisco prepared to close its second-quarter books. Analysts expected a profit of 19 cents per share. Cisco was scrambling. At the company's main San Jose warehouse that evening, employees were rushing to load as many boxed-up machines onto trucks as they could. CFO Larry Carter monitored the situation from a computer terminal in the warehouse that was counting the shipments in real time. One employee fell on the floor in full view of the CFO.

Ten minutes before midnight, Chambers called Carter's cell phone from Davos, Switzerland, where he was speaking at an economic summit.

"Did we make it?" Chambers asked.

Carter took a few more minutes to look at the numbers. Then he gave him the unfortunate news. For the first time in 11 years, Cisco had been below expectations—by a penny per share.

On the day that the quarter closed, Chambers, in an interview with the *International Herald Tribune*, urged American economic policymakers to act more decisively and speedily to stabilize the economy, which was slowing, he said, "faster than most people realize." He also predicted, though, that the turnaround would be "quicker, assuming the government moves with speed on tax cuts, including payroll tax cuts that are retroactive." Three days later, he was forced to admit to the *Wall Street Journal* that "we may not be as affected [as others] in the first or second waves of cutting" by companies of their tech spending, "but we will be affected."

Chambers candidly acknowledged that Cisco's revenues would probably drop as much as 30 percent for the year. "We were growing one day at 70 percent and within 45 days we were experiencing a negative growth rate. It didn't happen over three or four months, it happened immediately."

On February 6, Cisco announced its second-quarter results. Reporting its earnings per share at 18 cents, a penny short of the Street's 19-cent estimate, Cisco for the first time under Chambers had missed a quarter. "I had $300 million on the shop floor," Chambers noted sorrowfully. "I just couldn't get it through." The reason: a supplier had delivered a key product to him the last month of the quarter, when it had been promised earlier in the quarter.

Only one other time had Cisco missed an estimate, but that was prior to Chambers's ascension to power. It happened in the April 1994 quarter, when Cisco made its earnings-per-share forecast estimate but was a little light on revenue growth. Revenues had been forecast to grow at 11 percent quarter over quarter but came in at only 9.6 percent because of a halt in Japanese spending.

For that second quarter of 2001, Cisco's net sales rose a very healthy 55 percent, to $6.75 billion, compared with $4.36 billion for the same period the year before. Those revenues, however, were some $400 million below some analysts' targets. Cisco's earnings growth rate for that quarter rose by 48 percent. Impressive figures on paper, but short of Wall Street's expectations, and so the grim news sent the stock falling by $4.69, or 13 percent, to $31.06.

Chambers's view was that if this "bump in the road" was no worse than a two-quarter event, Cisco might still be able to achieve its 30 to 50 percent revenue growth target for the year. Still, analysts now predicted that Cisco's 2001 revenues would climb to only $26.4 billion, and not the once-expected $30 billion. In the end, revenues were $22.2 billion for 2001.

Chambers remained confident about market opportunities for Cisco over the next three to five years, but at the same time he changed his sales-growth projections, from 50 to 60 percent for Cisco's 2001 estimate down to 40 percent. On a conference call to analysts, Chambers acknowledged that Cisco was slowing, though not freezing, its head count. Rather than the expected 4,000 new hires for the third quarter, the figure would drop to 1,500.

While the company had committed itself to cutting discretionary spending, Chambers eventually realized that with such a large portion of variable expenses related to people, Cisco would have to trim employees.

I WOULD HAVE DONE ANYTHING

The news was so devastating that Chambers felt he had no choice but to consider layoffs.

As noted earlier, he had made it a personal goal to avoid the kind of layoffs that he had been forced to organize while at Wang Laboratories. He could not imagine that he would ever have to do it: "I, probably more than anyone else in this company, would have done anything to avoid ever doing a layoff again. I thought I never would have to. I thought I had the productivity high enough, the cash high enough; a disastrous quarter would have been down 5 percent, and we could have easily handled that without adjustments this way."

If he was going to do the layoffs, he promised himself, he would not do them halfheartedly, and then be forced to do a second or even a third round. He would take out 20 percent of the company in one sweeping decision and get it done with. Only then, he thought, would Cisco have a chance of getting close to a profit for 2001, given how precipitously revenues had dropped.

In early March, after key economic leaders in the United States told him that the slowdown would last at least another two to four quarters, he decided on the layoffs. He decided to fire 5,400 full-time and 2,500 part-time employees. It marked the first time that Cisco had been forced to dismiss employees. John Chambers called the day he took the decision the saddest of his career.

Chambers tried to put a good face on the dismissals. They were, he insisted, the most generous in the history of Silicon Valley (probably true, as employees were given six months' severance pay when the norm was one to three months'). He allowed dismissed employees to exercise vested stock options—worthless in that spring of 2001—for one year after they left the company.

When I spoke to Chambers six weeks after he had announced the first-ever layoffs at Cisco, I asked him if he felt depressed or frustrated.

No, not at all, he replied. Depression was simply not in his vocabulary. "I never get depressed. My dad helped to develop this in me. It's a philosophy. You deal with the world the way it is, and if you know what it is, whether it's an illness, or a business problem, or a personal problem, then you deal with it, and I'm very good at it. I have said often: The leader gets too much credit when it goes well and absolutely too much of the blame when it goes the other way. But that's life. So the blame, while it hurts, I knew would come. . . .

"But the only part that hurts, and it really hurts, and it's disappointing, and it was a personal failure, was the layoffs. It hurts. It hurts really bad. That's the part that churns at me and churns in my stomach. It was the part that I'm up running at 5:30 A.M. on the running machine, and have been running every day since then until we get through this. I normally run in proportion to how much I'm eating. I've been running every day for the last two months. It's the way I handle stress."

I mentioned to Chambers that others, such as Jack Welch, were less emotional when dismissing people, saying that it was the only choice.

"You don't have any choice, but at the same time I never want to rationalize that I missed a personal goal. This is one of those that is absolutely the right business decision to make. You've got to be aggressive. You've got to be decisive. You've got to make it happen. And you've got to tell people why you're doing it. But by the same token I almost never miss any goals, either business or personal. This is a personal goal that I missed.

"I'd be hard-pressed to think of one that I failed on. I knew I was never going to get an A in English. So a personal goal was a C-plus or a B. And I was satisfied with that. If I got anything less than an A in math that would be a personal goal I missed the other way. So I very rarely miss personal goals and have never missed on a personal goal that I can think of."

He had constantly vowed that he would do whatever was required to avoid, as his former employers IBM and Wang had not, letting people go. But when he made that vow, it seemed safe enough. Cisco was virtually printing money, and the very notion that the company would be forced to lay off employees seemed absurd. Then the "100-year flood" arrived, and try as he might, Chambers saw no way but to forge ahead with layoffs. The distressing turn of events gnawed at him. He could not forget how quickly Cisco had grown in recent years. Nor could he erase from his memory how much he had worked to gain employee loyalty. And now he would have to send some of them home. He believed that the economy was to blame, but he could not help but feel that somehow he had personally been responsible as well: "It was a personal failure to do the layoffs. When I set goals, you either make them or you don't. I said I won't do a layoff in my life. That was my goal. We set goals. And we missed this one."

It was 1:30 P.M. in San Jose on Friday, April 13, 2001, when John Chambers greeted me on the telephone with his usual friendly and enthusiastic hello. This conversation was bound to be different from the previous five we had held. He told me that he had reduced his yearly salary to a dollar a year "until we get this turned around." Reluctantly, the board agreed. Chairman John Morgridge followed suit.

When it came to the bonuses for the first half of the year, Chambers asked 700 employees at a birthday breakfast whether they felt executives should forgo them or perhaps take only half as much. Bonuses for most Cisco personnel depend on the company's meeting its revenue goals, customer satisfaction, and a few other metrics. Chambers noted that the company had "barely" missed those goals, by only 1 to 2 percent. He suggested paying half the bonus. He and his vice presidents would not get bonuses. Nearly everyone there voted to pay half.

It is May 8, 2001, a sad day for Chambers and his company: he delivers the earnings conference call. For the first time since it went public in 1990, Cisco reports a year-over-year sales drop. There are other dismal figures: even after the huge $2.2 billion write-down of excess parts, the inventory grew 60 percent. The picture remains bleak, as a number of its high-tech customers from the dot-com world as well as new-age phone carriers (which contributed 20 percent of Cisco's revenues in the second half of 2000) are going bankrupt.

With no other choice, John Chambers briefly reduced his public schedule. No longer did he meet with as many political leaders. He made few speeches. He declined many requests for media interviews. He issued few press releases. He knew that Wall Street was eager to hear from him on when the American economy and Cisco might turn around; but faced with such a dismal near future, Chambers chose to retreat into silence.

In a few short months, Chambers became a shell of the once mighty figure that we all had seen, devoting all of his energy to running his troubled company. He confessed that the period from January to May 2001 was the worst time of his career. It was supposed to be his best.

3 Grinding to a Halt: Who Is to Blame?

When I was shown around the Cisco Systems headquarters in San Jose, California, and watched John Chambers in action during the fall of 2000, the place had the feel of success. The late-model cars in the parking lots, the smiles on the employees' faces, the Cisco annual reports with their bulging growth statistics on the tables in the reception area—all reflected the magical ride that the 40,000 employees were on.

No one uttered a critical word against Chambers or against Cisco Systems. Quite the opposite. *Fortune* magazine, in its May 14, 2000, edition, was absolutely fawning: "On the way up to a stock market value of half a trillion dollars, everything about Cisco seemed perfect. It had a perfect CEO. It could close its books in a day and make perfect financial forecasts. It was an acquisitions machine, ingesting companies and their technologies with great aplomb. It was the leader of the new economy, selling gear to new-world telecom companies that would use it to supplant old-world carriers and make their old-world suppliers irrelevant."

A number of business leaders who knew John Chambers asked—always privately, never publicly—how Cisco was pulling off such incredible growth rates year after year. "When I listened to these people talk, it really lacked credibility with me," said one CEO. "No business is going to grow at 30 percent for more than four or five years. The question is: Are you building something that is really sustainable? I would listen to John tell me: 'Oh, we're buying a company every weekend. We close them in four days.' I asked myself: Are they that much brighter than I am?" Chambers would have been better off, he said, being "really disciplined," pursuing growth, but keeping one foot on the brake, or at least knowing where the brake pedal was. "So you don't talk about the fact that you can close your books in three nanoseconds, and then suddenly you have to write off billions of dollars of inventory. Hello?"

As John Chambers's 100-year flood began to wash over Cisco, the same Wall Street analysts and the same journalists at *Business Week* and *Fortune* who had gushed over Chambers and Cisco now wondered: What exactly happened to Cisco? Why did it fall so precipitously? What happened to its systems that were supposed to stave off disaster? How could John Chambers one day be the King of the Internet, and the next, its fallen idol? How could his seemingly foolproof vision suddenly and disastrously go awry?

Many guessed at the answers, but few could really fathom what had truly happened. All around Cisco, the high-tech world had been buffeted by slowdowns in discretionary spending, but most analysts had simply assumed that Cisco would escape being sucked into the vortex. After all, it had attained almost mythological status as the king of the high-tech world, the world's most valuable company for a brief period in March 2000. Just a year later its market value had plummeted by $430 billion in one of the most severe sell-offs in Wall Street history.

THE POSTER CHILD

It would take a while—at first the analysts and journalists were too shocked to ask many questions—but in time Chambers and Cisco were drawn into the spotlight and subjected to sharp scrutiny. The business world was clearly looking for an explanation. As John Chambers told me in September 2001: "We were the poster child of the Internet economy on the way up, and as it trips, we are the poster child when it got challenged." Chambers's neat attempt at euphemism—tripped, challenged—cannot disguise the remarkable chain of events that caused his vision to go awry.

The Chambers vision was to drive Cisco Systems to unparalleled hypergrowth by riding the marvelous new business tool, the Internet. In setting out that vision, Chambers promised that Cisco would help change the way we work, play, learn, and have fun—in short, the way we live. Fueled by his own irrepressible charm and a "sky's the limit" conviction about the company's growth potential, Chambers predicted that Cisco would become the first trillion-dollar market-cap company in the world. At the time, few scoffed at this prediction.

As I probed Cisco that fall of 2000, trying to pinpoint the success factors that turbocharged Cisco into the heavens, I listened to John Chambers explain that it was the sum total of Cisco's 12 business strategies—especially its reliance on listening to customers, developing a quality team, empowering staffers, and meeting stretch goals—that explained the company's success. Taken together, these strategies embodied the Cisco culture, which Chambers boasted was a prerequisite for becoming a great company. By the time I sat down with John Chambers that fall, he had received every imaginable accolade, and the media were speculating on whether he might not be the best CEO in America. However important the Cisco culture and strategies were in Chambers's eyes, to many outsiders it was John Chambers himself who was the determinant of Cisco's success.

To certain cynics, however, neither Chambers nor the culture he had spawned could satisfactorily explain Cisco's achievements. Rather, luck played a determining role: Cisco had simply been in the right place at the right time, making routers and switches for a market that in the mid-1990s took off dramatically because of the sudden arrival of the Internet.

Whatever was the true cause of Cisco's success, almost no one believed that Cisco might suffer a setback in the near future. As long as the projections of Internet users over the next five years or so panned out, as long as the demand for broadband continued to increase, it was a no-brainer that Cisco was unstoppable.

Indeed, much of Cisco's growth plans depended on the Internet's flourishing. At first, that had been a given. Although in its infancy in the mid-1990s, the Internet quickly came to be regarded as the greatest business tool of our era. Investors poured millions of dollars into Internet business ventures that often lacked any prospect of turning profits. Yet the bubble grew and grew.

In early 1993, the Internet had 1 million computers attached to it. By early 1995, there were more than 27,000 Web sites, with the number doubling every two months. In time, the forecasts for the Internet went off the charts: Forrester Research, an interpreter of Internet trends, estimated that on-line advertising would jump from an estimated $37 million in 1995 to $700 million three years later; Forrester soon raised its forecast for 1998 to $1 billion. In June 1997, the Internet had 35 million users, and the prediction was that the figure would rise to 150 million by 2000. As for the stock market, fueled by the high-tech bubble, some guessed that the Dow would reach 15,000 by 2005.

Internet euphoria reached its height in 1998. In 12 months, America Online's stock climbed 593 percent, Yahoo!'s jumped by 584 percent, and Amazon.com's stock went up 970 percent. Fueling the Internet boom were people like Henry Blodget, a stock analyst who on December 15, 1998, issued a $400 price target for Amazon.com when it was trading at $242; other analysts considered even that latter price absurd. By the summer of 1999, commentators were suggesting that the Dow was going to reach 20,000, 30,000, or perhaps 40,000.

High tech was the chief catalyst for the economic boom. Since 1995, spending had been growing at a 15 to 20 percent clip a year on computers, software, and networking equipment; high tech accounted for some one-third of all economic growth.

As already noted, by the year 2000, over 75 percent of all Internet traffic traveled over Cisco products, and the future looked bright. But even as demand remained high for Cisco's products in early 2000 and it appeared that the Internet bubble would last a good long time, seething under the surface was a new reality. The dot-com bubble was collapsing, and the frenzy among big businesses to incorporate the Internet was beginning to fizzle.

It took only until early 2000 for commentators to figure out that many Internet companies were likely to close down within a year simply because they were making no money and fast running out of cash. In one week, $2 trillion of stock market wealth was wiped out; the Internet bubble had burst. And indeed over the next year or so, numerous dot-coms simply vanished.

The glowing forecasts of Internet growth shrank overnight, and few believed that the Internet would grow at the speedy rate that had once been predicted.

The effect of the dot-com collapse on large corporations was enormous. Vacillating about whether to invest in the Internet, CEOs and CIOs now believed that the most prudent maneuver was to spend as little as possible on Internet infrastructure. Few companies would be as negatively affected by such a decision as Cisco Systems.

When the U.S. economy, and the world economy soon after that, came to a near-abrupt halt in the winter of 2000–2001, it seemed reasonable for John Chambers to assert, as he did, that Cisco got caught flat-footed by a turn of events that could not possibly be predicted. What he meant was that as long as technology and Wall Street analysts agreed that the Internet would grow substantially in the next few years, there was every reason to believe that Cisco's existing and potential customers would invest heavily in high-tech gear.

A heady euphoria set in. I saw it everywhere that fall, on the faces of Cisco executives, on the faces of its rivals, on the faces of Wall Street analysts. At Cisco, the growth opportunities seemed endless. It was simply left to the vaunted Cisco sales force to pick and choose which ones to pursue. Of course it wasn't as simple as that, but all that market demand kept the Cisco sales force busy, and no one running the show thought it wise or prudent to suggest putting the brakes on. Indeed, Cisco's growth machine worked overtime: there were people to hire, campuses to build, start-ups to purchase. The mantra was "growth, growth, growth." Catch the market opportunities as they fall from the sky. No one ever dreamed that it might rain.

For Chambers, the whole experience proved exasperating. He believes that he did behave reflectively, but the advice he got from the experts was not to change course: "Whenever we asked people what we could be doing differently, they said: 'You're executing perfectly.' That actually made me uncomfortable because too many people were saying that. Whenever everyone's in agreement, it's wrong." But armed with that advice, he chose not to apply the brakes. Although the Internet collapse was taking place for all to see during the year 2000, Chambers saw the orders still coming in to Cisco and chose to believe that everything would be all right.

Chambers believes that, if anything, it was his conservatism that got Cisco into trouble: "Some of the issues that I've been doing, like keeping my foot on the brake, about inventory levels, about how fast we could grow, etc., actually were what contributed a little bit to our problem. Because I went for six quarters being too conservative on the inventory, being too conservative on my manufacturing capability, and it cost us business. We were growing great but it was costing us business because our lead times were way too long; our competitors were taking advantage of that. When I finally said all right, let's get our capacity up to what the run rate is, even though to me it was abnormally high, it was fine for two quarters, I gained market share, but then two quarters later, when the market turned down, I had too much inventory, too much capacity, and too many people."

A LITTLE BIT EXUBERANT

Hindsight, as they say, is always 20/20. Chambers wishes he could have behaved differently—now. But the simple reality was that no one wanted to believe that the U.S. economy would run out of steam. One veteran Wall Street analyst who has watched Cisco for years explained: "It would have been better, obviously, if Chambers and the others at Cisco could have seen it coming. They became a little bit too exuberant, like the rest of us. They chased too many opportunities. They got a little too—you know the expression? They were drinking their Kool-Aid. We were all doing it. They were no different. They were spending all that money on expensive companies because they supposedly offered the next technology, and then their technology didn't turn out."

Urging that Cisco prepare itself for a rainy day would have sounded blasphemous, the equivalent of a sports team pulling out its star players for most of the season so they would have longer careers. Nor could John Chambers imagine issuing an order to his sales force to slow down on taking orders. Euphoria always trumps a rainy-day philosophy.

John Chambers spent agonizing hours wrestling with the question of what had happened in late 2000 and early 2001. Publicly, he would eventually say that Cisco had been caught off guard, a victim of a 100-year flood. But clearly he was disappointed that he and Cisco had been brought to this stage: "We don't want to mislead anybody," he told me in September 2001. "It surprised us. Maybe it shouldn't have. It did. We've been through multiple periods of time when there was uncertainty in the market, and we took good business risk and moved through that uncertainty pretty effectively. In this uncertainty we planned for a 100-year flood maybe being up to the first floor and a couple of feet around the house, and we had the sandbags in place."

For Chambers, the frustration came from the fact that everyone at Cisco had come to believe in the company's infallibility. That left the Cisco team open for a sucker punch. Chambers said the only way to avoid being caught off guard is to face reality—which Cisco simply did not do.

"You have to be realistic that a 100-year flood does happen. And a 100-year flood does not mean a couple of feet around the house that we handle with sandbags, because that's what we had—remember, this is a company that never achieved not only a negative quarter sequentially but never grew slower than three and a half percent sequentially, and so if I were to tell my CFO that we might have a down 5 percent quarter he would have died of a heart attack. [He laughs a little.] And if I had told him down 10 percent, he would have said that was mathematically impossible. Well, we went from 70 percent growth to −30 percent growth momentum in 45 days. No company that I'm aware of in history has ever had the sustained growth and then had something like that occur."

He was also taken aback by the fickleness of the business media, one day praising Cisco as the darling of the Internet business world, the next finding fault with its leadership and strategies.

"What was surprising about the media criticism was the move on the personal. We never anticipated that, and maybe we should have. We now understand that's part of life. Some of the comments were pretty brutal.

"But that goes with the territory. I was particularly surprised by some of the media that should have known us—who were saying one month we're the best, and then the next month saying this company doesn't get it. But they missed it too. And so we're all on a learning curve. You don't take it as personal. And you've just got to realize that it's part of the job. And realize you'll get more positive [comments] when things go well and more negative when it goes the other way [than you deserve]. And be prepared that they will make it personal."

WHO IS AT FAULT?

When it became clear to Chambers that the economy was faltering and it was beginning to affect Cisco, he asked himself a very tough question: Was the economy truly at fault, or had he been at least in part responsible? "Was it a macroeconomic capital-spending question or was it something you were doing yourself?"

He took time analyzing what had gone wrong "to be sure that it was largely inflicted by others, not by ourselves. And you really want to look closely internally to make sure it wasn't yourself because remember, there were people saying this was Cisco doing it to themselves. And you don't want to say just, 'They were wrong.' You want to say, 'Let's understand what the criticism is and weigh it.' Then we backed up and we said, 'No, we think this is an industry phenomenon. We think it is the 100-year flood. We think it's going to be much longer than people anticipate. Much tougher, and here's how we're going to react.' And we got second-guessed for that. It was very hard at the time."

He decided that the troubles had to do largely with the sharp decrease in capital spending, a by-product of the weakening economy. That led him to one key conclusion: "If it's a macroeconomic, capital-spending issue, you don't change strategy."

Once he concluded that Cisco's distress was due to the faltering economy, he felt there was no need to alter any of the company's strategies. Nonetheless, some adjustment was necessary.

And so he did not blame himself. He suggested that he had reflected on the company's behavior and had found himself and the company blameless. He turned Cisco into the role of victim, indicating that a biblical act of nature—a 100-year flood—had overwhelmed the U.S. economy and brought everyone, including Cisco, down. Chambers was saying: Hey, floods and earthquakes happen. When they do, they sometimes kill people. Don't blame us for not preventing the flood.

On the surface, it sounded reasonable. And during the Monday-morning quarterbacking, a number of Wall Street analysts, whose once-glowing forecasts now made them look starry-eyed, rushed to Chambers's defense. He could not have known. He could not have diverted the flood. He could not be held accountable for an economy that suddenly collapsed. The analysts had projected great things for Cisco's future, never suggesting that the Cisco growth machine was churning too fast and might benefit from pulling back a little. They had been caught up in the euphoria as well. When you're euphoric, you're not looking for or preparing for a sudden flood.

. . .

John Chambers had a vision that high tech was here to stay, that the Internet was the great new business tool of the age, that business executives in the United States and around the world could only benefit from investing in and taking advantage of this new Internet-based world.

For one glorious moment—which lasted five years or so—the Chambers vision took flight. The stars were aligned in such a way that Cisco Systems could do no wrong; it could only benefit from the Chambers vision. The vision produced the kind of hypergrowth for Cisco that led John Chambers and others to believe that the rocket ride would last forever. Cisco had all the right tools, the right attitude, and the right strategies to make it work forever. There was no need to question, no need to second-guess, no need to take a big, deep breath, certainly no need to pause.

Indeed, so the argument went around Cisco, for as long as the public wanted Cisco's products in such great quantities, it would have been foolish to behave cautiously. Companies who are too conservative, John Chambers likes to say, don't survive.

He became exceedingly comfortable with Cisco's enormous growth rates, convincing himself that he would always be able to cushion the blows of economic downturns. He always believed there would be sufficient warning, as did CFO Larry Carter, who, as noted earlier, confidently believed that any slowdown would take one to two quarters.

When the downturn came in the dreary winter of 2000–2001, Chambers, at least at first, decided that little could have been done about it. The growth machine had to be fed and fueled. Not to do so would have been perilous. And yet, in retrospect, there were warnings that trouble of some sort was looming.

But only in retrospect do the warnings look like flashing red lights. At the time they were shrouded in fog, not visible to the naked eye. Only a few people on Wall Street paid attention to one warning sign—the gradual shrinking of Cisco's free cash flow beginning soon after the stock peaked in March 2000, even as revenue and EPS growth were accelerating.

The fact was that Cisco required more and more cash to run its business. As the Internet bubble grew—the funding at any cost of Internet carriers—Cisco had to put more money into vendor financing, inventories, receivables, and capital expenditures to fuel the growth. With the scarcity of components and a lack of manufacturing capacity among its contract manufacturers, Cisco had to hold much more inventory to meet its production schedule.

The scheduling became a nightmare.

Analysts barely took notice of the diminishing free cash flow. "We all just assumed it was needed for growth," said one—noting, nevertheless, that there were a sufficient number of investors who *did* worry, and that as a result the stock kept dropping through the spring, summer, and fall of 2000.

A FLASHING RED LIGHT

Another flashing red light was vendor financing. It was a symptom of the Internet bubble. Starting in 1999, Cisco began lending money to help create a new carrier market based on the Internet Protocol concept. These IP carriers would compete head-on against the traditional phone carriers. Unable to obtain venture financing, they turned to their vendors for help, especially Lucent, Nortel, and Cisco.

There was nothing unusual about vendor financing; it had always been a part of large equipment purchases or leasing. What was unusual was that the new telecommunications start-ups began using vendor financing as venture capital. If the market was so good, Cisco should not have had to provide seed money for these companies. It was certainly a sign of strain that Cisco was operating at the margins and that it was being overly optimistic about its growth projections.

Cisco acknowledges spending $1.5 billion to finance these projects. When the crunch came and most of the start-up carriers went under, Cisco avoided a bigger nightmare by virtue of CFO Larry

Carter's strategy of not recognizing any revenue until the carriers paid Cisco. Because they recognized revenue much earlier, Lucent and Nortel got into much more trouble with vendor financing than did Cisco. Still, when the start-ups went under, Cisco was forced to take back the equipment in order to resell it, settling for 20 to 40 cents to the dollar. It was widely believed on Wall Street that Cisco would suffer large losses as a result of the downfall of the start-up carriers, but Larry Carter insists that Cisco lost no money. Still, the perception lingered that Cisco was employing all sorts of methods, including vendor financing, to feed its enormous growth, while that vendor financing itself was a sign that the market was not as robust as Cisco wanted to believe.

Whatever passed for warnings at the time, no one paid attention to them. Indeed, Cisco's positive outlook, based on presumed growing market demand, led the company down a path it would later regret. The excess demand encouraged Cisco's midlevel managers, empowered by John Chambers to act on their own, to double- and triple-order, incurring longer and longer lead times for delivery of Cisco's products. According to Larry Carter: "When you're trying to get so much market share, you're trying to meet customer needs, you may have a solution for one customer set that is what the customer wants; but it doesn't fit another customer, so you may create another platform for someone else that has the same functionality; one focuses on speed, another on quality of service; in an ideal world, you could have produced both products cheaper."

To deal with the longer lead times, Cisco built up a great deal of inventory.

The reason for the buildup of inventory had to do with the way Cisco manufactures its products. Cisco makes just 40 percent of its products. As for the rest, suppliers and contract manufacturers deliver Cisco-branded products directly to customers. The heavy emphasis on outsourcing was meant to reduce fixed costs, avoid the need for large inventory, and provide Cisco executives with real-time information on demand, shipments, and orders.

What the outsourcing model failed to take into account was customers who when tired of waiting lengthily for shipments, would double- and triple-order. To meet what seemed like genuine increased demand, Cisco started to stockpile parts and finished products in large quantities. It had to try to resolve a major dilemma: while its order rate was up 70 percent, its lead times had reached 12 to 13 weeks, five to six times what customers would tolerate. Not resolving the dilemma would mean losing lots of revenue. Plaguing Cisco were component manufacturers who were taking six months to provide their products. They themselves were having a hard time adjusting to excessive demand coming from a strengthened PC market and the fast-growing mobile wireless market. Stimulating further demand was the Y2K syndrome during that period.

The crunch came for Cisco when capital spending halted in late 2000 and the company was stocked with billions of dollars of inventory, which had grown much faster than sales. In April 2001, Cisco was forced to write off $2.2 billion of excess inventory and to cut 18 percent of its staff.

If the warning signs were actually in place, it was clear why Cisco was not heeding them. The very companies that were about to get into serious trouble, the dot-coms and telecom start-ups, were the great hopes in Cisco's hypergrowth plans. Even if some analysts were predicting flat spending on the part of the telecoms, large and small, Cisco kept seeing the orders coming in and did little worrying. The fact was that John Chambers and his senior colleagues were tracking the orders, but not other indicators that were telling a different, more ominous tale. Ron Ricci, Cisco's vice president for market positioning, was very candid in acknowledging that Cisco would have been much better off using a whole other set of metrics: "One tool we should have been tracking was debt load of the telephone communication service providers. That should have been a thermometer— how much debt have our customers taken on and how much has that affected us. If we had measured it, we would have known what was happening. It cut down investment. Operationalizing paranoia is something that is easier said than done. We operationalized different things."

Cisco saw the orders coming in and wanted to believe that the orders would continue endlessly. But there was, as it turned out, a serious problem with the nature of that demand.

Everyone, including the Cisco leadership, underestimated how much of the spending was frivolous, how much of it was based on what turned out to be excessively optimistic scenarios. These scenarios predicted that large numbers of people would be downloading videos from the Internet and using a cell phone with Internet access, and that many would want some kind of wireless device. A driving force in all of this was the immensely popular Napster music Web site (it once received as much as 13 percent of all Internet traffic).

The expectations over how much Napster and other sites like it might grow fueled a new wave of irrational exuberance. Many genuinely believed that millions of customers would want instant response times to the Internet and that consumers and advertisers would flock to the Internet.

But it eventually became apparent that it would be a long, long time before huge numbers of people would become serious customers of the Internet. Napster and a whole fleet of dot-com companies began to sink as the Internet bubble was fast deflating. As it did, CEOs began to lose the urgency they had felt—and Cisco had nurtured so effectively—to get on the Internet bandwagon.

Analysts were once projecting 13 to 15 percent a month growth for the Internet. But in October 2001, that projection dropped to 20 percent a year.

When Internet traffic projections did not materialize, some of Cisco's largest customers went under.

There are valuable lessons for business executives to mull over in looking at what happened to John Chambers's Cisco Systems. We will devote ample attention to these lessons later in the book, but we want to summarize some of the most important lessons at this stage.

The first lesson is that companies would benefit from adopting some sort of rainy-day strategy that would buffer them from the worst effects of a sudden stoppage of the national and world economies. Cisco Systems believed that a rainy-day strategy would hinder its march to growth; the very act of slowing down seemed an act of whimsy at a time when market demand for Cisco's products was so overwhelming. And yet, had Cisco heeded this lesson, it might have softened the harshest blows that were delivered to the company.

A corollary of this first lesson is to stay on the alert for a sudden deterioration in the economy. Cisco executives later acknowledged that they had simply not believed the economy would slow down so rapidly, so their strategies did not take into account that sales could drop overnight. Executives cannot afford to overlook such a prospect.

A second lesson to be gleaned from the Cisco experience is to avoid being too optimistic. Optimism can be an important business tool in seeking to convince Wall Street that you know what you are doing and are headed in the right direction; but it can trap you into adopting a mind-set that does not allow for sudden downturns in the economy.

Cisco's optimism was partly based on an excessively rosy belief in the infallibility of its forecasting systems. As it turned out, the company's forecasting capabilities, which it boasted about, looked very fallible indeed. And when the forecasts changed rapidly as the economy deteriorated in the winter of 2000–2001, Cisco found itself attacked by some who claimed that the company's systems for tracking business that had already been booked should have been able to accurately forecast the future as well. Nonetheless, there is a valuable lesson for business executives who are adopting forecasting technology: Take a hard look at what you are using, and check whether your systems are comprehensive enough to enable a fast, accurate read on sudden changes in the economy.

One of the most important lessons arising from Cisco's difficulties has to do with facing reality. John Chambers preached this lesson time and time again; yet, when the economy turned downward so drastically, he instantly drew the conclusion that the fault had been with macroeconomic forces, not with any defects within Cisco. Had Cisco faced reality, it might have asked probing questions: Why was it necessary to finance the telephone start-ups? Were they going to survive? What did the collapse of the dot-coms mean for Cisco? Later, as a healing process began, Chambers was able to acknowledge that Cisco had taken its eye off the ball in some important areas. Business executives can benefit greatly by acknowledging new realities on the business landscape and acting on them as quickly as possible.

One way to deal with reality is to make sure to use the proper metrics. Cisco's affection for growth led it to measure all the criteria that had to do with rising revenues. Meanwhile, it was not taking a close look at the measurements that would have shown danger looming on the horizon. Had it been looking at the right metrics, it would have spotted trouble much earlier.

To John Chambers, the explanation is straightforward: Fueled throughout the nineties by a seemingly unending hypergrowth, Cisco eventually encountered a 100-year flood for which there could be little planning or preparation. Floods just happened, and the only thing to do was to figure out how to recover as quickly as possible. To others, however, warning signs existed, and Cisco might have heeded them and thus lessened the damage that in time would bring the company low. The roots of all these issues date back to a time when almost no one had heard of the Internet, when high-tech networking firms did not exist, and when two academics who happened to be in love with each other began to have their own vision.

PART TWO

Flashback Mode

4 On Massive Hormones

The beginnings of Cisco have become the stuff of legend. Those beginnings are rooted in a love story.

In the late 1970s, the man and the woman involved, Len Bosack and Sandy Lerner, were computer nerds, both graduate students—Len in computer science, Sandy in political science and statistics. After receiving their master's degrees, they took jobs at Stanford University in Palo Alto, California.

Sandy was director of computer facilities for the Stanford Graduate School of Business, one of the few women in the male-dominated computer science fraternity. Friends who were using the various DECsystem-20 time-sharing computers around the Stanford campus introduced Sandy and Len to each other. Sandy took an instant liking to Len. He was in charge of the computer facilities at Stanford's computer science department, and, more important to Sandy, she found him quite clean compared to the other computer nerds. "I just didn't think that a more perfect man could exist," she noted.

Though they possessed starkly contrasting personalities—he was philosophical and nonconfrontational, she was flamboyant and in your face—they fell in love, and, so the legend goes, they wanted to e-mail each other from different ends of the Stanford campus. Len and Sandy were caught up in the exciting world of computer networking, and they agreed with the conventional wisdom among Stanford nerds that a computer was only useful if attached to a network.

But the technology stymied them. The computer networks that their departments used were not compatible.

Had Len and Sandy not been computer nerds, they would have carried on their love affair by less technological means, walking back and forth across campus or talking on the phone; but they lived for their computers, and in time it would bother them very much that Stanford computer networks could not "talk" to one another.

It bothered others at Stanford as well.

While local area network (LAN) technology, especially the Ethernet, began appearing at this time, users of the various departmental computer systems were stuck with computers that had very limited networking capabilities. LANs existed cheek by jowl on the Stanford campus, embracing 5,000 computers of all different kinds. And while computers were connected to one another within "local" LANs on different parts of the campus, the problem for Len, Sandy, and the other computer-savvy folks was that no campuswide network existed.

Whoever could figure out how to get the LANs to talk to one another would be sitting on an enormous technological breakthrough.

Describing the computer environment at Stanford during the early 1980s, Kirk Lougheed, who played a major role in getting computers to talk to one another, compared that campus environment to an archipelago, a set of islands (the LANs) that are relatively close together, though isolated, and whose inhabitants (the computers) often speak different languages.

THE "TOWER OF BABEL" ISSUE

The breakthrough—if there was going to be one—would address and solve the "Tower of Babel" conundrum that emerged in the early 1980s as a multitude of companies developed their own networking protocol or language. Any company that built an operating system for a network figured impractically that it had to have its own networking protocol: Apple had its own, and so did DEC, IBM, Xerox, Novell, and Microsoft.

The networking chaos in the outside world mirrored the situation back at Stanford. Routinely, the professors and students were forced to keep accounts on computers in different departments, with the annoying result that their files—students' essays, professors' research papers—were not convenient to access. Stanford professors would have loved to transfer course work electronically, permitting students to turn in their homework and have it checked on computer screens instantly. But without an integrated network system, without campus computers talking to one another, Len and Sandy's love life, as well as students' homework assignments and professors' research, would remain electronically challenged.

Prior to Stanford, Len worked at Digital Equipment Corporation, and he had a love affair with DEC-20 computers. In the mid-1980s, when DEC decided to build VAX computers instead of DEC-20s, Len left for Stanford, hoping to build and then sell desktop DEC-20 clones. Sandy adopted Len's way of thinking, and the two were decidedly DEC-20 "bigots" (quoting Kirk Lougheed).

Soon after arriving at Stanford, Len sought venture-capital funds so that he could build a DEC-20 clone, but was turned down. Disappointed that he could not sell the idea of the desktop DEC, Len became the head of a computer science department project to build an Ethernet interface for the DEC-20 that would permit someone to attach DEC-20s to the Internet.

It was at that time that Kirk Lougheed, a former physics student at Stanford who had been a systems programmer in the school's electrical engineering department, wandered over to the computer science department. Bored with his own work, he was intrigued to find that Len Bosack was working on early networking interfaces. Kirk began working on both the interface microcode and the operating system support for network protocols required for Len's DEC-20 Ethernet interface. Once the interface worked, copies were made for all the Stanford DEC-20s, as well as for a few friends at other universities.

The process of developing the DEC-20 Ethernet interface put a strain on Len and Sandy. Kirk Lougheed recalled that Len would get grief from Sandy for having to spend long evening hours debugging a DEC-20, available to them only at night. Len sometimes excused himself early, telling Kirk that he had to attend to "domestic politics."

At the same time that Len, Sandy, and Kirk were getting interested in networking, a parallel effort was occurring elsewhere on the Stanford campus. Graduate students and department staff were unofficially trying to connect their friends to a Stanford-based network that became known as the Stanford University Network, ultimately spending millions of dollars in the failed effort.

THE BIRTH OF THE CISCO ROUTER

The problem that Kirk and Len had to address was the limited nature of existing Ethernet wire technology, which, because it had a distance limit, kept the Stanford LANs from operating effectively, leading eventually to network instability. Kirk and Len tried to interconnect the Stanford LANs and to have them work effectively. The solution lay in a device called the multi-protocol router, a high-speed, reasonably cheap, highly specialized box filled with electronics that, acting like a kind of postal service, could move data packets from one computer to another.

Stanford researcher Bill Yeager had invented the multi-protocol router. Len and Kirk gained access to Yeager's source code. Kirk figured out how to turn the software into production quality, enabling anyone to install the software, not simply the software's author (in this case, Bill Yeager). Kirk added to his software the IP (Internet Protocol) that had been running on the ARPAnet, then the most important networking community in the United States. Kirk's add-on IP software became the Cisco Systems Internet Operating System (IOS). Its great technical advantage was that it enabled people to "talk" over a wide area network.

Len and Sandy, who were married right after graduate school, saw commercial prospects in what Kirk Lougheed had been doing to make the multi-protocol router a highly desirable network product. Hoping to get rich, Sandy wanted to start a company based on the router. She became the driving force. Neither Len nor Kirk had the same instincts; in effect, they went along for the ride. As it turned out, what gave the new product a distinct advantage was the team's ability to make it commercially available at a reasonable price. While router technology existed, it was either far too expensive ($80,000 per router) or too inaccessible for commercial use because it was tied up with government contracts.

Before Sandy and Len could progress much in setting up a company, they needed Stanford University's blessing for taking the router commercial. But Stanford officials said no. They felt that Len and Kirk, as mere staff members, did not have a right to leave and start their own company; academics, on the other hand, had that right—they were permitted to exploit the fruits of their research for commercial purposes.

Sandy was outraged. She could not understand Stanford's seeming obstinacy: it was obvious that Stanford, which would never build and sell computer equipment, had no interest in exploiting the technology on its own. She and Len, however, had every reason—and right, they believed—to create a private firm that would manufacture and sell their product.

Shocked at Stanford's rigidity, Len and Sandy decided to forge ahead, unwilling to take no for an answer, willing to let the chips fall where they may. That decision was inherently risky for Stanford was threatening to sue, angry that the Bosack-Lerner router had been developed on its nickel. And as long as Stanford's threatened suit remained possible, a dark shadow was cast over Cisco's future.

TEARY EYES

In late 1984, Sandy Lerner journeyed with Len to San Francisco, where, as she recalled, "with tears in our eyes we took our $5 up to the secretary of state's office in San Francisco and made Cisco Systems anyway." The name Cisco Systems was Sandy's idea—adopting the last half of San Francisco. She also designed the company's logo based on her impression of the Golden Gate Bridge.

With the new company duly registered, it was time to get to work.

While garages have become glamorized in Silicon Valley lore as the entrepreneurial cauldron of hot new start-ups, Sandy and Len in a middle-class sort of way established Cisco's first headquarters in their living room at 199 Oak Grove Avenue in the well-to-do community of Atherton. For the next two years, Cisco's manufacturing division was located in that living room, since it was the only room large enough to build and test the product. The hardware and software development units took over the spare bedroom.

One photograph from Sandy Lerner's Cisco scrapbook shows her and Len on the floor of the living room surrounded by boxes filled with routers, a piano and other pieces of furniture in the background. Len is on his knees and Sandy is sitting cross-legged. Another photograph shows Sandy, Len, and Kirk surrounding Cisco's first router, all looking proudly on; the router is enclosed in a white package with the Cisco logo on it.

Beneath the middle-class facade were the typical birth pangs of a Silicon Valley start-up: Cisco's first five employees—Sandy, Len, Kirk, Greg Satz, and Richard Troiano (who focused on sales)—spent three years working for Cisco before receiving any income. Until July 1985, they held full-time consulting jobs, turning up at the Oak Grove Avenue living room in the evenings. A sixth employee, Cecilia Strickland, was hired in the spring of 1986 to answer phones and perform other administrative tasks. (When the first Cisco badges were struck, Cecilia took the first; Sandy was number 2; Len, 3; Kirk, 4; Greg, 5; and Richard, 6.)

Len and Kirk quit Stanford in July 1986; Greg Satz followed a few months later. Sandy kept working full-time elsewhere for several months longer to keep up the cash flow for the nascent Cisco. Meanwhile, the new company was funded by personal loans, sales from Len's DEC stock, and the proceeds from various credit cards.

Always there was pressure on the team—to bring in cash and to find more "volunteers" to do the grunt work. (Kirk Lougheed's girlfriend, whom he eventually married, was an early recruit to help build the first routers.)

The first Cisco product was shipped in March 1986. As of that summer, the team was producing a few a week, selling them by word of mouth or via e-mail connections. Early customers were fellow academics at the University of Washington and Rutgers University, who were also using the Defense Department's ARPAnet networking system. Another early customer was Hewlett-Packard, for whom Len had been consulting. It was, Kirk Lougheed recalled, "basically a sell one to your friends sort of operation."

At the time, Kirk Lougheed had no idea that he was helping to produce a revolutionary product. "I must confess that I couldn't see that far in the future. It was interesting. It was stuff I had never done before. It was part of the Silicon Valley romance, if you will. I simply thought to myself, Gee I'm doing a start-up." Later, when Kirk knew how important his work in the living room would become, he began to sense the revolutionary aspects: "This was the first enabling technology [for the Internet] to go commercial."

In later years, Cisco veterans attributed most of the company's early success to being in a hot new market at exactly the right time. Robert Peters, the company's first vice president for marketing—he began in May 1988—recalled that "the initial product was so incredibly successful because it was a technically advanced product in a niche that was crying for the product, and it could be easily sold."

By the fall of 1986, it was clear to Len and Sandy that they needed more space. Orders were coming in. The product was an undeniable success. Revenues had reached $250,000 a month by the time the team got ready to abandon the living room that November. Scraping together the money to make a down payment, they took over 8,000 square feet of office space at 1360 Willow Road in nearby Menlo Park. Len sold some stock. Others took second mortgages on their homes. Kirk turned over part of his savings.

SEARCHING FOR A VENTURE CAPITALIST

Len and Sandy eagerly wanted venture-capital funding, and they looked under every rock—75 to be precise—but, remarkably, no one at the time thought it was wise to invest in a tiny start-up that was building and selling routers out of a living room. There was also the shadow hovering over the team in the form of the threatened Stanford University lawsuit. Few venture capitalists seemed eager to throw cash at a fledgling company that might well be sued by a major university.

But Sandy and Len never gave up on the VC community. They could not know that they were on the cusp of a revolution that would turn their product into gold. But they certainly had a good feeling about how the company was proceeding, for unlike other high-tech start-ups, Cisco had a viable product and a decent revenue stream. Best of all, it was on its way to an $83,000 profit in its first fiscal year, ending July 1987.

At the start of 1987, the Cisco cofounders knew that the business needed fresh leadership. Len and Sandy understood that they were not equipped to run a growing business. Sandy chose Bill Graves to be Cisco's first chief executive officer in January of that year. (Graves, a physicist, would stick around in that post for 16 months.) Two months later, Cisco appointed the first chief financial officer, Lloyd Embry, who served for just over two years.

That spring, Ed Leonard, a member of a Palo Alto law firm, was contacted by someone from Cisco, perhaps Len Bosack, and asked to help find VC funding. Leonard turned to Don Valentine, the general partner of Sequoia Capital since 1974. Valentine already had a long, distinguished career in Silicon Valley. With a good grasp of the technical details of networking, Valentine was one of the few VCs who understood the widespread problem of "broadcast storm," that is, the phenomenon of data packets colliding with one another because they lack the proper routing mechanism. Valentine's interest in Cisco Systems was instant because the company appeared to have a solution to this problem. Cisco was far more advanced than others with whom Valentine was familiar.

Valentine was under no illusion about the management skills of Len Bosack and Sandy Lerner, and he knew the company faced major hurdles, but he still wanted to make the investment: "This was a start-up that had no management. They had a great idea. They had an entanglement with Stanford University in determining the ownership of their product. And they were extremely bitter individuals about how the extraction process from Stanford worked."

None of that deterred Valentine. Cutting what some have called the deal of the century, he arranged for Sequoia Capital to invest $2.5 million in Cisco in exchange for 29.1 percent of the company. By the early 1990s, it certainly seemed like the deal of the century, for the return to Sequoia comfortably exceeded $1 billion.

THE STEAL OF THE CENTURY

Easing Valentine's entry into the Cisco family was the settlement that Bill Graves reached with Stanford University in April 1987. The terms of that settlement called for Cisco to pay 3 percent of its total revenue up to $150,000 for the license that allowed the company to use the router software. It was for Cisco Systems a spectacular achievement, for it meant that the company had to pay a mere $150,000 to Stanford in return for which it was now free to build the company. Reaching the settlement constituted one of the most important milestones in Cisco's early history. Though the amount of the settlement at the time seemed "astronomical" (at least to Greg Satz), Cisco had purchased its future at a very small price indeed. Cisco veteran Terry Eger called the settlement "the steal of the century."

What to some of Cisco's early leaders seemed a bump on the road always remained to Len and Sandy a festering wound. To Don Valentine, Stanford had displayed ample generosity, abandoning all rights and claims to the router product, and leaving the two cofounders with their ownership of the company intact. But to the cofounders, Stanford deserved no praise, because it had taken so long to end the dispute. Sandy and Len seemed to take the university's slowness personally, but more than a decade later they attended a ceremony marking Cisco Systems' donation of a chair in their names to Stanford University.

Though Sequoia's share in Cisco was just under 30 percent, Don Valentine wanted a significant amount of control over Cisco's daily operations. For all the zeal that Len had shown in seeking venture-capitalist funding, he and Sandy recoiled bitterly at Valentine's assertion of power. However vituperative Sandy became—and she was by all accounts a screamer when agitated—Don Valentine began to invigorate the tiny company with a sense of business professionalism that had been sorely lacking. Nakedly ambitious, eager to assume the presidency of the company, Sandy Lerner needed Don Valentine on her side, but even before he greeted her for the first time, he had shrewdly identified her as the company's main stumbling block. "Don's opening words to me the first time I ever met that man . . . were 'I hear you're everything that's wrong with Cisco.'" She retorted bitterly, "I'm also the reason why there *is* a Cisco." Maybe so, but Valentine knew that the company needed an injection of professional management or else it would never get beyond the struggling start-up stage. Undeniably, Cisco's product was popular, and revenues were heading for another good year in 1987—$1.85 million—but the company was top-heavy with engineers, and only by finding some sales and marketing talent could it continue to grow. Valentine decided to start by finding a sales manager.

The man chosen, Terry Eger, would have a profound effect on the tiny start-up. He had held various sales and marketing positions, first at Datapoint Corporation and then at Wang Laboratories. Appointed Cisco's first vice president of sales in January 1988, Eger was fiercely independent, perseverant, and incorrigible—qualities that endeared him to some, but added fuel to the already simmering cauldron of tensions and animosities within the Cisco group.

Eger was the 17th person hired at Cisco, and his arrival was a genuine relief to Don Valentine, who hoped the new man would bring stability to the organization. Paid a $90,000 salary, Eger also accepted 5.1 percent of Cisco's stock to compensate him for forgoing other extras, making him one of Cisco's largest shareholders at the time. Don Valentine owned, as noted earlier, 29.1 percent of the stock; Len and Sandy owned 17.6 percent each. (Terry Eger's stake would have been worth $27 billion in March 2000 when Cisco was America's most valuable company.)

Terry Eger was stepping into a can of worms. Battle lines were firmly drawn between Sandy and Len on one side, and Bill Graves and Lloyd Embry on the other. Graves and Embry felt they had the right and the duty to tell the two cofounders how the business should be run. Sandy and Len disagreed. Eger went to business sessions feeling that he should be dressed in full armor. ("At meetings, everyone would be fighting.")

There were more internecine subplots than in a Shakespearean tragedy. Soon after Terry Eger began working at Cisco, Sandy Lerner warned him that she and Len Bosack planned to ask Don Valentine to fire Bill Graves. As the price for performing that chore, Valentine asked Sandy and Len for the voting rights to their 35.2 percent of the stock.

Added to Sequoia's 29.1 percent, that gave Valentine a whopping 64.3 percent control of Cisco. But Graves's departure had little quieting effect, and by the time Robert Peters arrived in May 1988 to take on his marketing assignment, he was shocked to find the same old contentiousness. ("All the people were talented, capable people, but that place was anarchy.")

The selection of Chuck Sutcliffe, a Silicon Valley veteran, to replace Bill Graves that May did little to calm emotions. "A nice gentleman" (Terry Eger's cutting phrase) who commanded little respect, Sutcliffe ran the company for six months—long enough for a search to be conducted for a permanent president and CEO. Sandy Lerner remained as demanding as ever—the cofounder might have understood the need for professional management, but she had no desire to bend to that management. Significantly, despite the passivity at the top, Cisco's engineers were highly productive.

ANOINTING A CHAIRMAN OF THE BOARD

The strong man in the organization was Terry Eger. Everywhere, his influence was felt: He was setting up the company's first sales organization. He was cutting deals with major clients. It was he who huddled with Cisco's engineers to make sure that they included features in products that he had promised to customers. No one knew more about the inner workings of the company than he did, and that gave him enormous power. ("I didn't take over, but I had a big effect.")

Eger was even instrumental in choosing Don Valentine to become chairman of Cisco's board of directors. It came at the meeting when Valentine announced to the senior executives that Graves no longer worked for Cisco. Terry Eger expressed concern that Wall Street might be bothered that Cisco had neither a chairman of the board nor a president.

"What would you like?" Valentine asked Eger.

"Since you are the most well known of us, I want you to be chairman of the board," Eger stated.

Valentine gazed around the room, asking if there was any disagreement.

Hearing none, he said, "Fine, I'm chairman of the board."

And yet Terry Eger seemed a part of the problem at Cisco, rather than the purveyor of a solution. To those who knew him best at the time, he engendered mixed feelings. They admired his aggressiveness and fierce independence, and knew that it was largely because of Eger's bulldozer tactics that Cisco landed its deals. But they described him as a loose cannon and a one-man wrecking ball. He was volatile and wouldn't listen to anyone. But he got the job done. He brought in business. Eger would tell Cisco's engineers that he had an order for 30,000 routers, but he had promised the client some add-on features. He would then bark, "You want to build them or not?" He would sit in a customer's office until he came back with orders. Cisco's sales force took its cue from Terry, inundating customers with data, tearing through every level of the organization, if necessary, to get the sale. Robert Sweifach, a Cisco board member from 1989 to 1993, said simply: "Cisco developed the reputation of taking no prisoners. That was from Terry."

COUP AFTER COUP

It was Terry Eger who pulled off coup after coup. During the summer of 1988, Cisco landed its first big corporate sale. The customer was the Boeing Company. In quick succession, Cisco wrapped up deals with Motorola, Citibank, and General Electric, most of the seven Regional Bell Operating Companies, other phone companies, and some brokerage firms. Cisco also secured contracts with virtually all of America's major corporations.

Cisco's numbers were spectacular. In May 1988, sales climbed to $500,000 a month; in August, they rose to $1 million a month; and by November, $3.5 million a month. Revenues for 1988 jumped to $5.45 million.

The Boeing deal was the most significant for Cisco at the time. Boeing had (and still has) the largest private network in the world. As an early leader in networking, the aircraft maker had a large influence on the networking world as a whole. Its Boeing Computer Services did computer consulting for people everywhere, including the government, managing such projects as the Space Station Project Network. Relying on equipment from Vitalink, Bridge, and IBM, Boeing purchased tens of millions of dollars of networking equipment every year. Terry Eger's pitch to Boeing was that using Cisco's equipment would enable the aircraft firm to increase the capacity of its network. Testing the Cisco equipment, Boeing's officials liked what they saw. Boeing began implementing Cisco routers in its future networks. And, just as significantly, Boeing began recommending Cisco equipment, helping to boost the router maker's business. Eger was jubilant: "When the biggest and best network in the world uses your equipment, it is a great reference."

The Eger-led deals boosted Cisco into the stratosphere. The money kept coming in. "It was a company on massive hormones," said Ed Kozel, one of Cisco's early executives. "It was growing like crazy." But it was also a company with distinct flaws (albeit concealed from the outside world), a company that, if corrections were not made quickly, was nurturing the seeds of its own destruction.

In mid-1988, for all of the Cisco routers being sold, the company still lacked effective leadership. For all the deals that were being made, too many of the people at the top functioned within their own worlds, unwilling to take orders from superiors, disregarding chains of command, their emotions churning and grinding one another down. It was not a happy place.

Sandy Lerner and Len Bosack, two of the main culprits, grudgingly acknowledged as much. Neither had the desire or the talent to manage a business that was growing by leaps and bounds. Both of them grated on other employees. Ever conscious that he was the company's maverick, Terry Eger did not disguise his individualistic impulses. The folks who had the top titles, first Bill Graves, then Chuck Sutcliffe, could not keep anyone in line. John Bolger, who took over in June 1989 as Cisco's second CFO, realized how fortunate Cisco was to have such a great product. He would kid investors that "even the management team can't kill the product. Heaven knows they've tried. That wasn't totally a joke. We had a pretty dysfunctional management team before John Chambers came along. We had some very competent individuals, but we had some very wild personalities."

Don Valentine had to come up with someone who could take control of the dysfunctional Cisco family. He understood the urgent need for a strong new CEO. The man who might have seemed the obvious choice, Terry Eger, did not want to run the place.

Though the company was still small—it had 35 employees in November 1988—a leader was needed who could put some structure on an organization that was top-heavy with engineers (12 of the 35 employees). Most important, the new leader would be mandated to take the company public. Once a new CEO was installed, Don Valentine planned to give up his day-to-day role.

ENTER JOHN MORGRIDGE

Finally, Valentine found the right person to become Cisco's first permanent and professional president and CEO. John Morgridge, then 54, possessed just the right mix of managerial experience and knowledge of the high-tech world. He had spent 20 years climbing the ranks at Honeywell, where he ended up as vice president for marketing and planning. He then worked for a pair of start-ups: Stratus Computers, from 1980 to 1986, where he was vice president of sales, marketing, and service; and GRID Systems, a manufacturer of laptop computers, from 1986 to 1988, where he was president and chief operating officer.

With an eager eye on Wall Street, Don Valentine urged Morgridge to make his first task at Cisco taking the company public. But it took the new president and CEO little time to realize that he was entering a hornet's nest, and taming the hornets would have to take priority over the IPO. Even before he stepped foot in the office, Morgridge had been warned that he faced one seemingly insurmountable obstacle to his effectively taking charge: Terry Eger remained the company strongman and the favorite of the Cisco board.

"I want to get along with you," Morgridge told Terry at their first meeting.

Terry pretended that he did not understand the comment. "Why, John, you're the president. You don't have to worry about getting along with me."

Morgridge assured Eger that indeed he did have to worry, "because you have the support of the board, and I was told that if I get sideways with you they'll support you."

On the very first day he walked into the Cisco building, Morgridge got a whiff of the troubles ahead when he quickly spotted Terry Eger poring over diagramming requirements with eight engineers in a small conference room. To those engineers, Terry Eger seemed very much the man in charge, not John Morgridge.

Keeping Terry Eger in check became one of Morgridge's most formidable tasks. Terry was devilishly incorrigible. He rarely took part in meetings. If he had something to say to the engineers, he skirted Morgridge and went directly to them. Morgridge was ambivalent toward Eger, impressed with his sales skills, but daunted by the man's "I'll do what I like" attitude toward authority. "In his own way," Morgridge recalled, "Terry Eger was as much an evangelist as John Chambers is today. The only problem is: Terry was a very aggressive sales guy as an evangelist. So you either became a believer in the faith, or you didn't look upon him too favorably."

THE QUEEN OF EMOTION

Cofounder Sandy Lerner was indisputably the queen of emotion. "There was a wild energy in her that when focused was spectacular," Ed Kozel, a former chief technology officer, commented. "But she had zero tolerance and would yell and scream. There were no boundaries to her comments." Don Valentine encountered the same sort of intolerance: "She was brutally tough to work with. She had a blunt style, a perfectionist attitude, a very demanding confrontational technique, and absolutely no forgiveness for humanity."

If Sandy was a screamer, Len posed as much difficulty for Cisco employees by seeming, in Ed Kozel's phrase, "downright strange, eccentric, esoteric." Len's social skills were virtually nonexistent, according to Kozel. Len yelled at potential customers, telling them, "You're being stupid. This is the way it should be." But the customers needed Cisco's product, so Len got away with a lack of finesse and tact.

He seemed to have difficulty communicating clearly: "He would speak to you and you wouldn't understand a thing he said," explained Kozel. "Len had a tendency to start a conversation in the middle, and then wander off." It seemed that the only one he listened to was Sandy.

The only difference between the opening pages of Joseph Heller's hilarious novel *Something Happened* and the scenes that unfolded at Cisco in the late 1980s was that the Cisco eccentricities were true. Putting Terry, Sandy, Len, and some of the others in the same room was the business equivalent of lighting a match and throwing it on combustible material. Sandy Lerner, as founding engineer Greg Satz recalled, "had no trouble lighting fires if she thought it was in the interest of the customer. Terry had no problem burning anyone at the stake if he thought he could make a deal. So you get these people together and you get explosions." Among the three senior executives—Sandy Lerner, John Morgridge, and Terry Eger—alliances sometimes formed, but then just as quickly dissolved. Sandy was inclined to get along with

Terry Eger but not with Morgridge. "Sandy was born a barracuda, so she and Terry got along wonderfully," remembered Ed Kozel.

A realist, Morgridge understood that he could not just enter the fray and scatter the hornets: "It was a requirement to deal with what was there because you couldn't change it all." A way had to be found to keep the employees from coming to blows. Don Valentine pressed John Morgridge to bring in a "company shrink" (Morgridge's phrase), a man named Charles Kaufman. "He was kind of like the company priest," said Morgridge. "His role was not necessarily to cause us to love one another, but to avoid taking physical action against one another." He wasn't always successful. Some fisticuffs actually took place in full view of John Morgridge, who must have felt more like a boxing referee than a CEO. "It was a fairly dysfunctional family," he said. "Cisco's employees got along best when they weren't together."

The company priest-psychiatrist had little luck. In the end, Morgridge and Valentine believed that the best way to lower the temperature within Cisco was to give the group a common goal: taking the company public, they hoped, would at least make them forget their pet peeves. Morgridge explained: "Going public was the single unifying goal. That was about the only thing that the group agreed upon."

But before the company could go public, it would have to look more like a flourishing business and less like a zany, chaotic start-up. For starters, it would need to grow out of its engineer-focused culture.

RECRUITING A NEW TEAM

During the early phase of Morgridge's leadership, with Don Valentine's Sequoia Capital playing a major role in the recruitment process, a number of executives were hired who took over business chores from the engineers. One was Dave Ring, who became Cisco's first vice president for manufacturing in December 1988, serving in that post for the next five years. Another was Ed Kozel, who joined Cisco in March 1989 as market development manager. A third was

John Bolger, who became the company's second CFO in June 1989. Morgridge began to develop an international team, including someone to head up Cisco sales in Japan. He moved Cisco into Europe. Perhaps as an antidote to the vitriol that infected the place, Morgridge placed great emphasis on what he called "team building," and he was one of the first CEOs in Silicon Valley to offer stock options to a broad slice of the company. Until then, venture capitalists had frowned upon supplying stock options to anyone other than the founders and engineers. Morgridge debated the point vigorously with Don Valentine, and eventually Valentine was won over. "John Morgridge smoothed out this very, very sharp-edged organization," said Ed Kozel, "and to a large extent covered it up, so it would grow and people wouldn't just quit if they ran into this sharp edge [Sandy Lerner]."

Taking a seriously professional attitude toward the buildup of the company, John Morgridge served as a bridge between what Ed Kozel called "that nutty and unscalable small company" and the Cisco of the 1990s. But there was just so much structure that could be put on this "nutty" little start-up, and Morgridge appeared to understand that point quite well.

With routers all the rage and with a host of talented executives, Morgridge's loose control worked if only because the executives, when left on their own, performed masterfully. In Robert Peters's view, "You simply had to aim people at what they had to do and they would go off and do it. Morgridge was smart enough to let it happen."

But Morgridge's approach was not, as Don Valentine had hoped, a source of calm. Emotions remained high. Egos ran rampant. The most explosive force by far was Sandy Lerner. Her great virtue was in focusing the company on the customer. The significance of that strategy cannot be overstated. Other Silicon Valley start-ups, not to mention a host of corporate giants, self-destructed largely by overlooking the great value of listening to the customer.

In 1988, Sandy Lerner became what some believe was America's first vice president for customer advocacy. Doug Allred, Cisco's senior vice president for customer advocacy, suggested that the concept of customer advocacy "saved Cisco's bacon in the beginning."

Sensing how important it was to listen to customers, Sandy made sure that the company's engineers knew what customers wanted and needed. The engineers, the dominant element in Cisco at the time, might easily have promoted the devices *they* wanted to create; but Sandy wanted to keep them humble.

LOOKING AFTER THE CUSTOMER

So thinking about customers became a natural act for Cisco from its inception. Cisco employee number 4, Kirk Lougheed, recalled an early Cisco competitor named CMC that was based in Santa Barbara, California, a manufacturer of the first router that worked on the ARPAnet—a DDN-X25 router. When CMC delivered its router, however, problems arose that offered Cisco Systems the chance to excel. Cisco had problems with its router as well, but its product was better, Lougheed, indicated, "because we could fix it over the Net and get to and from our customers quicker."

Given all that he faced, it was difficult for John Morgridge to show Don Valentine that he was indeed doing a good job. Sandy Lerner and Len Bosack continued to feel that the company was theirs and that Cisco's spectacular sales were due to their wonderful routers. Terry Eger saw himself effectively running the business, or at least making all the key decisions. Morgridge wanted to make a splash, to get noticed. "I wanted to keep my job," he told me.

To keep his job, in March 1989 Morgridge decided to demonstrate that he had leadership talent. One obvious way was to increase Cisco's cash flow. Though sales had reached $3.5 million a month toward the end of 1988, Morgridge fretted over Cisco's future. With Valentine's blessing, Morgridge took the bold step of selling the right to license Cisco's code for its router product to Minneapolis-based Network Equipment Technologies for $750,000, at the time an impressive sum. NET acquired the right to sell Cisco's product for five years, with another five years at its option.

Furious that Morgridge was in effect giving away Cisco's family jewels, and believing that the arrangement essentially offered NET a chance to ruin Cisco, Terry Eger threatened members of Cisco's sales force with instant dismissal if NET began distributing the company's routers in their sales territory. Just as distressed at the amount of power NET had gained was Ed Kozel, who on his very first day at Cisco was given the NET contract to manage: "They had not only our technology but unlimited rights to fresh new Cisco technology. It was very broad and one-sided and in the wrong hands a very dangerous contract."

So one-sided was the relationship, recalled Kozel, that Cisco had every incentive to work against NET, and it did. "Terry beat the hell out of them," recalled Ed Kozel with undisguised glee. "It was head-to-head competition, going to the same customers with essentially the same product. It certainly created confusion. Terry gave all kinds of special incentives to kill NET. They were lousy partners."

With Cisco effectively its main competitor, NET was unable to sell many of the Cisco products. Ten years later, when John Chambers was president and CEO, the company negotiated back the code from NET. Eger believes that NET could have buried Cisco if it had succeeded in selling Cisco's products.

However misguided the licensing decision seemed to certain Cisco executives, they acknowledged that the company came out of the experience stronger. It would choose its partners far more carefully in the future. "I learned a lesson that I held for the next decade," said Ed Kozel, "and that is that a good business relationship can never be one-sided." Someone else would learn the same lesson, though he was not even in the company at the time. His name was John Chambers. As Cisco's leader in the latter half of the 1990s, Chambers embarked on a series of partnerships as part of strengthening Cisco's business. In each case, he had to make a strong argument for why the new partnership was a win-win situation to those Cisco executives who had been through the NET experience.

Another positive result of the NET sale was that Terry Eger had an incentive to build a strong direct-sales organization.

Nothing bolstered Cisco's self-confidence as much as watching NET, with its several hundred employees, diminish as a business over the next two years while Cisco, with its 35 employees, flourished. Talking about the incident 11 years later, John Morgridge seemed visibly uncomfortable. It was clearly a painful chapter in his days as Cisco's leader. In November 2000, he said candidly, "I don't know that it was a smart thing to do, but it was a case of the survival of the company at that point."

One way the company survived in its early days was by being frugal.

Though he wishes it were not so, John Morgridge is best known within Cisco's precincts as Mr. Frugality. He would rather be remembered for presiding over the company's spectacular growth. He emphasizes that thriftiness was always part of Cisco's culture: "This was not a venture start-up. This was a cottage industry. So frugality was fundamental to its existence. When I joined the company it had been profitable because they didn't spend money they didn't have."

Don Valentine put pressure on Morgridge to keep costs down. Valentine wasted little time telling him that the $2.5 million investment that his venture-capital fund, Sequoia Capital, had made in Cisco back in 1987 was in the bank purely as an insurance policy in case Cisco's working capital and debt could no longer finance its growth. In the event, Morgridge never touched a penny of it.

The example of frugality that employees cite most often is Cisco's policy requiring them to fly coach on air journeys. Saving money on airfare eventually wore on Cisco executives, who by 1993—three years after the IPO had made them all wealthy—were getting tired of flying coach. By this time, they felt they deserved a more comfortable journey if they were going to be sent overseas for the company.

One day a group of executives approached John Morgridge at an executive staff meeting and asked to travel business class on flights to Europe and Asia. Morgridge observed that Cisco had spent $700,000 on travel during the previous year. Had the executives traveled business class, travel costs would have risen to $1.2 million. Taking the $500,000 in savings and running it to the bottom line, Morgridge said, would produce an additional $5 a share for Cisco's stock.

Fearing the loss of that $5 a share—since they all had plenty of options—the group, without a great deal of cheer, quickly voted to keep flying coach unless they could upgrade to business class for free.

Matching the frugality in the skies was the policy of keeping office space spartan. Offices were small. Buildings relied on natural lighting. Morgridge boasted of finding a piece of office furniture for $25. Senior executives went without much office help. Terry Eger notes: "I never had a secretary. I handled my own day planner."

After a day's labors on a sales trip, Morgridge liked to challenge Cisco colleagues: "Okay, guys, let's look at our airline tickets. I got mine for a hundred bucks. How about you?" "The hundred bucks wasn't the point, or the embarrassment," suggested Ed Kozel. "It was to push this idea that money is valuable." Morgridge played the same game to discover who was occupying the cheapest hotel room.

It might have had as much to do with Morgridge's view of how Cisco should be spending its marketing dollars as with a sense of frugality, but during the Morgridge era the company spent almost no money on advertising or public relations. In that period, Cisco was marketing its products to the technical employees of a company, so it wanted to spend its dollars on reaching that audience. Neither advertising nor public relations was needed. Cisco *did* spend a good deal of money on trade shows and technical seminars, sending its engineers on these trips.

After only a year in office, Morgridge presided over a very different company. By December 1989, Cisco had 174 employees, of whom only 35 were in engineering. The rest were spread over manufacturing (42), sales and marketing (45), customer service (32), and finance and administration (20). The company's financials were looking good indeed: revenue was up fivefold from the year before, reaching $27,664,000 for 1989, and profits rose to $4,178,000.

On February 16, 1990, Cisco Systems went public. (By this time, Sequoia Capital owned 23.5 percent of the company, while Len Bosack and Sandy Lerner each owned 13.8 percent.) The Cisco IPO marked the first new technology issue of the 1990s. It was priced at a very reasonable $18 a share and closed at the end of the first day at $22.25 (the stock split four times between then and 1995). Just prior to the IPO, the company was worth $288 million.

Into the early 1990s, the company continued to prosper. Cisco's 1990 profit was $13,904,000, more than triple the $4,178,000 earned a year earlier. Revenue that year reached $69.7 million.

Notwithstanding the company's success, Cisco's executives had decided that summer of 1990 that enough was enough: either Don Valentine had to let Sandy Lerner go, or they would quit en masse. They had stood by while she screamed at them and berated them. She was getting in the way of conducting Cisco business, and the whole situation had become intolerable. The executives knew that their task of axing Sandy would not be easy. For one thing, she continued to have an ally in Don Valentine, who labored behind the scenes with John Morgridge to keep her in the company as long as possible.

Then came what Valentine referred to as "that fateful day." A half dozen Cisco vice presidents—including Terry Eger, Dave Ring, and John Bolger—approached Valentine, with John Morgridge's approval, to say they would quit unless Valentine fired Sandy Lerner. According to Terry Eger, the other vice presidents had been prepared for some time to have Sandy axed, and only he had been holding out because he appreciated the way she had been gaining the confidence of customers. But even Eger gave way when he watched in frustration as she lashed out venomously at a very good customer, Alan Greenberg, the head of computer science at McGill University.

On August 28, 1990, Valentine fired Sandy Lerner. Though the same Cisco executives who forced Sandy out did not want Len to leave, he did soon after Sandy's departure. That December, Len and Sandy, who had separated in 1988, sold their Cisco shares. At the time the company was worth $1 billion; their shares were worth $170 million.

James Richardson, senior vice president and chief marketing officer, joined the company around that time. He remembered Sandy and Len's departure as a defining moment for the company: "We really said that now we're going to be serious about making a business out of this."

. . .

It has been widely accepted that Cisco Systems was in the right place at the right time, which explains its market dominance during the company's early phase. It was not, however, entirely good luck.

Certainly, Len Bosack and Sandy Lerner placed a premium product in an ascending market that was about to explode. But one compelling reason for Cisco's triumphs in the late 1980s and early 1990s had to do with the complexity of the product. Former board member Robert Sweifach commented that "it was hard for corporations to change their networking protocols. Most guys running the company didn't know how the product worked, just that the company depended on it. Corporate information-systems people didn't need to study manuals. Cisco could come to them. Cisco's people would always say, 'Let us be part of the planning process. We'll bring in products that will help.' And none of the users objected to that."

That Cisco sold a complicated product that required a good deal of service and support played into the company's hands, since it meant that customers would become dependent upon their supplier of network equipment. It was not so much that Cisco had the best products in the early days; it simply had better products than anyone else. "We may have been deficient at times," acknowledges John Bolger, Cisco's second CFO, "but it was much better than anyone else had." Cisco benefited as well from the growing popularity of the Internet. John Bolger explains: "People thought they were making a million-dollar buy decision; but they were really making a $10 million decision. After they had a little bit, they had to have more. It was insidious. It was luckily insidious. It wasn't that Cisco was doing anything devious. It was that the customers didn't realize that you couldn't just do a little bit because the technology was so positive, so productive."

Cisco's great advantage in the marketplace was that it was first with a solution to networking. Suddenly, it became possible to communicate instantly with anyone in a large institution, or, for that matter, across institutions, across national boundaries. Everyone wanted the new technology.

PART THREE

John Chambers Arrives on the Scene

5 The Heir Apparent

The year was 1990. Cisco Systems was six years old. The once-tiny start-up was growing by leaps and bounds, and its main problem seemed to be whether it could handle the explosive growth in the coming years.

Weathering those early years had not been easy, but as a new decade was getting under way, the Cisco leadership was beginning to take shape. Cisco's chairman, Don Valentine, whose Sequoia Capital venture fund had become Cisco's sole investor two years earlier, had eased himself out of the day-to-day running of the company after John Morgridge took up CEO duties in 1988. Dave Ring was running manufacturing, John Bolger was well ensconced as CFO, and Terry Eger was in charge of domestic sales. But if the company seemed in good shape as far as leadership was concerned, it was illusory.

With the two cofounders no longer around, and with John Morgridge, now 57, uneager to serve as CEO until age 65, the stage was set for another major leadership transition for Cisco Systems. It was a precarious time for the company, no longer a start-up, but not yet certain that it could survive in the nascent marketplace of networking.

Morgridge promised himself that he would step down once the

company's revenues reached $1 billion. It was true that Cisco was doing well—its revenue had jumped from $27.6 million in 1989 to $69.7 million in 1990—but the $1 billion goal seemed far off. Perhaps Morgridge was not all that eager to step down so soon. After all, the company was going great guns under his leadership. (When he first took over, revenues were only $5 million.)

But the fact was that Morgridge was seriously thinking about who might replace him. Possibilities certainly included Terry Eger, the vice president for sales. But Terry liked to sell. He detested attending meetings. He was simply not the managerial type. Unwilling to consider Eger, Morgridge thought the way he ran the sales operation was not scalable.

The ultimate decision maker was Don Valentine, and on the surface that might have worked in Terry's favor. Valentine loved Eger's talents ("Probably the best start-up sales manager I've ever encountered in any company"). But the truth was that Valentine never thought of Eger as potential CEO material: "Terry is more of a backlog builder than an organization builder."

For his part, Terry Eger was increasingly frustrated over the leadership turn the company was taking. He truly believed that no one knew how to grow the company better than he did. He was pleased that Don Valentine had told others that the most important person in the company during Cisco's early days had been the vice president of sales (without mentioning Terry by name). Terry understood that many people outside of Cisco simply assumed that he was Morgridge's heir apparent. But grudgingly, Terry made it clear that the CEO post held no appeal for him.

Valentine felt that the company needed a new kind of leadership instead of the individual performers it had had until then (he was clearly thinking of Len and Sandy and Terry): "We were doing extremely well, but our results were largely the work of a tremendous amount of perspiration and not enough inspiration." Cisco needed people "who had the capability of building organizations now, not just individuals who were great individual performers."

. . .

The search for new people began in earnest, but not so much for a CEO as for new executives with specific responsibilities who could help the company prepare itself for growth. The Valentine-Morgridge agenda to find new people jolted Terry Eger into realizing that he was no longer happy working at Cisco Systems. Informing Morgridge privately in the summer of 1990 that he planned to retire, Eger stepped down in May 1992.

During that summer of 1990, Terry Eger learned that John Morgridge and Dave Ring wanted to hire someone with a manufacturing background to be the new chief operating officer. Terry balked. He wanted more of a sales or marketing person. Terry began looking around on his own. His views would go a long way: he had the ear of the Cisco board of directors, and especially its chairman, Don Valentine.

Then in late September 1990, Terry Eger received a phone call.

That call would set in motion a chain of events that would change the face of Cisco Systems.

A PRETTY DECENT GUY

On the phone was Kathryn Gould, then a partner at Merrill, Pickard, Anderson & Eyre, a premier West Coast venture-capital firm based in Menlo Park, California. The résumé of John Chambers had crossed her desk, and her firm was considering placing him in a sales job at one of the high-tech companies in which her VC firm had invested. Chambers had just left his job at Wang Laboratories and was looking for a job as vice president for sales. Though Wang Laboratories had gone through a dramatic decline lately, Chambers had escaped being stigmatized and was in fact "a pretty decent guy," as Gould recounted years later.

Gould knew that Terry Eger had once worked at Wang Laboratories, so she picked up the phone to ask him what he knew about Chambers.

"Tell me about this guy Chambers," she asked Terry. "Is he as good as everyone says he is?"

Hearing the name Chambers, Eger quickly remembered him from the time when Eger was a branch manager for Wang in Edison, New Jersey. The year was 1982, and the two men were attending a sales planning meeting in Lowell, Massachusetts. Chambers was in his early 30s, a young man who had come a long way, geographically and otherwise, from his boyhood experiences in West Virginia.

Born on August 23, 1949, John Chambers grew up along the banks of the Kanawha River in Charleston, West Virginia. His father was an obstetrician-gynecologist who delivered 6,000 babies, including the four children of Senator Jay Rockefeller. Later in life, Jack Chambers was a successful real estate developer. John credits his father with giving him his business acumen. John's grandfathers were business figures: a bank president and the head of a construction company. June Chambers, John's mother, was a psychologist.

When John was a youngster, he learned the meaning of trust from his father while the two were fishing in a river. The young boy slipped and began to go underwater, but was able to cling to a pole. Jack Chambers began running after his son, shouting, "Don't drop the pole." Eventually, his father rescued John. Later the boy understood that his father had wanted him to concentrate on holding the pole in order not to panic. He had trusted his father.

LIVING WITH A CHILDHOOD AFFLICTION

Chambers remained silent for years about one anguishing childhood secret: he was dyslexic.

He was deeply affected by the affliction as a child. His schoolmates kidded him mercilessly. His second- and third-grade teachers told him candidly that they doubted he would graduate from high school, much less go to college. He was, after all, reading backward! (To this day, he's not sure if the teachers ever raised such doubts with his parents.)

At that time, the teachers did not identify John Chambers's reading problem as dyslexia. They simply assumed he was unable to learn.

His parents, who were great believers in education, were relentless in getting help for their son. They arranged for young John to meet with Mrs. Lorena Anderson, an expert in learning disabilities, who helped him to correct much of the problem.

He went to Mrs. Anderson several days a week after school for several years. Incredibly, thanks to her and to his own determination, John Chambers received mostly A's in high school. He attended Duke University and then transferred to West Virginia University to be close to his college girlfriend, Elaine (later his wife), where he obtained a JD degree in 1974. A year later, he received an MBA from Indiana University in Bloomington.

He learned to deal with schoolmates who taunted him over his dyslexia and learned some valuable lessons for life: "Sometimes you do not realize how much you can hurt a person without meaning to. I learned that by dealing with a learning disability at a time when learning disabilities weren't understood. Having been through that, you learn to overcome major challenges, learn to treat others like you'd want to be treated. More importantly, if you find others in a tough situation, try to help them, like you would like somebody to help you."

Simply knowing that he had it within him to beat so great a handicap, Chambers acquired enormous self-confidence as an adult: "Once you learn you can overcome a major hurdle like that, you know you can do it again." He lowered his voice to a whisper. "And again."

It was only in 1998, when he was 48 years old, that John Chambers felt comfortable talking publicly about his childhood affliction. Cisco Systems was sponsoring a "Take Your Children to Work" event. A girl began asking Chambers a question but could not get the words out easily; she then tearfully pronounced that she was suffering from a learning disability. John Chambers strode over to her to offer solace. He knew what it was like to be embarrassed in front of your peers and for them to think that you were not very smart. He knew how much that hurt.

"No problem," he told her. "I had a learning disability too."

He then announced to the crowd what he had just said in a lower voice to the young girl.

After the event, he received e-mails from parents and children who had been present for his disclosure, offering him words of encouragement. He then realized that "if you could show that you had this and could overcome it, that was more important for others' ability to handle similar situations than it was for me not to share what I viewed as my weaknesses."

Though Chambers acknowledged that parts of the affliction never got fixed, as an adult he showed no outward signs of the dyslexia. He encouraged colleagues at Cisco not to give him long memos, and he worked hard to hone his listening and memory skills.

If he could overcome one personal difficulty, he told himself, he could conquer others as well: "You can learn what your weaknesses are, and learn to compensate by surrounding yourself with people who will help you turn your weaknesses into strengths." Later in life, for instance, he made a big effort to convert a weakness in public speaking into one of his great strengths.

He learned valuable lessons as well from childhood sports. Chambers described himself as a pretty good athlete in most sports. Sports taught him that with "hard work and discipline you could do almost anything to a certain level."

Chambers dreamed of eventually running his own company, assuming that it would be small, certainly smaller than the Cisco Systems of the year 2002. He put such dreams on hold, taking the advice of an IBM recruiter who told him that understanding technology would help him learn how businesses function. IBM had another attraction: the money was very good. Over the next 14 years, Chambers worked for two large companies—IBM for six years, then Wang Laboratories for eight—gaining more scar tissue than he cared for, learning as much about how businesses should *not* be run as about how they should be.

He was 26 years old when he embarked on his business career. He had job offers from companies in the Midwest, but none were in sales. While he was mulling over which one to take, someone he knew from his MBA program who had started working at IBM asked Chambers to interview with Big Blue. Reluctant at first to make the trip east, Chambers agreed after his acquaintance said that he had two tickets to a basketball game that they could attend after the interview. Totally uninterested at first in taking a job at IBM, Chambers changed his mind when the interview went well. The interviewer explained that he would be taking a sales job and therefore would not be using his education, but he noted, "If you sell technology the right way, it uses all your skills." Perhaps the greatest enticement was the guarantee that the interviewer made to John that within 18 months, he would be making twice the salary that he would have made in the Midwest. Chambers agreed to enter the IBM training course in January 1976.

One IBM veteran spent three weeks with Chambers in those early days taking the entry-level class in Endicott, New York. Here the new hires got their first taste of the vaunted IBM culture; mostly the class was designed to teach basic sales skills such as how to prepare presentations and how to make sales calls. The IBM veteran found Chambers "smart, very personable, and very attuned politically." Making a major effort to get to know the 25 members of the class, Chambers got himself elected to one of the class offices: "He was definitely a salesman. I don't know anybody who did not like him in the class," the veteran observed, adding that he had found Chambers more mature than their classmates.

Four years later, Chambers transferred from IBM's Charleston, West Virginia, office to Pittsburgh to take his first managerial job. A Chambers secretary from those Pittsburgh days, Lydia Blankenship, recalled that he was a "young lad with a bit of a West Virginia twang. He was a ball of fire, eager to learn, dynamic and exhilarating." As he became more comfortable in the job, he began looking for opportunities to diminish some of the tension that went with office meetings: he arranged for sundaes to be served at the end of one meeting and for popcorn to be dispensed from a rented popcorn wagon at another (a precursor, no doubt, to the fun part of the Cisco culture that Chambers would promote).

The six years at IBM gave Chambers a sense of unease about large companies, with their swollen bureaucracies and discomforting rigidities. Those rigidities often bred the kind of arrogance that left Chambers bemused. Early on, he tested IBM's famed open-door policy that permitted—in theory at least—any employee to pose a question to any executive. Given an unacceptable answer, the employee could take the query to a higher level. A company friend cautioned Chambers not to repeat such foolish behavior.

The same arrogance exhibited itself to a frustrated Chambers when he complained to a boss that unless huge resources were invested in a new product line, IBM would likely find customers rejecting that line. With the boss's own bonus riding on the products being sold, the boss encouraged Chambers to make sure he sold a great deal of it. Period.

On the positive side, Chambers came to admire the company's pride in its sales force as well as its strong competitive focus. Yet IBM was coasting on its reputation as the nation's premier computer company, drifting from its customers and losing sight of significant changes in the computer market. More than any other lesson from those six years, Chambers learned to become customer-obsessed.

The eight years he spent at Wang Laboratories reinforced that conviction. Managing Wang's Asia Pacific territory for some time, Chambers achieved a lot. When the company began to suffer, An Wang, the head of Wang Laboratories, brought Chambers back to the United States and elevated him to senior vice president for U.S. operations. An Wang—"the smartest man I ever met"—remained one of John Chambers's business heroes. Chambers was impressed with Wang's kindness toward others. ("You'd never have known he was one of the richest men in Boston. He was really very humble.") But it was An Wang's talent with numbers that left Chambers in awe: "I am really good in math. I love numbers. But he could do numbers faster in his head than I could do it with a calculator."

THE PAIN OF LAYING PEOPLE OFF

For all of his admiration of An Wang, Chambers was deeply embittered at the way his mentor let Wang Laboratories slip out of control and at the ax that Chambers was forced to wield as a result of the company's dismal slide. Coerced into laying off 5,000 employees, Chambers vowed to himself that he would never again be in the position of having to fire so many employees. It was, he would say later, until then the single worst experience of his career, being asked to lay off people who had families and who had been loyal soldiers for a decade or two, who through no fault of their own were being sacrificed because of some flawed corporate strategy. (As Cisco's CEO, Chambers believed that Cisco's exploding revenue and earnings growth would assure that he could keep his pledge.)

Cost cutting became a sacred principle for him: "At Wang, we made the classic mistakes. We had twice the organization size we needed. That's why [at Cisco] I'm so careful about adding facilities and adding people. Because I laid off 5,000 people at Wang. You wreck people's lives. You hurt your customers. You hurt your shareholders. But most important, you hurt your employees. When Wang built their buildings, they were ivory towers. And they couldn't be sold independently. You learn more from your mistakes than you do from your successes. Probably because they hurt a lot more."

Though one of John Chambers's mentors has been Jack Welch, it is striking that Welch took a completely different, some say more indifferent, attitude toward the dismissal of employees. While mindful of the pain he caused, Welch stoically downsized 100,000 General Electric employees in the early stages of his rein at GE in the 1980s. If the company required personnel cuts, Welch told his executives, they should carry out the tasks without emotion and with the conviction that they were doing what was right for the business. He never regretted the decision he took to downsize GE in earlier years. Welch undoubtedly thought little of Chambers's sharp distaste for dismissing staff.

In the summer of 1990, Chambers decided that it was time to move on. He notified a headhunter that he was available for a senior sales position at some other firm.

Chambers was ready to leave Wang. His strong personal relationship with An Wang was deteriorating because they held opposing views on which way the company should go. "At Wang, I knew our customer satisfaction was sliding and I pushed on it, but I didn't push as hard as I needed to. But when Wang wouldn't move from the minicomputer to the PC, I had the courage to really challenge Dr. Wang, and very few people did. But he got so mad at me his hand was shaking. It was clearly the only time in my career I saw him visibly upset with me. We were tennis partners, and yet his hand was shaking when I pushed him too hard on the PC issue."

Though it would not appear on his résumé, Chambers carried with him a mental list of dos and don'ts that would provide the nuts and bolts for the corporate culture he would want to create if ever given a chance to run his own company.

At both IBM and Wang Laboratories, Chambers learned not to fall in love with existing technology, not to let a reliance on any single technology prevent the company from listening to how customers feel about new technologies. IBM remained infatuated with its cash cow, the mainframes, and Wang swooned over minicomputers way too long. Had they only listened to their customers, they would have heard these two words over and over again: personal computers.

By not falling in love with existing technology, a company would be in a far better position to catch technology transitions. But only smart people could come up with those insights, so a solid leadership team was a prerequisite to staying ahead of the curve. An Wang dropped the ball on that score. Chambers recalled, "We got into trouble in part because our leadership team didn't have a breadth and depth of experience from outside the company. I was the newest member of the leadership team, and I had been there seven years. So we didn't have people who had seen the problems. I can still remember the article in the *Boston Globe*. It said that only Wang had yet to trip, although all the minicomputer companies had tripped, recovered, tripped, recovered. Wang never tripped. But when we tripped, we never got back up because we didn't have the experience."

From his Wang days, Chambers also learned the crucial lesson that the public remembers failures more than successes: "Dr. Wang had been very successful at transforming the company from one area to the next, but he missed on his fifth transition. I learned that people remember you not necessarily for your successes, but from your failures."

The name John Chambers was certainly familiar to Terry Eger. There had been that sales meeting in Massachusetts, and later Terry had contact with Chambers when John had become the regional vice president for Wang based in Chicago.

While speaking to Kathryn Gould, Terry thought John Chambers would be ideally suited to replace him as vice president of sales at Cisco. He sensed that Chambers would fit in well at Cisco "because he's hardworking and a great cheerleader."

Terry began to sing John's praises. Chambers had great people skills and great sales management skills, and those were the dominant thoughts in Terry's mind as he and Kathryn were talking.

Then suddenly he got quiet. Kathryn knew "I was done for." She knew that she had given Terry Eger valuable information: John Chambers was in play. She could not have known that Terry was looking around for someone to replace him as sales VP.

I'VE GOT A JOB FOR JOHN

"Listen, Kathryn," Terry said in a rushed voice, making up things as he went along. "You know, John isn't really that good. I've got to go. Oh, and don't even bother calling John Chambers, because I'm going to hire him. I have his phone number, but I'm not going to give it to you."

Recalling that phone call to Terry years later, Kathryn Gould was still upset with herself for making it: "Obviously, I wouldn't have called Terry for a reference if I had known he would pick me off. If I hadn't made that phone call to Terry, you never know."

Wasting no time, Terry picked up the phone to John Chambers's home in Andover, Massachusetts. John was away on a job interview in Atlanta, and Elaine, his wife, answered.

"I've got a job for John," Terry told Elaine enthusiastically.

"Where is it?" she asked.

"California."

"But there are earthquakes out there."

Terry turned up the sales pitch. He couldn't let a little rumbling in the ground keep Cisco from getting such a good find.

"You're going to love it."

Terry asked Elaine to have John call when he returned home.

Returning home, John Chambers heard Elaine say, "I got you a job."

Chambers said to her, "What do you mean, you got me a job?"

She suggested that he call Terry Eger.

"What are you looking for?" Chambers asked Terry over the phone after some initial pleasantries.

Terry explained the job to him and insisted, "This is a great opportunity."

Chambers seemed more than willing to entertain the offer.

"Terry, you know in the end I didn't make a lot of money at Wang. I need a great situation where I can make some money. But it's going to be real difficult moving to California."

"John," Terry replied, "this is the best thing you're ever going to see. Come out and take a look at it."

Eger contacted both Don Valentine and John Morgridge, recommending that they take a look at John Chambers. Terry knew that both Morgridge and Dave Ring were hoping to find a new chief operating officer who had operations experience. But Terry thought that would be a mistake. Cisco needed someone who could sell the company aggressively in public, and John Chambers seemed to fit the bill. Though Eger had some misgivings about Chambers—he had once thought him a bit domineering, a bit manipulative—he believed that he had assets that Morgridge did not possess: "Morgridge was dull and Cisco needed a cheerleader and John [Chambers] is great in an expanding market, which I felt Cisco would be in for years. Also, even though Chambers couldn't manipulate me, I saw how effective he was manipulating others."

Chambers was delighted to hear from Terry Eger, delighted at the prospect of a new job. He was becoming increasingly miserable at Wang: "I couldn't stay at Wang. It was killing me. I'd lost faith in the management both ethically and culturally, as well as the momentum of the company."

There were also a lot of questions about the California job dancing around in Chambers's head: Did he want to uproot his family? Could he work for a much smaller company than IBM and Wang? (Cisco had 500 employees at the time and some $183 million in annual revenue.) Was he willing to shift his career from the more formal business style prevalent on the East Coast to the looser style of Silicon Valley enterprises?

Chambers knew that he would be abandoning the big corporate bureaucracies in favor of a faster, more intense business culture. Although he would receive a good salary, he knew that houses were smaller and far more expensive than those on the East Coast. It was easy for him to get over the concern about fitting into a small company: "I'd already lived in 10 cities. And I was part of a lot of cultures."

GETTING A CLOSE LOOK-OVER

Don Valentine played a key role in convincing Chambers to accept the post even though their initial contact was somewhat chilling for the job candidate. Valentine had the reputation of being one of the Valley's most successful venture capitalists as well as a tough boss. "Don Valentine is both the best and toughest board member I've ever seen. His reputation," Chambers recalled, "was firing and hiring presidents in that order." Living up to his reputation, when he met

Chambers for the first time, Valentine spoke so bluntly that it startled Chambers: "This was the first time I realized how open the Valley was—Don Valentine knew about my other offers. He said, 'Tell me about them.' I was kind of hesitating. Then he walked me through them. He said, 'First, you have probably a little bit too much confidence. But if you're really that good, go to the company that's in the right growth time period,' and he walked me through where the other companies were in terms of industry group. He said also, 'If you're as good as you think you are, why go to a turnaround, or why go to a company that is a database company that has already done well? Go to one that is just about ready to take off.' "

Valentine liked what he saw in Chambers: "We had a guy who had been in a big company [IBM] and had gone to a smaller, very sales-oriented company that had crashed [Wang]. If we can find somebody who has failed and knows why he failed, we have a much better asset than someone who hasn't had that experience and is still full of himself." Chambers also possessed all the skills to help manage Cisco's expected high level of growth. Valentine did not then think of Chambers as Cisco's next president and CEO.

Chambers was interviewed for the job by a number of Cisco representatives. CFO John Bolger found him to be "sociable" and "a very positive person." He particularly liked Chambers's special blend of optimism and realism: "He wasn't a starry-eyed optimist. He had both feet on the ground. And he had a very high energy level."

Robert Sweifach was the Cisco board representative on the three-member search committee for the Cisco COO position (John Morgridge and Don Valentine were the other two members). Sweifach met with Chambers over lunch at Alexander's Restaurant at the Marriott Great America Hotel in Santa Clara, California. Sweifach wanted to prepare Chambers for the fast-changing high-tech environment of Silicon Valley. He would have to get used to rapid changes, Sweifach noted. He would have to be flexible and have the ability to make lots of decisions and not stew over them. Sweifach, who liked what he heard from Chambers that day, said later, "I was trying to scare him on the tremendous amount of change [found in the Valley], as opposed to the standard companies where the same things happen every day. I wanted to see how he reacted to it."

John Morgridge, upon meeting Chambers that first time, appreciated Chambers's years spent at large companies. That would be important, since Cisco was headed for high-velocity growth, and Chambers would have to help transform Cisco into a large company.

Once it became clear that Chambers was going to replace Morgridge, the outgoing CEO sought to give the impression that it had been assumed from the time Chambers joined Cisco that he would one day run the company. Indeed, in the 1994 news release announcing that Chambers would become president and CEO, John Morgridge was quoted as saying, "John Chambers was brought into Cisco with the expectation that he would eventually run the company."

Yet at our interview in November 2000, Morgridge acknowledged that back in the early 1990s he did not view Chambers automatically as heir apparent. At their first meeting he told Chambers that he might well become his replacement: "I think it was more than *could*, but less than *guaranteed*. It was put in terms of 'if everything worked out.'" Looking back, Chambers suggested that he was led to believe that the job was his barring anything unforeseen: "I was brought in as the number two to become the number one unless I messed it up." Then, at a dinner when he was formally asked to join Cisco, Chambers asked Morgridge what he was looking for him to be, and the CEO answered, "If you execute well, you're my replacement."

The pressure would be on John Chambers. For he knew that doing a good job meant running one of Silicon Valley's most promising start-ups well.

The Cisco Systems that John Chambers joined in January 1991 was doing spectacularly. The previous month it had showed year-to-year growth of 181.5 percent. It held a whopping 85.5 percent of the router market, while its only competitor, Wellfleet, held only 14.5 percent. In its founding days, Cisco had had a good deal of competition, particularly from Wellfleet, Proteon, and Vitalink. Eventually, its main competition came from Wellfleet. Then a series of mergers occurred and the number of competitors included Wellfleet, Cabletron, and Chipcom.

Underneath the surface, however, it was the same old Cisco: individualists going their own ways, enmities seething, and so little harmony that many wondered how the company sold so many products. Some continued to attribute the company's growth to just plain luck—and a world-class product. The business remained precarious.

For all the self-confidence that John Chambers would exhibit in later years as Cisco's president and CEO, he was filled with uncertainty as he moved through his early days at the company.

Chambers started work at Cisco in charge of customer service, customer support, and marketing. Terry Eger took over product marketing and continued to run business development and domestic sales, which constituted 75 percent of Cisco's sales and 80 percent of its profits. Because he was not interested in handling Cisco's overseas sales, Eger persuaded Don Valentine to hire sales executives for the rest of the world; in time, John Chambers began running international sales. His mandate was to bring sales in the rest of the world on a par with Cisco's domestic sales. At the time Europe had only 18 percent of total sales, and the remaining 7 percent came from Asia.

Slowly, Chambers took on more and more responsibility for Cisco's operations. Early in 1992, Eger turned over business development to him; a few months later, North American sales.

Chambers came in as a senior vice president. His first and greatest challenge was to figure out how to tame all the individualists. He would have to inject fresh managerial discipline and process into a company that seemed to be pulling in all directions.

A DIFFERENT BREED

The place seemed to Chambers more like a series of wrestling matches than a finely tuned business enterprise. He was walking into a "combative" culture (his phrase), but he was determined to get along with colleagues and to work hard at assuring that they got along with one another. The hard part was getting this combative culture to adjust to him. He was, by Silicon Valley standards, a different breed ("a lawyer and an MBA, with a sales background in an engineering company"). But he was confident that he was the right person for the job: "There's a point when you really need people who are entrepreneurial but understand how to manage large professional organizations. And you can't constantly learn on the job. Of equal importance is the ability to build a rapidly evolving and expanding organization. Very few other organizations have been able to achieve this like Cisco."

Unbeknownst to him, at first Cisco's executives were having a hard time adjusting to the new man from West Virginia. He seemed so different, plucked from West Virginia and Boston and cast into Silicon Valley, an obvious stranger to the laid-back California experience: "I talked very fast and had a southern accent and they had trouble understanding me. People tend to like people like themselves."

Ed Kozel, who joined Cisco nearly two years before Chambers and went on to become a board member, remembers how the naturally exuberant Chambers struck a discordant note with the more passive types at Cisco. Gregarious, eager to be one of the guys, appearing to say whatever was on his mind, Chambers was brimming with charm and enthusiasm.

Some of the executives who had trouble figuring out how to deal with Chambers joked among themselves that a southern preacher, a Jimmy Swaggart of sorts, had come to the company. With his thick, syrupy accent, many had difficulty understanding him. Then again, he employed phrases that were alien to the West Coast business culture: "I'm going to empower you." "I'm going to trust you." "I trust people." "We're just going to grow the organization." "I believe in partnering." The word *partnering* was particularly devastating to those who had been unable to partner with one another, let alone with another company.

NO SURPRISES, PLEASE

Some executives felt that Chambers was a phony. "But," insisted Ed Kozel, "John was who he was." He offered to trust employees to do their jobs, but he expected a superhuman effort in return. None of the leadership had mentioned the word *trust* before. None of the old guard had tried to get close to their subordinates, to help them through the difficult moments. Chambers behaved differently: he wanted to mentor others, to become friendly with them, to help them solve their problems. "The big difference," recalled Kozel, "was that if a person screwed up, for Chambers it was not the end of the world. There were second lives as long as it was an honest screwup. He defined an honest screwup as either something that didn't have to do with Cisco's core values, or a surprise." One of Chambers's mantras was: "I don't want any negative surprises and I don't want positive surprises. I don't want surprises."

Chambers demanded a very high level of performance from employees, noted Kozel, "but you didn't feel that it was fatal to make a mistake." Such tolerance was a welcome relief from the unforgiving atmosphere that prevailed in the Sandy Lerner days. Chambers was visiting some Cisco salespeople in San Ramon across the bay in northern California on one occasion. Mark Dickey, then an account manager, remembers Chambers saying, "The hallmark of a great company is not that you don't hit potholes, because every great company does, but how quickly you adjust and move out of that so that you don't let the pothole consume you."

Chambers planned from the beginning to make wide-scale changes among senior leadership. Seemingly a far-fetched notion—after all, the company was doing fine—getting rid of the more incorrigible types made eminent sense to John Chambers.

HE'S NOT PUTTING ON A FACE

Cisco executives began to sense that John Chambers was no phony, that he was serious about all this teamwork and empowerment and trust stuff. "The revelation," admitted Kozel, "was that he actually meant all of that. That gregarious, cheerful person was who he was. It wasn't just a face he put on for us. We all thought it was." Moreover, as a senior vice president and the heir apparent, Chambers carried an increasing amount of authority.

Chambers felt he had to work fast and aggressively because the very survival of the company was not guaranteed: "I realized that we could have very easily crashed and burned during those first couple of years. It was far from obvious to our customers and others that we had the uniqueness to break away. Any start-up that believes it has better than a fifty-fifty chance of being successful is unrealistic."

The problems for Cisco had actually begun back in late 1993, when the media began to question whether the company, in promoting itself as mainly a router company, had adopted the best strategy. The media pushed the notion that routers would soon be dead, and Cisco was just a router company.

John Chambers hired people to fill out management layers, introducing a new process into the sales and marketing side. He held people accountable and injected a fresh discipline into the company. Chambers displayed none of the volatility of Terry Eger, but he was still aggressive. Cisco had acquired through Eger the reputation of taking no prisoners; Chambers kept that reputation alive, but he managed the whole process of sales and marketing in a more orderly fashion.

The pressure was indeed on. The market seemed likely to get crowded, and Chambers believed that only two or three companies would survive. Moreover, large companies such as IBM, Hewlett-Packard, and DEC were giving thought to entering the network market. With so many horses in the pack, the frightening thing for Cisco—and for its competitors—was that no one had a breakaway strategy. No one could truly be sure what role networking would play in American business and how large a market it would generate. And so the pessimists held sway: "There was," recalled Chambers, "a mentality that Cisco would be just another good start-up as opposed to a breakaway company." Many predicted that Cisco's stock might rally in the future, but only for another two years, so it might be better to cash out quickly if the company was going to sink. Hardly grounds for optimism over the long run, even the cofounders had sold their shares. (And in fact from March through July 1994 the Cisco stock plummeted 50 percent.)

Still, Chambers had not moved 3,000 miles to preside over Cisco's demise. He had dreams for Cisco. He sensed that the Internet might become a mighty business force, and he had high hopes that Cisco might catch that wave earlier than anyone else.

From the very start, Chambers applied enormous pressure on his employees. He felt he had no choice. The challenges were mounting against the company: "From the beginning, we built the culture here at Cisco with the confidence that we could do almost anything, not missing goals, and with the healthy paranoia that makes [Intel's] Andy Grove looked relaxed."

Very much consistent with Sandy Lerner's customer advocacy effort, Chambers became obsessive about customers. (For a full discussion of Cisco's customer strategy under Chambers, see Chapter 8.) At Wang Laboratories he had watched grimly a steady decline in revenues that was of course attributable, directly or indirectly, to customer dissatisfaction. And in his first few weeks at Cisco he had listened to engineers who wanted to make only complicated products for smart customers to use. For these reasons and more, Chambers vowed to make customer "sat" the company's top priority.

NO DISTRACTION

Chambers set a tone in the company from the start, spending as much as half of his time with customers. For a high-level executive to devote so much of his energy and time to a single aspect of the business was a marked departure from the way most senior businesspeople functioned. Away from his desk continuously, Chambers seemingly created distractions that kept him from the critical task of supervising Cisco's field operations. He felt, however, that putting himself in front of customers was no distraction; it was performing a company's single most important business task. Chambers was confident that his presence would show customers that Cisco cared enough to send a senior representative to a meeting, which would result in more business for the company. (He also correctly believed that no one had a better chance of making a sale than he did.)

Seeing more and more customers, getting more and more business—it was all part of the John Chambers effort to pursue very ambitious goals, setting the stage for one of Cisco's key cultural features—the stretch-goal mentality: "Setting very aggressive goals forced you to think out of the box. The goal could be market share, it could be profitability, it could be specific to a product, or it could be people retention."

Setting stretch goals would energize the company for heightened growth. To meet the demands placed on a rapidly growing company, Cisco could no longer afford to rely upon the very people who were building its product—the engineers—to sell the product as well. Too often, that had been the case.

When customers cared only about "feeds and speeds" (how fast one company's computer equipment processed data versus the company's competition), then who could explain the equipment better than those who had built it? What Chambers perceived as the engineers' arrogance was, to the Cisco engineers, just doing their part to help the company: "We were asked to do a lot," recalled one of Cisco's first engineers, Greg Satz, "and we delivered on quite a bit. We were pulling ahead from everybody. We created a lot of technology and we came up with solutions that no one else had the opportunity to do because no one had gotten into it as we had. We enabled sales to close a lot of accounts."

Nonetheless, Chambers chose to give an entirely new impetus to the sales and marketing side of the business, giving it equal status with engineering. And that meant the introduction of a revolutionary approach to the marketing of its products. The entire company had to become conscious of customer needs. The tide was shifting: customers cared less about feeds and speeds and more about getting top-notch product service; they also wanted help integrating networking products into their businesses rapidly and efficiently. To handle these issues the entire company would be given over to the task.

As the head of worldwide sales, Chambers understood that only by strengthening customer service could Cisco expect to maintain and improve upon its high growth rates. One day, Chambers went to the customer service department and was frustrated to find only a dozen employees around. Where was everyone? he asked. "This is it," he was told.

Clearly, a customer service desk that totaled 12 employees was not sufficient to handle the volume of phone calls that was coming in to Cisco. If the company was going to continue its current growth pattern, it would require, Chambers estimated, at least another 2,000 people to handle the customer service desk chores, but Cisco had already allotted that many job slots for the entire company over the next 18 months. So Chambers decided that he would look into technology that might make the customer service operation more efficient.

In late 1992, Chambers assigned one of his lieutenants, Don Lebeau, to build a team of salespeople, including systems engineers, regional managers, and operations directors, and to beef up the existing sales channels, the resellers, as Cisco moved away from a reliance on direct selling. If, as seemed inevitable, Cisco was to become a broad networking company—selling more than just routers—it would need a large distribution structure.

Don Valentine, the key decision maker, still clung to the hope that John Morgridge would abandon his plan to retire. Thus, John Chambers did not weigh heavily in his mind as the likely new CEO. Valentine was still "wedded to the idea that Cisco was Morgridge's company to run, that he was doing it well and that the board was exceptionally happy with the result. So we were all going down this high-speed track hoping to have Morgridge run the company indefinitely." As Morgridge became more and more insistent upon retiring sooner rather than later, he began to state openly to Don Valentine that Chambers was the obvious choice to succeed him. "It was," said Valentine, "certainly more John Morgridge than me who advanced the idea that John Chambers was his logical replacement." Valentine refused to think about a successor. He wanted John Morgridge to stay in place: "It was hard for me to imagine that someone would want to give up running a company with this kind of momentum."

THE GROWTH MACHINE

And indeed, the momentum was spectacular. Revenues grew from $183.1 million in 1991 to $339.6 million in 1992, an 85.4 percent increase. Profits for that period nearly doubled, from $43.1 million to $84.3 million. By 1993, revenue had soared to $649 million and profits to $171.9 million. These were spectacular numbers indeed.

The commonly held view in Silicon Valley, particularly among engineers, was that acquisitions were a kind of cop-out. Engineers, not surprisingly, believed that only they could build first-rate products, so there was no reason at all to purchase other companies—to acquire someone else's product. The Cisco culture reflected such hesitancy well into John Morgridge's tenure. (For more on the Cisco acquisition strategy, see Chapter 9.)

Then something happened.

In the spring of 1993, Morgridge was attracted to the idea of a prospective merger with a Cisco rival called SynOptics Communications. Cisco and SynOptics were the two main providers of networking products.

Cisco's routers had been aiding customers to make their networks communicate with one another. But the customers' need to scale up those networks was fast becoming a major issue. In the 1980s, scaling was a luxury—most customers simply wanted equipment that would not crash. When it was developed, the intelligent hub proved less likely to crash and had the added advantage of significantly lowering the cost of operating the network. SynOptics Communications pioneered the market for intelligent hubs. Cabletron Systems, Chipcom, and 3Com joined the market soon thereafter.

But for all its benefits, the intelligent hub had little chance of replacing Cisco's router, because intelligent hubs had scaling limits and routers were very good at scaling. Moreover, only routers could establish network connections over a WAN such as the Internet.

SynOptics and Cabletron dominated the intelligent hub market; Cisco remained wedded to its routers. Ironically, the growing intelligent hub market helped Cisco: by spurring the growth of network traffic, intelligent hubs made it a requirement for customers with large networks to use routers. Put simply, routers were the key to scaling. Intelligent hubs could not do the trick. However, corporations were inclined to choose an intelligent-hub vendor prior to choosing a router vendor, encouraging Cisco to seek comarketing agreements with SynOptics, Cabletron, and Chipcom. No one spoke of a merger at this early stage, just comarketing or partnering agreements.

A DEBATE ON ACQUISITIONS

The physical layout for networking gear had hubs placed in closets on each floor of an office building, with routers down in the basement; the routers were tied into the hubs—and all the gear was tied into desktop computers around the office. If Cisco could partner with hub vendors and integrate its router product with the hub, it would be able to sell more routers.

John Morgridge, Ed Kozel, and Terry Eger spoke with executives from SynOptics, Cabletron, and Chipcom to check on the prospects of partnerships. Deals were made with all three vendors, first with Chipcom, then SynOptics, and finally Cabletron.

By entering into such deals, Cisco hoped to gain a foothold in the hub market, 90 percent of which had been controlled by three vendors. In that way, Cisco would overcome the disadvantage it had with regard to hubs. Now, thanks to the deals, Cisco would be assured of 90 percent of all the business, since the three vendors would push Cisco as the proper vendor for routers (that is, the most compatible with their equipment).

With those partner agreements in place, the three vendors began promoting Cisco's products. It was as a result of the partnering deal with SynOptics that John Morgridge got to know Andy Ludwick, the SynOptics leader. Ludwick wined and dined Morgridge and proposed a merger. The appeal to Morgridge of buying SynOptics was its hub business, along with its management team, and, most important, the fact that the combined Cisco-SynOptics enterprise would clearly become the dominant player in the hub market.

GETTING INTO THE CLOSET

Morgridge was also convinced that the new merged company would be able to build the next-generation product to replace the hub integrated with the router. It was increasingly clear that the hub would eventually by replaced by a new product because it had limited bandwidth.

The next-generation product turned out to be switches, but that would occur a year or so later. Switches would turn out to be far superior to hubs, which concentrate terminal connections (wires) and bridge the data between those connections using software loaded into the hub's memory. A switch essentially does the same thing, except it switches the data through the use of a chip that is much faster than software.

Morgridge thought Cisco would benefit from SynOptics' network management capability with software designed to put all the network data in one place so that reasonable decisions could be made about the data.

John Chambers disagreed with Morgridge about the need to merge with SynOptics. He disliked combining two companies of roughly the same size, preferring smaller technology acquisitions. Don Valentine also frowned upon a merger of equals, and noted that Morgridge's frugality contrasted sharply with the far more free-spending style at SynOptics.

Ultimately, the issue that proved the most divisive was the succession question. It appeared that SynOptics' Andy Ludwick intended to take over the merged enterprise. Ludwick, however, never made it crystal clear to Morgridge whether he wanted to run the new company.

None of Ludwick's waffling mattered, since the perception lingered among the merger's dissenters, Chambers included, that the job was Ludwick's for the asking. Morgridge contended in our interview that he and Ludwick did not come to an agreement on succession, but the dissenters believed otherwise, sensing that Morgridge was preparing the way for Ludwick to run the new company; that provided the dissenters with strong incentive to try to quell the deal.

The behind-the-scenes maneuvering during the proposed Cisco-SynOptics merger has remained a Cisco secret for years, in large measure because it was until then the company's darkest moment. To be sure, Cisco had gone through inner turmoil in the past, yet relative tranquillity had now replaced friction and disarray. But the planned SynOptics merger exposed the company to something it had never faced before—an unbridled rift between its two top leaders. It sundered relations between John Morgridge and John Chambers for the first time. And that rift threatened to cause enormous upheaval. No wonder Ed Kozel remembered that period as "the most difficult time, because this otherwise very tight group of people never had such dissension in the ranks."

The episode was significant not as much for being Cisco's first major attempt at an acquisition, but for the chasm that developed between John Chambers and John Morgridge, which at times seemed unbridgeable and appeared to be leading toward Chambers's departure from Cisco. Suddenly, Morgridge and Chambers were pitted against each other in a battle that many thought was being waged for the soul of Cisco Systems. At stake was the question of how Cisco would deal with one of its chief adversaries: Would it enter into a marriage of convenience with SynOptics, or remain a major rival?

When both Morgridge and Chambers addressed the issue in interviews eight years later, the dust had settled, they were on good terms, and the merger seemed like ancient history, no more than a minor blip on Cisco's radar screen. But at the time, the Morgridge-backed proposal split Cisco's leadership in two, as the Cisco board appeared almost evenly divided over the idea. (Ultimately, the merger's fate would be decided by one vote.)

For John Chambers, the episode proved a defining moment. Never before had he been tempted to go up against John Morgridge. Never before had he felt so strongly about an issue that he was prepared to endanger his prospects for replacing Morgridge. Never before had he seriously contemplated leaving Cisco.

Chambers understood how much was involved. He could have decided to sit quietly, leaving his role as heir apparent unaffected. But if he went up against Morgridge—especially if he won the battle, keeping Cisco from merging with SynOptics—he would probably lose the war.

Morgridge's way of dealing with controversial issues had been to resolve them before bringing them up at a board meting. With the two top leaders of the company in disagreement, there were further arguments to avoid entangling the entire seven-person board in this mess. But Morgridge displayed unusual tenacity despite suspecting that his chances of carrying the day at the board were no better than fifty-fifty.

John Chambers had operated cautiously in the past as well, knowing that he could cruise into Cisco's leadership by retaining the strong image of a team player and by keeping his own personal qualities on display without any attendant controversy. But the SynOptics events placed him in a wrenching dilemma: If he did not stir, he could keep the image of a team player, but, given the rumors swirling around Andy Ludwick, he might wind up the chief sacrifice in the succession contest. And whichever side he supported on the merger issue, he was bound to have some of the controversy stick to him. He had, in his view, little choice but to pick up the cudgel against Morgridge and hope that he could escape without too much personal damage.

By all accounts, despite the strong convictions within Cisco, this was a battle bereft of emotion. No verbal slugfests, no slamming of doors, no threats to quit on the spot. Instead, the merger debate remained gentlemanly, despite the high stakes.

EATING SYNOPTICS' LUNCH

John Morgridge was laboring aggressively to soften up the Cisco board in favor of the merger. He arranged for Cisco and SynOptics teams to meet, but as Ed Kozel noted: "Just putting the people in the same room didn't make them like each other." Morgridge knew that the plan was in trouble when he announced a board vote.

When the board finally met to decide the issue, Robert Sweifach opened the discussion and recalled being "pretty vocal" against the merger. Ultimately, Morgridge discovered that had a vote been taken, it would have been four against the merger, three in favor. Morgridge found only two other board members to support it; Chambers joined Don Valentine, who thought the merger was way too expensive for Cisco, and two other board members in quashing the deal.

Morgridge suggested with an embarrassed look that he had only been talking about a straw vote, and even that wasn't necessary.

The more the debate had gone on, the more the open wound between Morgridge and Chambers had festered. (Asked in our interview to describe his relations with Chambers during the SynOptics fray, Morgridge chose to play down the anguish he obviously felt: "I don't remember it painfully. It wasn't painful, but it was one of the few times we disagreed. Chambers said he would have left if we did it.")

The clear winner was John Chambers. Eight years later, he was pleased that, knowing the risks to himself, he had persevered—and ultimately emerged victorious: "I had the courage to realize that the

merger probably would not work." It was a defining moment for
Chambers, and for Cisco: "What really iced it was looking back later
and realizing we had called it right as a team." Reinforcing his conviction was the subsequent failure of SynOptics and Wellfleet to
create a successful merger. Once the Cisco-SynOptics merger evapo-
rated, it became clear to both SynOptics and Wellfleet that their
main relationship to Cisco would be that of rivals. That realization
led the two companies to merge in the summer of 1994, joining the
number one intelligent-hub company (SynOptics) with the number
two router company (Wellfleet) to create Bay Networks. After that
merger, Bay Networks was larger than Cisco, but Cisco swept past it
rapidly.

For Chambers, that triumph removed any doubt that he would
eventually take over Cisco Systems. "In practical terms," asserted Ed
Kozel, "it was when he became CEO of the company."

To be sure, scar tissue remained, and Chambers would have to act
rapidly to repair the damage that had occurred in his relations with
John Morgridge. Because their differences were largely over varying
approaches to business, and not personal at all, in time the two men
put their dispute into a far corner of their respective memories. (So
much so that Chambers hoped I would not write that the SynOptics
issue had been resolved by a majority of only one.) With John Morgridge still a few doors down from him and still chairman of the company at the time of one of my interviews with Chambers in
September 2000, John Chambers seemed intent on keeping private
the hard-fought, tightly contested battle over SynOptics.

In the same interview, Chambers talked about the SynOptics
episode with a certain degree of sadness at the divisiveness that had
swept through Cisco's leadership, but with a certain satisfaction as
well: "I've learned the hard way at Wang and before that a much
deeper lesson at IBM: When there's a transition occurring in the
industry and you're doing the wrong thing, you do a disservice to
yourself, to your employees and your shareholders and customers, if
you don't stand up and are not willing to risk financial ruin. I did not
think the merger would work. I thought the strategy was better to seg-

ment the market than go with one or two in the market and use a partnership and acquiring type of approach."

With the merger dead, Chambers knew that the Cisco presidency was now within easy reach. "By that time, it was clear that it was mine," he said, though he would not be tapped for two and a half more years.

In June 1994, Chambers was named executive vice president. And beginning with that summer, Morgridge began to transfer his remaining responsibilities to Chambers, setting the stage for the grand announcement that would signal the transition. Until then, Chambers had been in charge of sales, marketing, and customer service. That summer he was given manufacturing. Chambers effectively became chief operating officer, though the title was never given to him. During that same summer, one moment appeared to signal more than any other that John Chambers was effectively in charge of Cisco Systems and would soon be getting the title to go along with the power. To Wall Street analysts who listened to that first-ever Cisco analysts meeting, the fact that Chambers was running the session was foolproof evidence that Morgridge had made up his mind to step down soon. Selecting Chambers to run the meeting was not, however, John Morgridge's idea. He was fishing in Ontario and learned from his secretary that Chambers planned to take advantage of the presence of a number of analysts in the area for other meetings to hold the analysts' conclave.

NOT IN THE BAG

As it turned out, the meeting was memorable more for what Chief Financial Officer John Russell said than for anything noted by Chambers. With Cisco two weeks from the end of the first quarter, Russell felt impelled not to mislead the Wall Street crowd, but his words sounded shocking: "The quarter is not in the bag." ("We had rehearsed it more than a million times," said an exasperated John Morgridge years later, "but Russell said it's not in the bag.")

Chambers later acknowledged that he almost fell out of his chair when he heard Russell say those damaging words. With two hours to go before the market closed, the room emptied out as analysts rushed to alert their home offices to what Cisco's CFO had just said. Ten minutes later, Cisco's stock dropped 4 points, losing $1 billion in value during that brief span, closing at 19, one point above its lowest level ever. Though Cisco actually beat Wall Street's consensus earnings estimate for that July quarter, it proved to be short for the first time on the whisper number. By the fall, most analysts had returned to their heady view of Cisco's stock, and the stock rose accordingly.

Part of Cisco's maturing process entailed getting to the right people to sell its product. From its earliest days, the company's sales force did business with the customers' technical people. CEOs and CIOs were not interested in listening to a Cisco sales pitch because it was selling Internetworking, while the customers' top-level executives were making arrangements to buy equipment from such established networking vendors as IBM and DEC. IBM's SNA product was everything that the Internet was not: SNA was planned, predictable, absolutely reliable, and entirely inflexible. Cisco pushed the Internet, which was ad hoc and didn't always work, but it could be changed easily.

A huge culture clash existed within Cisco's customers. Cisco needed to reach higher into the organization and required someone who was effective at those levels. That was where John Chambers came in. The higher-level executives had been Cisco's enemy because Cisco was selling multi-protocol Internetworking; but they wanted IBM and DEC because they were familiar with those vendors. So Cisco represented a challenge to the model of the strong, centralized information technology (IT) group; the last thing Cisco's sales force wanted was to come to the attention of the CIO or CEO. Once that happened, the high-level executives who made IT decisions would issue orders to a junior department that had taken on

Cisco's networking, demanding that it stop buying from Cisco and start buying from IBM or DEC.

But by 1995 and 1996, the market was changing. Cisco's Internetworking products were beginning to have a profound effect on the enterprise side, and corporate executives were eager to learn more about what Cisco was selling. They were beginning to get Cisco's point: that by using the Internet in their businesses, they could make their businesses far more productive. It was the perfect opportunity for John Chambers to take advantage of his selling skills and knock on the doors of the CIOs and CEOs of Cisco customers. Happily for Cisco, these senior figures were eager to meet the man who had just become president and CEO of Cisco Systems.

John Morgridge was closer to the time when he would actually step down. One important event had occurred to ease his decision: in 1994, Cisco's revenues reached $1.2 billion, a 91.5 percent increase over the previous year's $649 million. Having vowed to run the company until that feat was accomplished, he could happily contemplate retirement. That summer he let Don Valentine know that the time had come for the transition. If Chambers had seemed his likely replacement, he was in fact not a sure thing at all. After the SynOptics episode, Morgridge became decidedly cool toward Chambers and even talked to board members about looking elsewhere for a new president and CEO. Morgridge was chilly as well to two of Chambers's allies, board members Robert Sweifach and Bill O'Meara, who had been against the SynOptics merger. They were not reelected to the Cisco board in 1994.

JOHN CHAMBERS TAKES OVER

But, as he neared his retirement, Morgridge grew increasingly comfortable with Chambers taking over for him. In November 1994, Cisco Systems held its annual shareholder meeting. John Morgridge announced that he was stepping down as president and CEO and that John Chambers, the executive vice president, would replace him in both posts, effective at the end of January 1995. Morgridge would become Cisco's chairman of the board, and Don Valentine would be vice chairman.

John Chambers had been waiting impatiently for the Morgridge announcement. Asked in our interview why it took four years for Morgridge to elevate him to CEO, Chambers burst into laughter, then said, "I think I was ready in two." Then, more seriously: "John [Morgridge] would probably say I was ready in three. And in four he knew it was time to change."

John Chambers took over as president and CEO of Cisco Systems on January 31, 1995. He was 45 years old.

Compared to what the company would become over the next six years, Cisco was small: 3,000 employees, and on its way to $2.2 billion in revenues that year, up from $1.2 billion the year before, a 67.3 percent hike. Cisco's market cap was $9 billion. The transition came at a time when Cisco was doing remarkably well. It was not in need of major overhaul or instant repair. Its annual growth rate remained astronomically high. It was hard to imagine, but a mere six years earlier Cisco's revenues had been only $27.6 million!

The transition to Chambers seemed like almost no transition at all. He had been all but running the company on his own, with most executives reporting directly to him, and with Morgridge quietly fading into the background. (The only new area that Chambers would head as a result of the promotion was finance.) But it was not only that Chambers had been running the internal side of Cisco for some time; increasingly, he had became Cisco's public face, as he handled analyst conferences, took questions from the floor, and essentially became the company's spokesperson.

Don Valentine recalled the transition as being "totally painless" because all of the difficult transitional relationships had been worked out long before John Chambers finally became president and CEO. The one potential obstacle in Chambers's quest for a successful transition was John Morgridge. Traditionally, the person retiring as head of a company disappeared from the scene so that company personnel would treat the new leader as the one and only decision-making authority. But Morgridge was staying on as chairman of the board and would keep an office at Cisco. Valentine and Morgridge sought out others who had experienced recent successful transitions, among them Intel's Robert Noyce and Gordon Moore. The two Cisco men spoke to still others whose transitions had fared poorly.

CHAMBERS IS IN CHARGE

Morgridge pledged to steer clear of Chambers: "I intended to stay in some role in the company, but I wanted to make it very clear that John Chambers was in charge. I didn't want people coming to me as an alternative channel. It was clear to me that sticking around does not work if you meddle at any level operationally. The best way to make it clear that you are no longer in charge is just to leave."

Morgridge spent three weeks in Vietnam with his son in February 1995. Then in May, he spent 10 weeks bicycling across America with his wife. During Chambers's first year in office, Morgridge was away a majority of the time. "That was the plan," said Valentine, "and it worked very well."

With Morgridge largely out of sight, an unfettered John Chambers took command. Chambers credits Morgridge with executing "one of the smoothest, if not the smoothest management evolution transitions ever carried out in our industry, in terms of handing the ball off. We didn't miss a beat."

Chambers was now ready to alter the face of the company in ways that would enable Cisco to grow way beyond its current size. He planned to upgrade the management ranks, to build up the organizational structure, and to empower executives to carry the ball on their own. In short, under Chambers, Cisco would cease to be a start-up and begin to have the look and feel of a major corporate enterprise.

During his first few weeks in office, Chambers made it clear to everyone that he planned to preside over a much larger Cisco in the coming years. Soon after becoming president and CEO, Chambers met with executives from Visa International to gain new business at the Executive Briefing Center at Cisco headquarters in San Jose, California. As soon as Chambers walked into the meeting, he explained to the Visa contingent that he was Cisco's fourth president. Mark Dickey, the Cisco executive who had asked Chambers to attend the meeting, remembered thinking, "Oh my gosh, they're going to think we're unstable." But within seconds, Chambers added, "And let me explain to you why that's a good thing." Chambers showed the group a couple of charts of Cisco's dramatic hockey stick–like growth, and noted that at each stage of that growth a different kind of president with different kinds of skills was required. "I'm here to make Cisco a multibillion-dollar company," he said matter-of-factly. Dickey was struck by how "logical and smooth" Chambers sounded. He seemed "clearly in control of the strategy and direction of the company."

Chambers knew from the start that building Cisco Systems into a multibillion-dollar company—in his own parlance, "one of the great companies in America"—required an attitude toward business and toward one's own company that few chief executives had the skills or patience to develop. He had both, and he was eager to get started.

6 Evangelizing the Internet

"What great routers you have!" It was always unlikely that customers would make such an endearing statement to Cisco's sales team. Clearly, the Cisco team needed another selling point, something more alluring and more exciting, a feature to make customers sit up and take notice.

Cisco found the selling point right at home.

The point turned out to be the Internet. More specifically, Cisco used the Internet to make its business functions more effective. And it then promoted the idea that every business needed to use the Internet to enhance its business capabilities.

Cisco's leadership became convinced that the Internet was a remarkable new tool that could speed up all sorts of business functions and automate business processes that had required human resources. It was right on the mark in understanding the great promise of the Internet for business; indeed, it was a pioneer in its use of the new business tool. But in its zeal to "sell" the Internet to the business community, Cisco never asked itself a critical question: Are we overpromising on the Internet? There was no reason to ask such a question. The Internet seemed to be on a growth path that was unstoppable.

Beginning in the mid-1990s, Cisco put more and more of its business functions on the Internet, casting itself as an E-company.

The strategy of working toward becoming an E-company has become a critical part of the Cisco culture. It developed into one of Cisco's great talking points in explaining how the company was different and why it had become successful throughout the nineties.

The way Cisco defined the new concept, an E-company would exploit the Internet to reshape and reinvent business relationships with Cisco's core constituents, whether they were suppliers, partners, customers, or employees. It looked to the Internet to provide speed, agility, and, most remarkably, a real-time global reach.

John Chambers said unhesitatingly that Cisco Systems had in the late 1990s become the best example in the world of how to use Internet technology. Therefore, he decided to turn the strategy of teaching how to become an E-company into a core competency at Cisco.

For Cisco's first decade, it was purely a manufacturing company. It made routers and switches, and it sold them in huge numbers. By the mid-1990s, the company began to develop this new core competency, which other companies could have developed on their own without the help of Cisco Systems, but did not. Either these companies did not understand the Internet, or they did not appreciate its power, or they failed to listen to colleagues who pleaded with them to take a modern approach to business. Whatever the case, they created a huge vacuum into which Cisco Systems came rushing.

The transformation of Cisco into an E-company coincided with the decision made by John Chambers to build a larger public profile for the company. At the top of the list of talking points detailing the company's achievements was the development of Cisco Systems into an E-company.

John Chambers was able to convince many of the leading businesspeople in the United States and around the world that there was something important to learn from Chambers and Cisco: "What we do now is teach people how to use the Internet to run their businesses better. So now I don't just sell products. I now show people how to transform their company—both in terms of the applications that go with it and the way that you change your culture."

These businesspeople wanted to learn how to use the Internet productively and efficiently for the benefit of their companies.

PROFESSOR OF THE E-COMPANY

And so John Chambers became a kind of professor of the E-company, teaching the virtues of the Internet as a business tool. Chambers was thrilled to take on the teaching role. The more businesspeople who listened to his speech about the wonders of the Internet, the more customers he would pick up for Cisco Systems.

"We are the company that goes out and teaches others to do it, and that is our business," John Chambers asserted proudly, adding: "If we teach people how to use the Internet, they buy it. But if we teach others and get productivity, and [the] standard of living increases, they buy a lot more of our product, and we'll truly earn their trust."

Keeping a certain perspective, Chambers acknowledged that Cisco still wins or loses on the basis of selling its products. "We don't lose track. The way that we get paid is by our product. But if I teach others how to use the Internet and help them transition over, they will buy a lot more of our product."

Cisco had an obvious advantage over older companies in striving to become an E-company. Because it was a new company, because it was unencumbered by old technology and old attitudes, Cisco adopted a very open and welcoming approach to the wonders of the Internet. And it seemed perfectly natural for a company that was supplying the key elements of the Internet's infrastructures (routers and switches) to adopt the Internet as its most valuable business tool.

Cisco did not have a heritage of using mainframe-based equipment dating back to the 1970s. Companies that were saddled with those legacy systems remained behind the curve because they had no other choice than to maintain their existing systems for as long as they could.

A young company could start with a clean sheet of paper and ask, How can we build an information technology system from scratch? Far removed from and not dependent on those legacy systems, Cisco was a member of the founding class that came to life in the mid-1980s, relying on the new technology of personal computers, local area networks, and eventually, the Internet. Not stuck in the past, Cisco's leadership team, both on the engineering and administrative sides, was eager to tackle new ideas, to do things differently—and nothing was more new or exciting than Internet technology.

NIFTY ELECTRONICS

But even Cisco took time to catch on to the excitement of the Internet. "When I joined the company in 1989," recalled former Cisco board member and Chief Technology Officer Ed Kozel, "I asked for a telephone. This guy reached into a box and dragged out a recycled telephone and gave it to me. It had the wires hanging out. You had to wire your own phone. So there wasn't any infrastructure. There was no information systems guy. This guy who had handed me the phone was the information systems guy, but he was doing everything. He kept the mainframe going, so putting in phones was the least of his concerns. We went on this real ad hoc do-it-yourself kick for a couple of years. There was hardly any paper, but there weren't any nifty electronics either."

As Cisco began to grow, its executives started to think about how to handle its business processes more effectively. Management consultants were invited in for chats. The executives knew that they really had to get organized. "When new hires came in," said Kozel, "we didn't want to give them phones with wires hanging out."

Kozel explained another great advantage that Cisco had over older companies: "We probably had a little bit of paper, but we never institutionalized the paper because we never had the processes. When we decided to create the processes, it was just the right time to say, 'I wonder if there is a better way to do it.' This was before the Web. But since we were never paper-heavy, when we needed to scale and put in that process, we sort of went to electronics early on."

The man who decided to put some "nifty electronics" into Cisco's business systems was Peter Solvik, currently senior vice president for information services and formerly chief information officer. He joined Cisco Systems in 1993. Solvik's insight was that it made little sense for Cisco to provide highly sophisticated products for the Internet, and then consider the Internet to have minor value to Cisco's business: "We shouldn't be going to customers with all these great slogans and then operate things the old way. We made a fundamental decision that we would have no credibility if we said 'Do as I say' and not 'Do as I do.'"

Part of that fundamental decision entailed upgrading most of Cisco's information technology staff and getting John Morgridge to increase information technology spending. For some time no one thought it would be possible to sell routers over the Internet. Cisco was growing 100 percent a year, and its main challenge was being able to scale while retaining customer satisfaction. The way to scale was by hiring people. That was the traditional view. But it would require Cisco's hiring large numbers of engineers. With competitors seeking talent as well, hiring all those engineers was not going to be easy. The clear incentive existed to look at the emerging Internet technology. (In time, Cisco did hire in large quantities, believing that it needed a much larger infrastructure to support its hypergrowth.)

Cisco's initial baby steps in using the Internet centered on customer relations. During the early 1990s, the company was using a simple text "bulletin board" on the Internet for customer questions and comments. The customer-help Internet site, called "Cisco Information Online," was not a great success although a good deal of money had been thrown into it.

Meanwhile, the number of customer calls coming in to Cisco was growing rapidly. It was not possible to hire technical people to solve customer problems fast enough.

Then, late in 1993, Cisco's engineers, searching for a better way to interact with customers, turned to Mosaic, the first Web browser. The new technology made getting information from the Internet easier. It was still before the commercial Internet, so customers had to dial directly into Cisco's computers. Most people could not connect to the Internet. At least the Mosaic software, existing in the public domain, was free.

Meanwhile, Cisco's Technical Assistance Center, which provided after-sales service, was experiencing a major staffing crisis. With complex network gear, customers required continuous contact with the supplier. That resulted in Cisco's highly trained service engineers handling routine questions about minor problems rather than devoting themselves to truly technical issues. At times mistaking the engineers for salespeople, customers sought to place orders.

The problem grew acute: Cisco executives realized that they would have to hire more engineers or reduce the time that its engineers were wasting on small issues. Otherwise, sales of routers and switches would suffer.

Brad Wright, the head of the Technical Assistance Center, decided that the answer was to automate all of the routine issues on the Internet. At the time, it seemed like a logical move. But to some it was fraught with danger. For instance, when Pete Solvik approached Don Valentine, then chairman of the board, to suggest opening up the Internet to customers, Valentine expressed concern that customers would discover Cisco's bugs. Solvik assured him that this was not a problem.

GOING BEYOND VANITY WEB SITES

The greatest leap toward becoming an E-company came in early 1994, when Cisco put up its Web site specifically to deal with customer issues. Whereas other companies over the next few years would put up what Cisco executives called "vanity Web sites," with little more than product and company information, Cisco created a site on which there could be actual business transactions. That was revolutionary.

At first, the transactions were limited to customers solving their technical problems, but that in and of itself was a trailblazing use of the new Internet technology. The beauty of Cisco's bold move onto the Internet was that the company was able to hire another 1,000 people, none of whom had to be employed at the Technical Assistance Center. Half went to the engineering side and the other half into sales and other areas. "Customer satisfaction went up," said Rick Justice, senior vice president for worldwide field operations. "Our competitors needed to pony up more for support or let their support deteriorate."

Cisco's engineers were asked to create new programs that could deal with queries on-line. Even if a network engineer was given a vague complaint such as "Cannot connect to remote server," the new software program would translate that comment into a description of a familiar problem, and the four most probable explanations would appear on the computer screen. It took another three months for a set of frequently asked questions (FAQs) to go on the Internet.

Customers took to the Internet eagerly. They no longer had to seek out engineers over the telephone. Unlike the old system, in which engineers were available on the phone only during daytime business hours, it was now possible to seek out answers over the Internet 24 hours a day. The site, accessible via special passwords, was only for customers who had Cisco contracts. It proved to be popular, and phone calls and faxes decreased.

Happily for Cisco, during the mid-1990s it increased its support staff by only 800 people, while sales quadrupled. Without the Internet, Cisco would have required 1,000 more engineers for the Technical Assistance Center. The Internet turned out to be another great cost saver with respect to customer-related software: that software could now be distributed over the Web rather than transferred to disks and mailed to customers. Cisco estimated the savings at $250 million.

The automating of the customer service segment of Cisco's business operations was the first major step toward the creation of an E-company. By saving so much money, Cisco could devote those resources to other aspects of the business that would yield remarkable dividends. "When we got involved in E-commerce," observed Rick Justice, "our cost structure was so far below our competitors' that it enabled us to invest more aggressively, and therefore we had a higher profile in the market, and that increased demand."

Pete Solvik was not prepared to attribute Cisco's first steps toward becoming an E-company to shrewdness or intelligence. It was, rather, a case of falling into a very good thing: "A typical company spent many years using the Internet as a generic tool. We started with it as a customer interaction tool and emphasized revenue. As our support got better, customers used it more. It made customer support a profitable business. So we tripped over it. There was a lot of dumb luck. We didn't say the Internet is going to change everything in 1993. Our first experience was luck because another project failed."

The shrewdness came when Pete Solvik and his colleagues began to exploit that good luck. He and the new director of customer service, Linda Thom Rosiak, were aware that a third of Cisco's orders, most of which arrived via fax, contained major mistakes—not surprising, given how complicated Cisco's products were. Each product had as many as a dozen features, including the power supply, memory, software, and cables. Cisco offered many choices for each feature. The trouble was that customers sometimes chose combinations that did not work together. A customer might select a piece of software but then choose too little memory to handle the software. To find prices, customers were expected to wade through a catalog the size of a thick phone book, containing 13,000 items! When the wrong orders came in, whether related to configurations or prices, Cisco simply faxed the wrong order back to the customer for adjustment—more wasted time. Customers grew angry and frustrated.

In remarkable contrast, one-third of Cisco's problems with customer complaints were being solved over the Internet. It seemed logical to conclude that the ordering process would benefit from automation. In May 1995, Cisco began studying how to put its ordering system on the Internet. Two months later, the new system was already being used widely around the company.

Most companies had not even set up a Web site yet. Meanwhile, Cisco created more and more programs, putting more and more business functions on the Internet. The Order Status Agent was the first such program, permitting customers to track the progress of their orders on-line. Then came a program that allowed for the posting of prices of all Cisco products on the Net.

Cisco learned of another software program—perhaps the most critical—that would allow customers to select compatible parts not only for PCs, but also for high-priced items such as routers. The software had been created by a small start-up called Calico Technology. Hearing of the company, Pete Solvik asked John Chambers for several million dollars to purchase Calico. Chambers quickly agreed, and Solvik now had the main element required for Internet selling: the on-line configuration of every Cisco product, accessible in a customer-friendly manner.

Eventually, Cisco's networked commerce agents became the best known of Cisco's Internet business solutions. These agents enable users to configure, price, route, and submit electronic orders directly to Cisco Systems, and permit more than 10,000 authorized representatives of direct customers and partners to configure and price Cisco products on the Internet.

As of June 2002, over 90 percent of all Cisco orders were booked on the Internet, and 90 percent of all customer calls were resolved over the Net. Brad Boston, senior vice president and the current chief information officer, commented that since arriving on the job in the year 2000 he had signed only three documents. The rest was done electronically.

Cisco was far ahead of other companies. "No other company has gotten this," Pete Solvik commented, "to be at 90 percent E-commerce. HP may be touting its E-service and Oracle may say that its software powers the Internet. But the fact is that when I want to buy big sophisticated equipment from those companies, I can't do it on the Web."

A BROAD USE OF THE INTERNET

Cisco's Internet business solutions make Cisco the most sophisticated user of the Internet, which is a competitive advantage. These solutions include virtual manufacturing, the virtual supply chain, and E-learning modules. Cisco is entirely paperless for employee functions: E-paychecks, E-benefits, E–stock administration, E–vacation time, E–performance management, etc. Even before they are hired at Cisco, prospective employees explore the Cisco E-company: almost all job résumés arrive over the Internet, allowing Cisco to screen with great efficiency the thousands of job applications it receives monthly. Clearly, such automation saves a huge amount of time. At one point, Cisco was getting 100,000 applications each year. Just finding room for all that paper in someone's office would have been problematic.

Cisco's CFO, Larry Carter, had an idea of how to make the lives of the company's sales force more pleasant. They had been grumbling about the amount of time it took to file expense reports and how long it took to get reimbursed. Moving expense reporting onto the Web, Carter eventually required, instead of hundreds of employees, only two people to audit the company's employees. The automated expense-reporting system is empowering: When an employee submits an expense report, the program checks to make sure that no expense rules have been violated. The person is then automatically reimbursed without a signature or other form of higher approval. The manager is notified that the expense report has been submitted and that there have been no policy violations. "The program helps to make the company real-time," says an obviously elated Pete Solvik.

What if an employee violates an expense rule? It happened to a Cisco employee who was on a 10-day business trip and was submitting expenses each day via the Internet. On the fourth day, he submitted an expense for getting his laundry done at his hotel. The program rejected the expense because Cisco policy permits a traveling employee to be reimbursed for a laundry charge every five days!

He would have to wait one more day to submit the charge! To correct this violation might have taken weeks without the Internet.

Larry Carter has been behind many of the E-company features. Besides expenses, he automated the payment of commissions and systematized the company's accounting procedures on the Web. The goal was to create real-time management accounting. It took him four years. The purpose of the entire exercise was to empower management teams to use real-time information to improve decision making. There are plenty of examples: The real-time system alerted Cisco executives to the ups and downs of Japan's economy. At one point, when Japan was rebounding, Cisco threw in new resources to exploit the improved economy. On another occasion, Carter and his colleagues noticed an improvement in the growth rates of European countries, which had previously been flat. They immediately authorized the hiring of more employees long before competitors caught on.

THE VIRTUAL CLOSE

The feature that has gotten the most public attention is the virtual close. The company can close its books within 24 hours of the end of its quarter. That means it has real-time hard numbers, not estimates. Considering how many companies are still unable to match that feat, the virtual close ranks as one of Cisco's most impressive technical achievements.

John Chambers enjoys pointing out that Cisco can do even better. He told a meeting of new Cisco salespeople on September 11, 2000, "Actually, I know three weeks before the quarter is over what our earnings will be. We can close the books anytime we want. It's the biggest productivity application on the Internet. The competition finds this data out a month after the quarter closes."

When Larry Carter joined Cisco as John Chambers's first chief financial officer in 1995, the company was earning a little over $1 billion in revenues. Carter noted: "My concern at that time was this: Here's a company growing really fast. How do you maintain control in a fast-growing environment and avoid surprises and also improve the timeliness and integrity of information to financial management. Control side was very much on my mind. I believed financial process is like manufacturing. When you shorten cycles in manufacturing, good things happen. No different in financial process—you reduce close, quality should improve, timeliness of information is better, and you have better controls inherently."

At first, Carter called the process "quality and close" because he was focusing on quality. Having real-time information available every day was almost unheard of for most companies. Carter knew he was onto a good thing.

"So as we got pretty good at this, we were closing in about four hours, whether at the end of the month, quarter, or year. As we got to the end of a quarter, it was no different; we watched orders every day, margins, backlog, lead times go out, all that information was available. We knew where we were and we also knew that at some point things would have to slow down. You can't grow 70 percent at our size year after year forever."

In 1995, it took 15 days to close Cisco's books, which was not unusual. Recognizing that companies cannot get the numbers together quickly, the Securities and Exchange Commission allows companies 45 days for filing 10-Qs and 90 days for filing 10-Ks.

The slow process had inherent flaws. By not having control over its own data, Cisco could cause unnecessary jitters on Wall Street, affecting its stock negatively. Given that Cisco needed a good deal of that stock to make its acquisitions, such jitters could have brought one of the company's pivotal strategies to a stop. But with all those numbers available at a second's notice, Cisco was confident that it could prevent any negative financial surprises that might depress the company's stock.

Though the information was literally at the fingertips of John Chambers, Larry Carter, and other senior Cisco executives, not every financial metric was checked daily: Market share was looked at quarterly. Order/revenue status was checked hourly, daily, weekly, monthly, and quarterly, as were discounts and product margins. Expenses were perused daily, weekly, monthly, and quarterly. Head count was observed weekly, monthly, and quarterly. Revenue per employee, after-tax profit, and the balance sheet were examined monthly and quarterly.

The perception grew that Cisco could actually forecast market developments so quickly that it would have ample warning to make corrections that would avoid harm to the company. In an article it published on May 24, 1999, *Fortune* magazine wrote: "With a couple of mouse clicks and a password, CFO Carter can call up his company's revenues, margins, orders, discounts given on those orders, and top ten customers—all for the previous day. . . . This doesn't just cut down on the need for number crunchers or on those 'negative earnings surprises' that freak out Wall Street. It makes for a company that reacts more quickly to market shifts and competitive threats. It allows execs of a big corporation like Cisco . . . to stay in tight control. . . . Thanks to this 'virtual close,' as Carter calls it, he and CEO John Chambers can detect changes in market conditions almost instantly."

Did the virtual close help Cisco forecast changes in the market? At times, Cisco said it did. At other times, it backed off from such a claim.

In its 2000 annual report, for instance, Cisco certainly gave the impression that its virtual close helped it to react: "Five years ago it took Cisco 14 days to close its books each quarter. Now, with the 'virtual close,' using powerful Internet technology, Cisco executives have real-time, daily access to company financial information, empowering them and their employees to instantly react to market shifts and changing business requirements."

Chambers liked the virtual close for its capacity to help his senior colleagues make decisions that he didn't have to make. After a quarterly close, for example, a product-line manager could learn what gross margins were on his or her products, whether they were below expectations. It became easier to determine the cause if margins were too small. That was the theory, at any rate.

Cisco executives acknowledge that it is difficult to indicate Cisco's savings because of the virtual close. Pete Solvik asks: "How can you put a value on knowing the exact status of the business when another company takes 14 days to close their books? You can't put a solid dollar on that." He did estimate that for the year 2000 the company was saving $1.4 billion in improved productivity. That figure rose to $1.7 billion for 2001.

Taking on the characteristics of an E-company has changed behavior patterns of Cisco employees in intriguing ways. Solvik said that the E-company approach "creates an Internet time culture where we're less meetings-oriented. I may have five meetings in a day but 15 transactions via e-mail and voice mail that in a lot of companies would have required meetings. We don't have written memos. Our communication is much more in real time. We don't honor the hierarchy. So people acting for me can interact with John Chambers. The real-time aspect has created a networked culture. We have a networked organization, a networked way of getting things done, a networked way of communicating. It's faster, more customer-focused, more employee-focused."

Throughout the second half of the 1990s, John Chambers enjoyed the spotlight, and he enjoyed serving as the spokesperson for the Internet business world. Just as an actor gets high on standing ovations, Chambers was positively ecstatic over the reception he and Cisco were getting wherever he went.

In earlier days, it had been much more difficult to find an audience for his message that the Internet was here to stay.

All through the early 1990s, Cisco's sales force sold its equipment to the technicians, or at least to the network managers, who had to build the network for their companies. But getting to see the top brass was almost out of the question.

CIOs did not think that networking was that important. Nor did they have a sense of how important the Internet was, or would become.

The real breakthrough for Cisco was getting to the CIOs and CEOs. Once those senior executives latched on to networking and the Internet, Cisco was going to sell more and more products.

Over the next five years, Chambers found it easier and easier getting to see the CEOs and CIOs of American corporations.

Don Valentine believes that Chambers's greatest contribution to Cisco has been his ability to get his foot in the door of heads of corporations. "As we switched from one John [Morgridge] to the other, we were still at that style of trying to reach up and learn how to do business with the head of General Electric and Hewlett-Packard and General Motors. John Chambers's background at IBM and Wang had provided both a comfort and a style of being able to do that. If you are going to become a serious company where you have huge revenues, you have to do business management to management."

Chambers has provided Cisco with access to the leaders of the top 500 companies of the world.

What compelled the CIOs and CEOs of corporate America to talk to John Chambers and his colleagues was the power of the Internet. These business leaders began to believe that the Internet could bring miracles to their companies: it could deliver productivity gains never before imaginable.

Cisco could now point to the way it had automated its own business functions and then show how its revenues had multiplied. Just as important, it could demonstrate that as those revenues rose, the number of staff it employed in certain vital sectors remained flat. "We became an example for the CEOs," said Ed Kozel.

"They didn't want to see a box. They wanted to see how a company could be run. They couldn't have cared less that we had all these gray boxes all over the place. If they liked the company, they bought millions of gray boxes. The beauty was we were first. All of our competitors were saying, 'My box is faster, it's cheaper.' They were competing at the level of boxes. They weren't talking about what you can do with the boxes.

"When we met with a CEO, we never talked about the box. We would explain what the CEO could do with a box. The CEOs and the CIOs began to realize that it's what you do with the box that will determine whether you succeed or fail as a customer."

Cisco did not create the Internet market, Kozel notes. "We were there and we saw it happening before others. We went to a CEO who didn't realize the Internet was important and we said that the Internet *will* change your company. Later, we went to government leaders and said this will change your country."

As word spread that Cisco Systems had embarked on revolutionary work in making itself over into an E-company, John Chambers became more and more in demand as a public speaker. And the more he appeared in front of audiences, the more the media began to sense that he was unique in the high-tech world. He was not only running his company spectacularly well, but he was also a great promoter, a great explainer of the hottest magic in town, the Internet.

GETTING THE MEDIA'S APPROVAL

Virtually from the first moment that journalists began to hear of Chambers, they liked what they saw. He was photogenic, he was smart, he was hip, and he was brimming with self-confidence. The media liked the fact that Chambers spoke with an unmatched authority about the Internet and the entire networking industry.

Chambers's good fortune was that the media began latching on to the networking industry at a time when Cisco Systems, personified by John Chambers, had become its most glamorous and successful icon. Almost every major story on the networking industry had to pay its respects to Cisco Systems. Journalists seemed to recognize that few of their readers knew, or for that matter cared, what Cisco did. Most of the articles focused on the personality of John Chambers and on his business strategies. When routers and switches were discussed, they got passing mention, and only grudgingly. Who wanted to dwell on plumbing?

Chambers's photo appeared on the cover of most business magazines, and though no one quite understood or appreciated what it was that Cisco Systems did for the Internet, Chambers had gained sufficient respect to speak on behalf of the entire industry. Indeed, these cover stories sometimes portrayed Chambers as perhaps the best business leader around: "Is John Chambers the best CEO on earth?" asked *Fortune* on its May 15, 2000, cover. The articles noted that Cisco supplied networking equipment; they noted that Cisco provided the "infrastructure"—whatever that was—for the building of the Internet. Since it was hard to explain precisely what the Internet was, few bothered to go into great detail on what the Internet's plumber did.

What media audiences did care about was the man at the top. Touted as something of an icon of the high-tech world, Chambers had an easy time converting that popularity and respect into the role of an evangelist. Audiences wanted to know why the Internet was important, and they didn't want to hear too much technical lingo. They wanted the Internet served up to them in straightforward terms that they could understand. And since the audiences were mostly businesspeople, they wanted to know how the Internet could help their businesses. Chambers was superb at transmitting uncomplicated but sweeping messages that made it almost instantly clear just what was so terrific about the Internet.

He had so much going for him, it was no wonder that his following grew, and that people were willing to travel thousands of miles to hear one of his speeches. When he spoke of the marvels of the Internet, he was much more than some academic type who had followed the high-tech world in an ivory tower environment. When he explained to business audiences how information technology was the key to success and how the Internet would change the world, he was no business school professor who had been perusing *Fortune* and *Business Week* and had just found the Holy Grail. Chambers had been in the trenches. He had built the most powerful high-tech company of the decade, and he truly seemed to understand what the emerging technology could do when applied properly.

Chambers seemed to understand better than almost everyone else that his audiences didn't care about how the Internet works any more than they cared about how a car gets up to 60 miles an hour or an airplane gets off the ground. They wanted to know what they could *do* with the Internet. And so Chambers always kept his message simple and straightforward: The Internet is here to stay. It will grow in dramatic terms over the next decade or two. It will change everything, from the way we work and live, to the way we learn and play. It is a fact of life, and it's not going away. Every device in our homes will be connected to a network. Every device at work will be connected as well.

One of the corporate leaders to whom John Chambers spoke was Jack Welch, the chairman and CEO of General Electric, and a Chambers mentor. It was a big moment for Chambers, and he pulled it off. When I spoke to Jack Welch in December 2000, he remembered the day well: "John came to speak to us and had an enormous impact. We were going full speed on the buy side and sell side, but he really lit a fire under us. We were diddling with the make side. And so he lit a fire under us on the make side. The fact is that Cisco's impact on General Electric was enormous. John talked about how to digitize a business. Now it's our job to do better than he's doing. He's shown the way. His products are right at the heart of what digitization is all about. They are in the middle of this global shift. These guys are right on the sweet spot. They have the products, and the world is coming to them. He was very smart to have digitized his own company. Some companies who have the right products and processes haven't done the job that he's done. He's made his company into a role model, and he was able to show the benefits."

Chambers speaks to government leaders, who are potential customers because the more information technology in which their governments invest, the more interest they show in the Internet, and the more business will accrue to Cisco. Chambers's message to government heads is that if they want their country to be competitive economically, they have to go with the Internet. These high-level visits do not come in place of visits to corporate customers in a foreign country; they are an important adjunct. Nothing makes a greater impression on a customer in a foreign country than saying, "I've just been to see your prime minister."

Visiting China's leadership gave John Chambers the chance to have an impact on a country with which he was intimately familiar. Indeed, he was in his element in China. He had been there many times before. And so when Chambers was ready to sit down with the president of China, Jiang Zemin, in September 1998, he had years of experience and knowledge to take with him into that crucial meeting. Chambers was something of a business icon in China. He liked the culture and the people and enjoyed the business atmosphere. Bill Nuti, the then Cisco executive who accompanied Chambers on his visit, sensed that Cisco faced an uphill challenge, for the Chinese business atmosphere was unlike others that he had known: "Where everything is horizontal or vertical, China's business atmosphere is diagonal. That is challenging to your mind. The mix of politics and business and social behavior has a lot to do with how you construct a sales cycle in China. That means that the government plays a significant role in business, and business plays a significant role in government. And popular opinion has a great opportunity to shape which players are successful and which are not."

With his vast experience in China, Chambers suggested that the best way to deal with the Chinese business environment was to be very careful: "With over 16 years of experience in China, always very profitable, I would say this: Let's start with the most basic premise, which is that you're better off as an American company putting your money in a safe-deposit box than you are investing in China, because if you don't know what you're doing and how to make money there, you will end up regretting the investment. What you have to understand about doing business in China is that you make money as you go. That doesn't mean you shouldn't partner with local businesses and local government, and we do that very well. But anyone who has been successful in China will tell you: You should make money as you go. And you build partnerships and trusts for life. Not just for a year or two."

Moreover, it is best to keep in mind, said Chambers, "that the Chinese are capitalists at heart. They are very astute and very good busi-nesspeople, including the government leaders."

The president of China rarely gives more than 30 to 45 minutes of his time to any business figure, Bill Nuti notes, "even when he meets Bill Gates." But when Chambers and the Chinese leader met that fall day in 1998, the meeting lasted one hour and 40 minutes. The president was knowledgeable about Cisco and eager to find out how the Internet could help him shape his country's economy, how it could reform education, how it could manage long-term growth through higher levels of productivity. He peppered Chambers with questions about how Cisco could advise them on their Internet strat-egy, less from a business standpoint than from an overall political and economic point of view.

Cisco has built strong relationships with the Chinese. "Cisco is seen in China," says Bill Nuti, "even though it is a Western company, as a Chinese entity, because it's created such a close relationship with China and it has access to government leaders regularly."

HE DIDN'T GET IT

In his frequent public appearances, John Chambers rattles off the names of world leaders with whom he has recently met. It is an impressive list. He always mentions the Japanese prime minister, whom he saw in 1996, two and a half months before his political defeat. That prime minister failed to understand John Chambers's message. He didn't "get it," as Chambers likes to say. In 2002, Cham-bers was happy to say that the current Japanese prime minister got it.

The ousted Japanese prime minister did not understand that gov-ernmental leaders have no other choice but to adopt information technology, specifically the Internet, as the single best means to improve their national economies. "The point that I made to the prime minister was this: He was building off of the Industrial Revolu-tion with less than 20 percent of his capital expenditures going into IT. His global competitor [the United States] was up to 47 percent.

He was building highways. The United States was building Internets. And while he understood it intellectually, he did not change. Often the most successful companies and countries are the most difficult to change. But when I showed this same chart to President Jiang Zemin of China, President Kim Dae-jung in Korea, Prime Minister John Howard of Australia, and Prime Minister Tony Blair in the United Kingdom, they got it. And the point is whether it's government leaders or business leaders, they now realize there's a one-to-one correlation between economic growth and infrastructure."

Chambers pauses for a moment. "Why do government leaders want to talk with us?" he asks rhetorically. "They understand the one-to-one connection between the economic strength of their countries and their infrastructure build-outs. Think of the infrastructure of the future like the highways and the railroads and the airports and the harbors and the education system of the past. The companies in the Industrial Revolution that invested right in that area were the ones that did not get left behind. The same thing now occurs with the Internet, whether it's a company or a country.

"When I was at IBM, information technology was important, but less than 10 percent of capital spending was being spent on IT. Today it's 60 percent." Chambers points to a PowerPoint chart that correlates productivity and IT spending. "Here's why CEOs didn't like spending on IT from 1980 to 1990. Even though IT expenditures were going up dramatically, the productivity of the country did not change. It was 1.5 percent per year, 1.6 percent per year. It's only with the advent of these Web-based applications that productivity went up to 2.6, even 2.9, and at high peaks even to 5.3 percent. We started saying four years ago that this was going to occur. We projected economic growth at 4, 5, 6, 7 percent. People thought we were crazy. If you grow your productivity at 5 percent, you can grow your gross national product at 5 to 6 percent with nominal inflation." Chambers believed that in 2002 productivity would grow at 3 to 5 percent. He liked to tell audiences that when he had made that prediction five years earlier, people thought he had lost it.

If the media have been kind to John Chambers, a few of his rivals are less generous in their thoughts about his evangelizing of the Internet. Craig Benson, the cofounder of Cabletron, minces no words: "I think it's a bunch of crap. He goes out and talks in broad terms about how we will work and play, but there aren't a lot of specifics. It sounds good, but it's what he's heard from others. He does it very convincingly and he gets people to buy into it. But it's totally self-serving. There's no meat to it. I don't mean to denigrate him. But his pitch to corporate America is basically that yesterday's stuff is obsolete. The whole idea [of Chambers as evangelist] is Cisco's strategy: It obsoletes its products fairly rapidly to get whomever he's talking to into this buying cycle. Chambers gets people on the [Internet] treadmill and gets them comfortable being on the treadmill, when in effect they don't have to be on the treadmill. John's strategy is to make incremental small steps in the technology, tell customers they can't wait, they have to keep moving, and get them to buy the stuff. He tells them that your competitors will do more than you do and you can't afford to wait. That's a scare tactic. That's his pitch. If you offer small incremental steps in the technology, it really builds a recurring revenue stream that is attractive. He's done a terrific job in that."

PART FOUR

The Strategies and the Culture

7 Doing Things Differently

John Chambers has the highest aspirations for Cisco Systems. He wants Cisco to change the world. He has looked at other successful companies and concluded that all of them have strong, tightly knit cultures. When the elements of those cultures are in place, companies have a chance to attain greatness.

Great companies, he believes, also require a whole set of rewards and punishments that assure that employees adhere to the culture. The punishment for not adhering to Cisco's culture is clear, as Chambers notes: "Any Cisco manager or executive who can't implement our culture, who can't be a team player, who can't be customer focused, will be changed." ("Changed" is a euphemism for being fired.)

Chambers had his own bitter experiences at IBM and Wang, which provided him with ready-made laboratory experiments in erring companies—and drawing from those experiences, he wanted to make sure that Cisco Systems did things differently. "We're not saying we're going to be smarter, but we are saying how we do it differently in order to accomplish our stretch goals and to achieve goals others have been unsuccessful at."

In Chambers's view, what Cisco does differently is the sum and substance of the company's culture. What John Chambers does not include among the elements of Cisco's culture is his own personal role in driving the culture. Yet, in the end, someone has to devise the culture, explain it to employees, and ultimately make sure it is implemented. Someone has to orchestrate it and tweak it, and that has been John Chambers's crucial role in the company's culture. It is almost as if he would like all of us to believe that the culture works of its own volition, on its own steam, if you will. But it is hard to imagine Cisco's culture holding together without the person at the top devoting so much energy and time to make it work.

Implementing all aspects of Cisco's culture is not easy. Chambers knows that inculcating the culture into each and every one of Cisco's employees is no simple matter. Getting the culture across became especially challenging for a company that was growing as rapidly as Cisco in the late 1990s; for a while it was adding 1,000 employees every month. So Chambers has instructed every employee to clip to their clothing a wallet-sized card with the elements of Cisco's culture written on it. It is easy to distinguish the Cisco employees from guests at San Jose headquarters: the male employees are the ones with the culture card clipped to their belts; the female employees are those with the card clipped to their clothing. Beyond insisting that all employees wear those cards on the job, Chambers makes sure to discuss Cisco's culture in every appearance he makes before employees. He also requires every Cisco manager to spend at least one minute of every meeting with colleagues discussing the culture.

Chambers breaks the Cisco culture into 12 discrete elements: customer success, quality team, empowerment, stretch goals, drive change, no technology religion, open communication, teamwork, market transitions, trust/fair/integrity, frugality, fun.

He deliberately puts the first four elements at the top of the list, for in his mind they are the most important aspects of the culture. He does not prioritize the last eight items. The 12 elements that made up Cisco's culture appeared to hold the best explanation for Cisco's success during the latter part of the 1990s. When you asked John Chambers to explain how the company had achieved such spectacular growth, he automatically pointed to these 12 elements.

But then came the economic downturn of late 2000 and early

2001, and at least some of the Cisco strategies appeared flawed. In this chapter we will discuss these strategies.

CUSTOMER SUCCESS

Nothing mattered more to John Chambers than customer success. He felt that his former employers at IBM and Wang fell down on the job by ignoring what customers were telling them. Keeping tabs on what customers think, what they want, and what they don't want is a full-time exercise.

It was Chambers's view that customers can be fickle and therefore need to be cultivated all the time. Chambers believed firmly that not having your fingers on a customer's pulse could drive that customer somewhere else instantly. In the high-speed Internet business world, he explained, missing the market because of a failure to listen to customers could wipe out a company in as little as two years.

He vowed that he would not make the mistaking of disregarding customers.

Other key figures at Cisco believed just as firmly that Cisco was on the right track in emphasizing a strategy of listening to customers. To Don Valentine, Cisco's vice chairman, the single aspect of Cisco's culture that distinguishes the company from other Sequoia Capital enterprises "is the nature and depth of commitment to the customer. Cisco evolved a technique of very proficient listening. If you've ever been at an IBM management facility, you notice the management people have this sign in their offices: THINK. That, however, is something you do in abstraction and you do alone. Listening you do interactively, and it requires other people. So the cornerstone of Cisco was to develop a widely orchestrated capability to listen."

Chambers boasted of being rigorous about listening to customers. He made sure that he heard about criticisms from the company's most important accounts on a daily basis. Executives were judged, and indeed compensated, on how well they handled customers. They received a sizable part of their bonuses on the basis of customer satisfaction surveys. We will spend much more time on this critical part of the Cisco culture in Chapter 8.

QUALITY TEAM

To achieve customer success, John Chambers believed, Cisco had to have the best executives and the best "individual contributors" (the nonexecutives). Recruiting the best talent was vital: "If I recruit and develop the best team and I'm a reasonably good coach, we'll win. That's what we drive throughout our whole culture. When people ask me what I'm most proud of, it's the customer focus and the quality of the leadership team."

By quality team, Chambers meant not just executives, but the rank and file as well.

Cisco's goal in the fall of 2000 was to find the top 10 to 15 percent in the industry and offer them jobs. At that time Cisco was one of the most desirable places to work in Silicon Valley. It was receiving 100,000 applicantions a year from people who were competing for 12,000 or so new jobs.

The hiring process is grueling. Cisco employees spend a considerable amount of time with job candidates to make sure the candidates are as good as they appear. Once the right kinds of candidates are selected, the actual hiring process begins. A candidate must have at least five interviews at Cisco. Two of the interview sessions must have Cisco employees who will not work directly with the candidates. Some people come back 12 times!

Cisco is not simply looking for intelligence; that is a given. The company wants problem solvers, people who are creative, who can perform quickly, and who are results-oriented.

In 2000, fully 67 percent of Cisco's personnel was new—due in large measure to a substantial increase in acquisitions during that year. Finding employees who will fit easily into Cisco's culture becomes a priority at the job interview stage. Prospective employees are asked what books they have read lately. They are quizzed on whether they have focused on customers in their careers and whether they are empowering types.

Once a Cisco recruit is hired, the real effort at creating a quality team kicks in. Located in one of the most competitive labor environments in the world, Cisco Systems decided early on to spread the company's wealth among employees as a way of securing employee loyalty. In an arrangement that began under John Morgridge and was expanded under Chambers, Cisco was giving stock options every year to certain nonexecutive employees. Under Morgridge, a secretary might have been given 300 shares over a 40-year period. But by December 2000, 42 percent of Cisco's options went to nonmanagement employees who were rewarded for solid performance and high customer-satisfaction ratings. For as long as Cisco's stock was rocketing off the charts, the shares were worth far more than ordinary dollars.

To Chambers, the stock incentive program was something that he was still getting used to: "If somebody would have told me in MBA school that we were going to give 42 percent of the stock options to individual contributors, not managers, directors, or VPs, I would have called it socialism. In fact, it's the ultimate form of capitalism—it really works."

The whole thrust of the stock options program was to build a company for the long haul. "At a time in the Valley when everyone was taking their stock options to shorter and shorter vesting periods," noted Chambers, "we said you're never going to build a company to last doing that. You're going to end up mistreating your shareholders. Your employees will not be motivated to stay, and the company risks coming apart. So at a time when everybody else was shortening options to three-year vesting, we took our options to five-year vesting. We said this is going to be a company that is built to last. Don't come here unless you want to be a part of it. Now the Valley is following our lead."

The stock options program, designed to keep Cisco employees loyal, will only work when the stock does well, as it did throughout the 1990s. In the year 2000, Cisco's retention rate (the number of employees who stay with the company) had been 97 percent; a year earlier it had been 95 percent. As of the third quarter for 2002 it was at 89 percent, bouncing back from the 79 percent level of 2001, the year of the layoffs. Cisco executives were not worried, noting that the average annual rate of retention varied from 67 to 83 percent for high-tech firms in Silicon Valley. The relatively high retention rate gives Cisco one significant dividend: the number of Cisco employees who leave to start or join other businesses that compete with Cisco is low, and those who do join Cisco's competitors usually remain on friendly terms with John Chambers and his team.

As long as Cisco's stock soared upward, Chambers could count on the loyalty of his team. One ex-Cisco veteran thought that it was sinister on Chambers's part to manipulate executives that way. To Chambers it probably wasn't sinister. He had the stock to give to his employees as a reward. It was a way of assuring their loyalty, a sine qua non of building a quality team, and of trying to impose some discipline in the company (by keeping people from running away).

In return for the rewards that Cisco could give his senior colleagues, Chambers insisted that his senior executives be high achievers: "The number one measure that I use to determine our executives' leadership ability is their attitude toward reaching for 100 percent of goals. This is the minimum success acceptable. And 110 to 120 is really what is expected in our culture."

They must also be able to build teams; they must be fanatical about customer success; and they must display teamwork. "If they are not team players," says Chambers, "they will be asked to leave."

When I spoke to Chambers in May 2002, he was clearly reluctant to discuss how this cultural element had fared in the past two years; but from what he did say, it was obvious that he was sorely disappointed with the way some members of his senior team were functioning. Reading between the lines, it seemed likely that the problem had largely to do with executives who were looking out for themselves rather than adopting a team attitude. While highly reminiscent of the internecine fighting that went on at Cisco in earlier days, the individualistic temperament displayed by current Cisco executives had one major difference: back then Cisco was doing well despite the difficulties in interpersonal relationships; this time these individualistic displays could well be pointed to as a source of Cisco's woes.

EMPOWERMENT

John Chambers came to Cisco as a sales specialist, not an operations man. He was not an engineer, not an Internet or computer expert either. It was perfectly natural for him to eschew hands-on management. It became very important to him to encourage his fellow executives to empower themselves.

Ray Bell noticed this when he was recruited to Cisco from Oracle in 1996 to work in the Internet business unit under Ed Kozel, then the chief technology officer. Bell's job was to help Cisco figure out how to integrate more closely the network functionality it was building in routers and switches with desktop operating systems. Bell understood that Larry Ellison at Oracle and Bill Gates at Microsoft were technologists. But John Chambers was not. Chambers always wanted to know how the technology fit into the company's business strategy. The net effect, said Bell, was that the technology and product focus at Cisco got pushed down to the vice president and director level: "So there's more empowerment in the organization to have product and technology decisions at that level. At Oracle, all of the decisions are driven from the top. But at Cisco, the various business units are empowered and entrepreneurial. They own budget and production decisions where they are knitted together at the executive level into a cohesive strategy. So you wind up with a more entrepreneurial spirit in the organization. And that helps business strategy."

At Cisco Systems, the result was that people were empowered at the lower management levels to make decisions. Unlike those at other companies, Cisco employees were given the opportunity to feel as if they were making a difference. They sometimes found themselves regarded oddly by the outside world. On one occasion, as part of the discussions Cisco was having with another, much larger company to form a partnership, a meeting took place between one of Cisco's director-level employees and, for the potential partner, someone at the vice presidential level. At the first meeting, the vice president of the other company said that he did not want to talk with the Cisco director. He felt it was beneath him to engage in a conversation with someone not at least his business equal. Then the vice president learned that the Cisco director had the same decision-making power that he had. The meeting went on as scheduled.

Chambers understood that a nexus existed between top-level employees and the notion of empowerment. The higher the quality of executives, the easier it would be to empower them. And one of the most important ways to attract great people, Chambers believed, was to let them know that they would be expected to function more or less autonomously. He was not alone in this view: within the high-tech world, it was generally accepted that the new high-speed, ever-changing, high-pressure world of Internet business required a full measure of empowerment among executives.

Mike Volpi, a senior vice president for the Internet Switching and Services Group, suggested that empowerment was deeply embedded in the company. He cited several examples. One concerned junior employees who thought the company's expense reports could be improved. They proposed a Web application that was quickly put in place. Another had to do with Volpi's own team, which made 17 investments in companies making optical components. "I hadn't asked them to do it, but they figured that to beat Nortel, we needed a lot of relationships."

Cisco rewarded executives who showed empowerment, Volpi noted. "We applaud executives who can make numerous decisions. I'd rather make 10 decisions and get two wrong, instead of making only five, and getting all five right. We might make bad investments, or a sales guy will overcommit on the features of a product."

Empowerment, of course, placed a great deal of responsibility on senior executives. For some time, the extra burden that Chambers's colleagues carried fit well into his own busy personal schedule visiting customers, political leaders, and others. Some Wall Street analysts believe, however, that it was the very empowerment of Cisco's executives that placed them in a bind when market demand shot through the roof in 2000. These executives were then forced to make quick and frequent decisions about products and markets that solved many problems, but by no means all. In their quest for going after products and growth, these executives left Cisco open to the kinds of problems—long lead times, overlapping of products, the excessive buildup of inventory—that became very visible only in early 2001. It was not that John Chambers was unaware of what was occurring, say these analysts; it was, however, left to the executives to deal with the problems, and they could only solve some of them.

STRETCH GOALS

To John Chambers, the concept of stretch goals is "that philosophy of doing what other people think is impossible." Chambers's goal has been to make Cisco the most powerful and influential company in history. To reach that goal, he required employees to do more than their best. They had to figure out how to go beyond that.

A very definite link exists among the top four elements of Cisco's culture, in Chambers's view. Customer success trumps every other facet of the culture: to achieve customer success, the best possible team must be assembled and then empowered; once in place that team must strive for results that are off the charts. Assembling a quality team means attracting employees who want to make a difference in the world, who want to improve technology, to be great at business. People like that would respond when asked to seek and reach stretch goals.

To set stretch goals and expect them to be carried out required the most aggressive and demanding attitude toward sales. Cisco employees were conditioned to believe that losing a deal was a very bad thing. The Cisco sales team was supposed to figure out how *not* to lose deals.

CAN-DO IS IN CISCO'S DNA

Going hand in hand with the stretch-goal mentality at Cisco is John Chambers's strategy of striving to be number one or two in any market that Cisco enters—a concept that he openly acknowledges he took from Jack Welch, the former chairman and CEO of General Electric. The assertion of that strategy places great pressure on Cisco employees to pursue their stretch goals relentlessly. Chambers observed that, "the importance of stretch goals plays a key role in our company's evolution. If you don't stretch the organization, you don't achieve your destiny or reach the opportunities ahead of you. If you ask your team to just improve 5 to 10 percent, they will do it in the same old way and just work a little bit harder. But when you begin to stretch the organization and think about improvement of 100 percent, you realize it's only possible if you do things differently. We're not smarter, we're not going to work harder—but Cisco does constantly do things differently than other companies."

But Chambers's approach differs from Welch's in one significant way. Welch urged GE executives and managers to introduce stretch goals into their thinking and their plans, but he did not insist that they meet those stretch goals, only that they do their best to reach them. Chambers notes that he and Welch differ "in our philosophies toward stretch goals. As I understand it, Jack sets stretch goals that require very hard work but are difficult to obtain. I believe you make them obtainable and then achieve stretch goals. You have to ask, 'How can we do things differently?' When we set a stretch goal, we almost never miss it. We've got to truly do it differently to accomplish that stretch goal. Otherwise, other smart, hardworking people will have already done it."

While uneager to destroy its opponents, Cisco wants to acquire market leadership in all that it is doing. Its overriding strategy is to manufacture products and product lines that will be either number one or number two in their markets.

Throughout its 18-year history, Cisco Systems has managed to conquer its markets. In March 1990, Cisco had 86.3 percent of the router market, while its chief competitor, Wellfleet, had only 13.7 percent. In the year 2000, Cisco was selling more than 80 percent of the routers and switches used in the key junctions of the pipelines of the Internet and of corporate networks.

It was vital to Chambers for Cisco to lead its markets. "We decided to segment the market like HP had done, to be one or two like GE, and to do it by ourselves, partner, or acquire."

Indeed, Cisco's acquisition strategy would play a major role in fulfilling the number one–number two approach. Acquiring Crescendo Communications in September 1993 to build market leadership in switches became an early part of this strategy. Chambers and his colleagues began seeking out companies that were among the five best in their markets for partnership or acquisition.

Acquiring market leadership via the number one–number two strategy was no walk in the park. Chambers acknowledged, "Most people thought that was a nice saying, but they didn't think that would happen, including inside our company." But he pushed hard at it. Early on, he was emphatic that Cisco would not try to be everything to everyone. Rather, it would pick only those areas where it had a good chance of becoming number one or number two.

Ultimately, this strategy worked amazingly well. By October 1999, Cisco was number one in 16 of its 20 product areas and number two in the other 4. In December 2000, appearing at a Cisco-sponsored conference for analysts in San Jose, California, Chambers detailed the company's market position and market share in product categories. In most categories, it was number one; in a few, it was number two. There was no product category in which Cisco fell below this level.

A company cannot rely simply on good or even excellent products. It must count on its sales and marketing efforts, and those efforts cannot be relaxed. From the moment he joined Cisco in January 1991, John Chambers made this point, and he set a personal example for everyone in the company to follow. Being aggressive in pursuit of a sale has traditionally been unpopular, usually drawing negative comments.

Chambers says he's quite aware that introducing change, which stretch goals are part of, makes people uncomfortable. Change is great when it happens to others, but not when it happens to you. But change—getting people to attain stretch goals in particular—is crucial: "You deliberately make people uncomfortable doing business the way they currently are and get them to focus that energy constructively and explain to them the advantage of doing it differently. Most of the time when I set the stretch goals, most of the people do not believe that we will be able to achieve them. But that is only at the beginning. And after they get over the shock and get over saying it's impossible, they begin to think out of the box, and that's really what you're after. Stretch goals are all about figuring out how you do it differently, most creatively, and how you build the culture and confidence to do things differently."

Chambers found hesitation from employees when he established the number one–number two strategy as a Cisco stretch goal: "When we first set the goal of becoming number one or number two in each product area that we entered by doing it ourselves, partnering, or acquiring, many people thought it was a nice stretch goal. I don't think anybody thought we could do that in the majority of our product areas. Many people now understand that when I set stretch goals, I expect we'll reach each and every one of the goals. This is the approach that Jack Welch used very successfully to really get GE to a leadership position. And only when it became a limitation for future growth did he change. If you think five to 10 years out, you've got to figure out where the market is going and where you want to play in it. In my industry, if you're not one of the first five to market with at least 20 percent market share with a product that really works, you can be displaced very quickly."

Using the old IBM approach, Chambers suggested, where a company enters a market late and becomes number one or number two, might have worked during the Industrial Revolution, but it could not work operating at the current Internet pace: "So we enter and we just don't miss." He likens Cisco's self-confidence to a sports team that knows it will win even when it's behind.

The stretch-goal mentality has seeped into the Cisco culture, and each Cisco executive with whom I spoke noted that two sets of objectives influenced the work year: the original goals and then stretch goals: "We always have two numbers," says Carl Redfield, Cisco's senior vice president for manufacturing and worldwide logistics. "It's a real healthy element." Of course, meeting stretch goals has its hazards: "If you get known as someone who always achieves stretch goals, it's not good, because John Chambers will ask you to stretch even more."

With respect to Cisco's stretch goals, it is the Japan example of which Chambers is most proud: gaining a foothold in the Japanese high-tech industry is something that no other American high-tech company had ever done. Chambers had worked out the arrangement in September 1994, just a few months before being named Cisco's new president and CEO.

Prior to Chambers's seeking an overall deal with Japan's high-tech companies, Cisco had been using a third-party channel to distribute its products in Japan—a most unsatisfactory arrangement because it prevented Cisco from going after Japanese customers directly. When Chambers entered the fray, he set a stretch goal for Cisco: he wanted to achieve the same market share in Japan as Cisco enjoyed in the rest of the world. "Everybody said you can't do that," Chambers noted. Among the skeptics was Ed Kozel. Challenged by Kozel's doubts, Chambers asked him to visit Japan to sort out the details, adding: "We're going to make a joint venture with all of the 14 most important companies there. And, by the way, they hate each other and us as well, because we're going to be a threat—we're going to go over and dominate the Japanese market. But they're going to open the doors for us and buy equity in our company, although we're going to give them only 1 to 2 percent."

Kozel was stunned. "Explain this to me, John," he said politely. In time, Kozel was won over because the deal concluded successfully, though not without a great deal of squabbling with the Japanese: "John had a total belief that this could be done. No one else believed it could be done except John. I didn't believe it. But he got it done."

Chambers knew that using the same techniques that other American companies had tried in Japan would diminish the prospects of reaching the stretch goal: "We knew that if we did it the way it was done before, we'd wind up with half the market share in Japan that we have in the rest of the world. If all you're trying to do is work harder and do the same thing others have done, you're going to get the same results. And so we approached it saying how do we do it differently."

BANGING HEADS

In the past, American companies (including Cisco) had been banging their heads against the Japanese wall, going into the Japanese market and trying to create a direct distribution system without the approval of the Japanese high-tech firms and without those firms sharing in the American companies' success in Japan.

Chambers wanted to try a different approach. Cisco proposed to the Japanese government a first-time joint venture with 14 Japanese high-tech firms. The Japanese companies agreed to invest some $40 million, representing about 25 percent ownership in Cisco's Japanese subsidiary. The new Cisco-Japanese alliance planned to work on multimedia Internetworking.

The result was astonishing: Cisco's annual revenues in Japan jumped from $40 million to $600 million from 1994 to 1997. Cisco became the number one company in the electronics field in Japan. No American or European company had ever accomplished this before. Cisco's market share reached 60 percent in 1997. In 1999, Cisco won the Prime Minister's Trade Award.

Chambers credited the outcome largely to setting stretch goals and then pursuing them aggressively: "Setting an impossible goal, not trying to do it traditionally, doing it differently. No one thought we could be successful."

Without going into the specifics of what he offered the Japanese, Chambers explained: "Many companies in their negotiation style and culture try to create a win for them and by default a loss for the partner. Our philosophy is exactly the opposite. We have no desire to ever create a win-lose—in the end those arrangements always come apart. I always try to create a win-win. So I always try to understand the win for my business partnership, communicate that win for them and what we expect in return."

Chambers knew that the individual Japanese companies were reluctant to establish their own Internet protocols (as American companies had done in the early days of the Internet) because of the high cost involved. He explained to the companies why, even if they could afford to take such a step, the approach made little sense. Helping Chambers's case was the fact that none of the Japanese companies wanted any of their Japanese competition to create a standard. "So we were the neutral party who would not be in their territory," Chambers noted.

The icing on the cake for the Japanese was Cisco's willingness to share in the profits. When Chambers put on his professor's cap and began explaining to the Japanese how the industry was moving away from mainframes (the Japanese had been very mainframe-centric), they liked what they heard, and soon the deal was done. But not before one very bad moment for Chambers: At one point he encountered such antagonism from the Japanese executives that his interpreter blurted out: "Now I know how you Americans felt at Pearl Harbor."

The deal was finally concluded in the fall of 1994. The Japanese media had trouble with the deal, suggesting that the country was surrendering the marketplace to Cisco. After 1997, the faltering Japanese economy kept Cisco from doing even better. The $600 million a year in revenues might have grown to $1 billion if the Japanese economy had not stagnated and if Japanese corporations had invested more in information technology.

Undoubtedly, getting one's company to achieve more, to go beyond one's stated goals, is a noble, if daring, pursuit for any CEO. For John Chambers, it became an essential part of his growth strategy. To keep Cisco's growth machine operating at full steam, he needed his executives to have their numbers fly off the charts. This created all sorts of pressures on executives that some could tolerate and some could not.

These executives, sensing how much of a priority growth was to the Cisco leadership, did their best to meet the stretch numbers, with the inevitable outcome that other issues received less attention than they deserved. Cisco would correct much of this, but it would pay a serious price before making those corrections.

The Cisco culture, as articulated by John Chambers, contains 12 distinct elements. We have touched on the four most important ones: customer success, quality team, empowerment, and stretch goals. The other eight are drive change, no technology religion, open communication, teamwork, market transitions, trust/fair/integrity, frugality, fun.

While these aspects of the Cisco culture may appear to have little in common, each one of them performs two separate but connected functions: each is meant to serve as a driver of Cisco's performance as well as a way of explaining the company's success. Some features are clearly connected. The need to drive and embrace change means, first and foremost, that Cisco must not become wedded to one technology. Also, in order to catch market transitions, there must be teamwork and open communication, and all of those efforts must be based on trust, fairness, and integrity. Frugality has been part of the Cisco culture dating back to its earliest days. It is so much a part of Cisco's DNA that it seems self-explanatory. Finally, there is fun—a part of the culture that John Chambers added to the list only in November 2000. He included it to remind Cisco employees not to take everything they do too seriously.

DRIVE CHANGE

Change has become one of Cisco's constants. "Most companies and individuals struggle with change," John Chambers explains. "Companies that thrive on change are the ones that break away. During the Industrial Revolution you could change slowly, but changes that occurred over a decade now take place in a few years in the Internet revolution. Great companies make change part of their culture."

Chambers acknowledges that change can sometimes be painful. During his public appearances, he asks audiences whether they like change. Lots of hands go up. But then Chambers looks someone in the eye and asks, "But you wouldn't like change if it meant that your boss was going to change things by letting you go next week, would you? Change can be pretty difficult, can't it?"

Change, however difficult, is vital to Cisco's future, and that's the point that Chambers makes repeatedly. He recalls how companies that did not make timely changes suffered. At Wang Laboratories, Dr. An Wang, Chambers's beloved boss, transitioned the company five times but did not make the next and crucial transition to personal computers. And so Chambers learned that if companies don't make changes, if they have too many layers of bureaucracy and get too far away from customers, a terrible price will be paid.

Embracing change means being as fast as possible—in getting products to market, in understanding how markets are shifting, in hiring the right executives and other employees. Cisco has acquired a reputation for fast decision making. Chambers promotes a go-go environment and always seems pleased at how many people he has seen in a day, at how quickly he has successfully read market changes, at how fast the pace is at Cisco.

No one gets a pat on the back at Cisco for researching a problem for a long time or for slowly making a decision. The sales team is aggressive, and Cisco executives receive credit for speedily scooping up acquisitions. The culture seeks to make everyone at Cisco comfortable with change—not the slow kind of change, but the kind that happens in the flash of an eye.

Above all, the culture urges employees to drive change by looking first and foremost for market transitions.

THIS INTERNET PACE

In the case of market transitions, it is the customers who are embracing change, and Cisco's job is to recognize when that change is occurring. Indeed, that is precisely what has happened. Each time that customers have changed their minds about what is important to them, Cisco has restructured the company. It has gone through seven transitions in a decade: "Changes that used to take place in the Industrial Revolution at one per decade now take place five or 10 times faster. This is an Internet pace," Chambers said.

The changes during the second half of the 1990s were startling. Every year thousands of new employees were hired. Indeed, for part of that time, every 18 months half the company's employees were new.

Senior executives come and go at a furious pace. Cisco is on its third to sixth generation of leaders in each category, and John Chambers has made almost all those changes. He hired every vice president at Cisco. Products are created, manufactured, and sent into the marketplace at a dizzying pace. Cisco is on its third, fourth, or fifth generation of products in nearly all categories.

He sets three-to-five-year goals but keeps them purposely vague out of fear that being too specific would put pressure on employees not to engage in change when the opportunities arise. Customers are bound to change their tastes long before the five years are up, and Chambers wants everyone at Cisco to be able to respond quickly to the change in those tastes.

One long-range goal at Cisco is to become the most powerful and most influential company in history, but that is vague enough to embrace all kinds of change as Cisco moves toward that goal. Chambers believes that the nature of the company—relying on a horizontal model that envisages partnerships and a full-blown ecosystem—gives Cisco a great competitive advantage, since it can enact change and move more swiftly than its competitors, who often rely on vertical business models.

NO TECHNOLOGY RELIGION

Driving change means being aware of what is going on in the marketplace. It means being prepared to integrate the changes that are occurring in the marketplace into the company. Above all, it means not getting bogged down by relying on one product when better ones have come along.

When a company puts a product into the marketplace and it sells well, the tendency sometimes is to stay with the product no matter what other market trends are emerging. IBM's love affair with mainframes remains the single best example of such rigidity. Wang Laboratories' clinging to minicomputers is a second example. John Chambers vowed to himself that he would not make the same mistakes at Cisco.

He would not make a religion out of technology. He would not fall in love with a certain technology and blindly push it at the expense of other, potentially more successful technologies: "Many leaders in the high-tech industry fell in love with an element of technology. My approach is exactly the reverse. Cisco will not make the mistake of missing a technology evolution. We have a culture that is technologically agnostic, where you build and deliver whatever our customers ask for."

WE ARE AGNOSTICS

By listening to customers, Cisco Systems could make sure that it had the right products in the marketplace at the right time. "If customers say, 'This is what we want,'" Chambers indicates, "we build it regardless of what we think or regardless of what the market is saying. That doesn't mean that we don't bet heavier on some areas, but being agnostic from a technology perspective has such a huge implication for the whole [Cisco] culture."

OPEN COMMUNICATION

For Cisco to manage its rapid growth, to make sure that it was keeping up with the rapid changes in the market, to utilize all the resources within the company optimally, there had to be camaraderie and harmony. One of the best ways to guarantee that everyone was pulling together was to keep the lines of communication within the company as open as possible.

Open communications meant candid communications. John Chambers encouraged everyone with whom he came into contact to give him an honest appraisal of how Cisco was doing. In public and private meetings, Chambers asked, "What could we do better?" It was a question that startled many people. But Chambers was serious. He said he did not want to be caught off guard. Seeking candor, he would often get it. Executives pressured him to move in certain directions. Employees did too. Since Chambers puts himself in front of executives and employees on a regular basis, it's relatively easy to raise issues with the CEO.

To Chambers, the open-communication policy means not just that executives and employees can raise issues with him easily. It means that he can drill down deep into the company easily without having to go through layer after layer of his own bureaucracy. And Chambers loves to talk to his people. Few CEOs spend as much time and effort as he does getting in front of employees. In earlier days in American corporate life, CEOs made videotaped presentations and distributed them to employees, who often put the videotapes in desk drawers where they gathered dust. Chambers will have none of that. He loves engaging people in person, and he finds it of great value to stand up in front of hundreds, sometimes thousands, of Cisco employees all at once, offering them a verbal snapshot of Cisco at that moment.

GETTING IN FRONT OF EMPLOYEES

Routinely in those appearances, Chambers spends an hour taking the employees through a slide show of Cisco's latest business initiatives, its market challenges, and its future opportunities. In the fall of 2000, when I had the chance to attend some of these sessions, he talked extensively about the Cisco culture and told employees over and over again why he believed Cisco had become so powerful, so influential, and so successful. He almost never took personal credit for the company's then superb record. He talked about "my team" and described himself as its coach, urging the team on from the sidelines. Every month Chambers hosts a birthday party for Cisco employees with a birthday that month. When the practice started, these were small, intimate affairs. By the fall of 2000, some 400 employees filled Cisco lecture halls at each birthday party. Excluded are Cisco vice presidents and directors, on the grounds that Chambers will hear more candid thoughts from the audience without them. Chambers dispenses with the hour-long talk at these events, taking questions from the audience for 90 minutes.

At the September 15, 2000, birthday party, employees asked Chambers questions on a host of issues.

One woman wanted a larger office cubicle. (He was against it.)

Another woman felt that Cisco employees on maternity leave should be credited for the time on leave in their stock option program. (He said he would look into it.)

Other questions: Might Cisco harm itself by adding so many employees so quickly? Chambers admitted that 5 to 10 percent of employees hired should not have been hired. "We need to be more effective on that."

How long would he be president and CEO?

Eighteen months earlier, he noted, he had committed himself to five more years as Cisco's leader, "and maybe five years after that."

Did he aspire to a government post? Chambers said, "No, when I retire, I'm going to teach. Maybe I'll teach business ethics."

What about running for office? "You never say never, but as close to that as I can."

Four times a year, Chambers appears before company meetings, where he talks to several thousand employees in person, and countless thousands of others watching over Internet television. Here he makes an hour-long presentation. Many employees walk away from the meetings not absorbing every single detail Chambers has thrown their way, but they are pumped up at having heard a personal report from the president and CEO. Chambers would like each one of them to memorize all 12 features of the Cisco culture, but he knows that's not realistic. The chances are, however, that they will hear Chambers personally a few more times over the next several months, and the cultural features should begin to seep in.

Chambers works at open communication with his senior executives as well. There are quite a number of them—160 vice presidents—but he has figured out how to get to them one-on-one on a regular basis. Every Friday, the vice presidents are invited to wander over to the lobby outside Chambers's office in the main building at headquarters, where lunch will be served (each week a different vice president picks up the bill for the event—one more stab at frugality!). On one Friday in May 2002 some 50 vice presidents showed up for lunch.

A FORMER COMPETITOR SPEAKS HER MIND

The open-communication feature refers not only to the internal life of the company, but to relationships outside as well. As noted earlier, Chambers strongly encourages his Cisco colleagues to listen closely to what customers are saying. That form of open communication should have a direct bearing on the company's ability to forecast market transitions. Listening to competitors is far more difficult. Most are unprepared to divulge the slightest morsel of information that might be useful to a Cisco employee.

Chambers was able to convince a former competitor of Cisco's, Carly Fiorina, to appear before the company's annual off-site meeting of directors in the summer of 2000. She offered comments on what Cisco salespeople had done right and wrong, and what it was like to compete against Cisco. There were 500 people in the audience at a hotel in Monterey, California. When she served as president of Lucent Technologies' Global Service Provider business (annual revenues: $20 billion), Fiorina was one of Cisco's staunchest adversaries. She has been ranked as the most powerful woman in

American business by *Fortune* magazine. By the time of her appearance at Cisco, she had left Lucent to become the head of Hewlett-Packard. Fiorina told Cisco's audience why she thought it had won certain deals against her, and why it had lost some. "When you lose," she said, "it's because you have become cocky, and that's when we could beat you." She noted later, "I told them they are so good, so focused, so on a roll, that where they got beat is when they stopped listening and we could find something that they hadn't heard that we could exploit. It is true of everyone. The time of greatest success is the time of greatest danger." (Early in 2001, Carly Fiorina joined the Cisco board of directors.)

TEAMWORK

Much of the Cisco culture is aimed at getting employees to work together productively. Always focusing on the customer, employees know that a lot is expected of them (stretch goals) and that a good deal of autonomy will come their way (empowerment). It is John Chambers's job to build the best possible team and to make sure that everyone at Cisco pulls together for the common cause. That has not always been an easy task.

The Cisco Systems of the late 1980s and early 1990s was a place of constant bickering and a lack of teamwork. When he arrived at Cisco in 1991, John Chambers vowed that he would bring harmony. He would not tolerate the infighting. He made it clear to executives that if they got along, if they collaborated with one another, they would be substantially rewarded. But if they put themselves above the team, he would discard them without any hesitation.

To make sure that the executives behaved like a team, he let a number of executives go, especially on the sales force, and replaced them with people of high quality. During the second half of the 1990s, Chambers distributed substantial stock options to the team, perhaps the greatest stimulus to teamwork.

MARKET TRANSITIONS

If the Cisco culture is functioning as it should, that is, if a top-quality team has been put in place, if employees have been empowered, if everyone is working beyond his or her presumed capabilities, then a mighty growth machine should keep pumping out the revenues and profits. But all of these cultural elements aim at one larger goal: trying to understand exactly what the customer wants at any given time. While the most important part of Cisco's culture is called "customer success," that element alone does not truly explain what Cisco employees are compelled to do to win the day.

They must acquire a sense of where the market is heading! Or, in one of John Chambers's favorite phrases, they must catch market transitions.

CATCHING THE MARKET TRENDS

Guessing what those market transitions will be has given Cisco a huge competitive advantage, according to John Chambers: "We've caught almost every trend right in the industry because we listen and we have a healthy paranoia. It's that confidence on the one side and healthy paranoia on the other that really results in the type of performance you see. So much of what we've been able to accomplish is how we tie it all together."

Transitioning the company seven times in a decade is one of Chambers's proudest achievements. Here are the seven market transitions that taken together form Cisco's customer-driven strategy:

Single Pinpoint Product. In 1991, when Chambers joined the company, Cisco was still a single-product company focused around routers.

Products and Company. In 1993, Cisco's customers became less interested in a company that played up feeds and speeds, and more interested in one that emphasized the support of its products. "We really began to make ourselves more of a support company, selling the company as much as the products," notes Chambers.

Strategic Vendor. In 1995, customers were looking for very few vendors, as was Cisco. It looked for vendors with whom it could partner. These partners, who sold their own products but not Cisco's, gained access to Cisco's internal information, including access to the company's increasingly automated supply-chain effort. They received special preference from Cisco, which purchased a lot of the strategic vendors' equipment and resold it to its own customers.

End-to-End. As Cisco began to concentrate on strategic vendors, it also began hearing that vendors preferred dealing with Cisco and only Cisco for its networking products—going "end-to-end." In January 1996, two Cisco customers—the financial institutions Merrill Lynch and Citicorp—told John Chambers that they wanted to go end-to-end with Cisco. "What I didn't understand about the end-to-end architecture was that customers were saying [we] already had the majority of elements in the network, so by building [ourselves] or by acquiring, we could fill out the rest of the network. I thought maybe 10 percent would follow this lead. I didn't realize it would be over 70 percent of customers that went this way."

Data/Voice/Video. In 1997, Cisco began to hear from customers that they would probably integrate their networks, but they needed a single infrastructure called IP (Internet Protocol). Beginning that year, Cisco made sure that every product was thus enabled.

Internet Solutions. In 1997, Cisco introduced a new business unit that taught business solutions. From selling technology only, Cisco moved into helping others understand how the technology changed the business.

Business Partner. In 2000, Cisco's customers were expressing a desire not only to go end-to-end, but also to work with only a few vendors on the integration of networks. Cisco was entering into more and more such partnership arrangements with vendors who were prepared to sell Cisco's products, as well as handle the integration of those products.

Chambers boasted about how effectively Cisco had made these market transitions: "In the Industrial Revolution you make one change in a decade. When we made the key decisions that really determined the company's history, there were only one or two of us who knew where this thing was probably going to go if we did it right."

Cisco caught these seven market transitions by listening to customers, thereby transforming itself from simply an engineering company that had some sales to a sales/marketing/engineering company that was globally based, not just American-centric. Don Valentine, Cisco's vice chairman of the board, noted that Cisco's virtue was in being a tactical, not a strategic, company, which could therefore capture market transitions much better than strategic ones: "By remaining tactical and listening to customers, Cisco has been able to hear the timing of the transition. Despite what was going on in the press, when customers said we should employ gigabit Ethernet, Cisco was aware of what customers wanted to do. Huge energy has gone into the listening program and the constant involvement of listening to the product planners and customers."

Robert Sweifach, a former member of the Cisco board, points to the example of Cisco's entry into optical networking as an excellent illustration of the company's ability to capture market transitions: "Three years ago with respect to optical networking there were whispers, and all of a sudden Cisco was making acquisitions in this area and emerging as a leader. A lot of companies would have taken a much longer time to become a leader."

TRUST/FAIR/INTEGRITY

This cultural feature might seem obvious. Business leaders disagree. There has been simply too much unethical behavior and too much public scrutiny of American corporate life to ignore the issue of integrity.

Corporate leaders like John Chambers add this feature reluctantly. For one thing, including integrity as a cultural feature may draw attention to issues that were better left unspoken. For another, a company that promotes integrity as an important part of its business may seem as if it has something to hide. Sweeping aside such considerations, John Chambers makes trust/fairness/integrity a part of Cisco's culture.

How has Cisco acquired so much business? What tactics has it used to defeat competitors? These questions dominated the business news in the year 2000, when the U.S. government prosecuted Bill Gates's Microsoft in one of the largest antitrust cases in business history. Cisco has rarely been accused of engaging in monopolizing activity, but the company is all too aware that it is being watched more closely than ever.

Cisco has been largely immune from the inquiries surrounding the accounting practices of major corporations, inquiries that emanated from the Enron and Arthur Andersen scandals of 2002. In January 2002, *Business Week* did do a cover story in which it raised questions about Cisco's financial reporting. It cited Michael Porter, a Harvard Business School professor, who was completing a major research project into what the magazine called "massive distortions in financial reporting." According to *Business Week*: "One astounding finding: He and his colleagues can't figure out how much money Cisco really made in the 1990s. After spending billions on buying companies, Cisco routinely wrote off massive amounts of acquisition-related charges — $5.4 billion in the past five years alone — making it nearly impossible to piece together how much Cisco actually invested or how much it earned on its capital. Says Porter: 'When the historians actually plow through all the data, we will likely find that even during its so-called heyday, Cisco wasn't nearly as profitable in terms of return on invested capital as many believed.'" In response, a Cisco spokesperson asserted, "The *Business Week* story rehashed the past year's news in a way that made the events look new. Unfortunately it was misleading to individual investors and it failed to acknowledge that Cisco has always followed the guidelines for pro forma reporting developed by FEI [Financial Executives Institute] and NIRI [National Investor Relations Institute], which are endorsed by the SEC. Cisco has always provided full, timely, and accurate disclosure on our financial policies. We're a company that takes risk on the business side and on the accounting side we're a very conservative company."

Large companies have discovered—to their peril—that the larger they grow, the more exposed they are to integrity issues among employees. It is not surprising therefore that John Chambers has included this element as part of the Cisco culture.

SQUEAKY CLEAN

Chambers points to his own personal record. He notes proudly that he has never had an expense report questioned in his life. "I try to be a role model for the industry in ethics and in dealing with people. Squeaky clean in terms of my expense reports, for example, because ethically it's the right thing to do, and secondly, most of the time when a person takes advantage of somebody, they never get challenged on it, and people form [a negative] opinion of them."

In the late 1990s, as the U.S. government went up against Microsoft, eyes focused on other large companies that dominated their markets. Naturally, Cisco came under scrutiny. There wasn't much John Chambers could do about it. He wasn't going to be any less aggressive in winning customers. He had a good healthy fear of failure, which drove him to push himself and his employees hard and to win as many deals as possible.

But the problems wrought by that official scrutiny don't go away so easily. In the fall of 2000, Don Valentine, Cisco's vice chairman, worried openly about that scrutiny from various governmental agencies and the effect it might have on the company: "Now, we have to worry about the government. We never used to be on their radar screen. We're big now. If you look at the SEC in the last 18 months, there's a whole bunch of initiatives dealing with options, pooling, particular kinds of accounting, research and development."

At Cisco, the Microsoft suit was carefully watched. Arguing that "you had a persecutor, not a prosecutor," Valentine added that Microsoft's "crime to me was hubris and lying on the part of a couple of major executives in dealing with the government. So our approach is open kimono. We've lived in geographic isolation from the usual aspects of these forms of government, who are not elected, who have an unknown agenda, who have a permanent bureaucracy. They've taken shots at Intel and at Microsoft. We're in business with these companies, and they don't seem to be populated with criminals and bad guys. They are populated by great guys." Valentine also worried what would happen to the regulatory environment in Washington as Cisco's rivals became less effective, and Cisco becomes larger and more powerful. "We never had to think about problems like becoming so big. We never did anything that people would be interested in."

But in the view of Cisco executives, the company was vulnerable to government scrutiny if only because it had been growing at such a rapid pace and brushing past competitors with such seeming ease. John Chambers does not apologize for Cisco's aggressiveness, and he admits that what drives him above all else is winning. But he makes a point of saying that he does not have a killer instinct. He has learned that while competing is good, there is no point in trying to kill off all competition. Having no competition can seriously harm a company. IBM and Wang got into trouble, he submits, because they had no competitors for a long time. Some competition is healthy to keep a company from becoming complacent or surprised.

Starting in 1996, John Chambers decided to take a proactive stance toward the Washington regulators. "We learned that you needed to work with government and educate them."

OPERATING IN AN OPEN ENVIRONMENT

Dan Scheinman, Cisco's senior vice president for corporate development, explains Cisco frequently in Washington, D.C. He suggests that companies with proprietary markets, such as Microsoft and IBM (in earlier days), have a harder time defending themselves than Cisco, which operates in an "open" market. The proprietary companies get Washington's attention when they try to keep others from getting access to their products.

Chambers points out that "many companies have a government-relationship staff of a hundred people in this [regulatory] area. We have six in total. The Justice Department is an example: when they raise issues that we think are valid, we figure out how to accomplish the goals."

On one occasion, Chambers openly favored Cisco's partnering with rivals Lucent and Nortel. Government regulators had probed into whether Cisco had violated antitrust laws in 1997 by discussing partnerships and cooperation agreements with these two major competitors. Negotiations with Lucent and Nortel broke down not long after starting. In October 1998, Chambers described the conversations in the media, noting that the talks had faltered because of cultural differences among the three companies. The news accounts of those talks had prompted a lawyer at the Federal Trade Commission to look into the meetings, wondering whether Cisco was trying to divide up markets by working out a truce among competitors. Unlike the usual practice, when such probes are opened and closed without getting into the media, Cisco itself described the probe to journalists, concerned that keeping quiet would give the impression that it had something to hide, and worried that it might appear to be contradicting its policy of openness and full disclosure.

According to the *Washington Post* of June 2, 1999, as communication networks moved toward data and away from voice traffic, and as Cisco began to take on Lucent and Nortel in that field, Chambers sought out his two rivals, reportedly promising to forgo certain markets if Lucent and Northern Telecom ceded the high-speed Internet switch market to Cisco. The *Post* cited Cisco officials as saying that they were merely trying to develop industrywide networking standards. In our interview, Chambers admitted that he and his colleagues had not "educated" Washington sufficiently in advance of his partnership statements: "We had to understand that an inquiry can result from a single lawyer—this is what a lot of people don't realize. It wasn't a top-down let's look at this. It was a single lawyer who said I want to look at this. We responded to it and it was dismissed."

FRUGALITY

Frugality.

The word has a negative connotation, as if the people who keep expenses down are the cheapskates, the negativists, the folks who are raining on everyone's parade. And yet, for people like John Morgridge and John Chambers, there is something sacred about the word.

John Chambers learned about the Morgridge predilection for cost cutting in a most personal way. Soon after he began working for the company in 1991, Chambers filed his first expense report, seeking reimbursement for parking in the short-term parking lot at the San Francisco airport. "I wanted it to be not only approved, but if anybody ever looked at it, they would never have any question about my integrity." Morgridge wrote him a note on the expense report saying that he generally parked in the long-term lot, which was $2 a day cheaper.

Chambers was quite bothered "because that parking garage would probably have cost me a half hour's time." Though he would not take Morgridge's suggestion—"I wasn't going to give John the satisfaction"—he got the message: "Here's one of the richest people in Silicon Valley, and he's telling me: 'You not only want to spend the money like it's your own, but you don't want to create an expense run rate that will get the company in trouble.'" Chambers has told this war story frequently, always pointing out that Morgridge "didn't bounce my expense report. He just gave me a nudge."

James Richardson reels off the "frugal" list at Cisco without missing a beat. John Chambers pays for his personal jet out of his own pocket. Richardson himself flies first-class out of his own pocket. There are no splashy dinners for customers. If a Cisco employee orders three bottles of wine for dinner, only the first can be treated as

an expense. Everyone has the same-size office. There are no elabo-
rate conference rooms.

Barbara Beck, when she was Cisco's senior vice president for
human resources, visited a company up the street from Cisco, one of
Silicon Valley's most successful start-ups. As she conversed with a
vice president there about how the company sought to retain its people, she was struck by the fact that "the desks were made of
mahogany. It was as if they were saying: 'Look at us. We don't want to
keep people here, because we invest in buildings.'" Later, she took a
careful look at her office: "I do not have the world's nicest desk. It's
not mahogany. We invest in people. John Chambers's office is the
same as others."

MY CUBICLE IS TOO SMALL

Sometimes an employee grumbles about the tiny cubicles. One did
so on September 15, 2000, when Chambers appeared before a group
of employees. Speaking politely but firmly, Chambers told the
employee that she would just have to get used to the cramped quarters: "I don't believe in overextending the company. I was with two
companies who behaved like Santa Claus. I'm not going to do that in
my life. Other companies have huge offices. You could play Ping-
Pong in some of them. My office is 12 by 12."

Visitors to Chambers's office get a kick out of its small size, and his
having a conference room off the office that is not much larger than
the office. "My office is larger than his," one analyst observed, noting
that he was an analyst and that John Chambers ran a company of, at
that time, 40,000 employees.

The company's frugality policy shows up everywhere. The buildings at Cisco headquarters in San Jose, California, are painted the
same brown and green shades to create a campuslike atmosphere; in
the event of a Cisco downturn, individual buildings can be sold to
high-tech companies attracted by the campuslike decor.

The frugality message is pushed routinely. At a company meeting in September 2000, held in a tent at the Great Mall near Cisco headquarters, a Cisco executive preached the value of saving the company money on travel. It seemed that $500 million had been spent on travel in the previous year, a 76 percent increase over the year before. It was one of Cisco's highest expenses. The executive urged employees to figure out how to save the company money by using the Cisco Travel Network more and by planning trips further in advance.

FUN

In much the same way that a company cannot flourish if it's not careful with expenses, John Chambers has concluded, Cisco employees need—and should not feel guilty about having—more fun in their lives. It should be fun to work at Cisco.

His favorite greeting is "Are you having fun?" He is eager to convey to everyone that there should be more to life than work. (He's not saying, however, it's okay not to work hard.) To emphasize that he wants to lighten the atmosphere at Cisco, in November 2000 he decided to add "fun" to the list of features that make up Cisco's culture.

Given the pressures at Cisco—the long hours, the stretch goals that must be met, the need for aggressiveness and competitiveness—it's hard to figure out where the fun comes in. Somewhat paradoxically, Chambers worries that all the hard work he expects from his employees will drain them of a sense of enthusiasm and pleasure at coming to work every day. He's not prepared to ease up on the pressure, but he is eager to inject some fun into their daily lives: "I'd always talked about having fun, but I had never put it on our badge. But I've always believed you want to enjoy your work as well as enjoy your personal life. You ought to have that right balance, and it's plain good business. If the person burns out in business, doesn't have a personal life, they'll eventually burn out their home life or they'll leave the company."

200 POINTS A GAME

"I want them to have fun in both [work and leisure]. You want to make Cisco fun. It should be. This is a company that plays better when it's relaxed and having fun. We are the fast-break basketball team. We score 200 points a game. Nobody else will score 100. We play better when we're loose and relaxed. It doesn't mean we can't handle pressure."

What message is Chambers trying to convey to employees? "I'm saying don't take it too seriously. That when you have meetings, make them enjoyable. I have fun in my job. I like to rib people and I expect it back a little—in a nice way and fun way. I am not a typical CEO in terms of the formality, nor would I want that. I like to enjoy what I'm doing, and I don't mind people teasing me or me teasing them. And so I want to make sure that people understand that I expect them to have fun here."

Chambers has dressed up as Santa Claus at the office Christmas party and passed out candy and ice cream or pushed a hot-dog cart at other company parties. He takes a few hours each day for several days before Christmas to wander around Cisco's campus to wish employees a happy holiday, passing out candy, and asking, of course, "Are you having fun?"

At the senior level, it's the Friday lunches for Cisco's vice presidents that seem best to exemplify Chambers's wish to inject some lightheartedness into the place. On one Friday afternoon, 20 vice presidents were seated in the lobby outside Chambers's office, munching on sandwiches. One of them made a remark that evoked laughter on everyone's part. It was one time when John Chambers didn't have to ask, "Are you having fun?"

Fun becomes a requirement in a company that expects a lot of employees, right?

Chambers agrees. "We don't want you to break down from all this—so enjoy it. This is the only company where I've ever told people to slow down or actually forced people to take vacations. It's a work-hard culture, but it should be fun and stimulating when you're here. Stimulating is even more important than fun. When people start to run too hard, I worry about them getting sick."

But he is pushing them to work hard too, isn't he? "Absolutely. You look at companies that are made to last. They have all the same common characteristics: customer focus, an entrepreneurial nature, regardless of their size, and empowerment. They hold people accountable. Change is an integral part of the culture; companies that can adapt to change quickly have strong cultures and are intensely performance driven. You want to be intensely performance driven if you're going to win, but you can do that and have fun." He wants Cisco employees to work and play like a couple of his basketball heroes, Larry Bird and Kevin McHale of the NBA's Boston Celtics. "They were not only intense and focused, they worked very hard, they liked each other, and they had fun."

8 Go Bleed with Them

Listening to what customers want may seem a self-evident strategy for any business, but as John Chambers learned both at IBM and at Wang Laboratories, it is not. Some companies, for example IBM, arrogantly believed that the customer should listen to them; they knew best what the customer should buy! Other companies, for example Wang Laboratories, simply ignored what customers were saying: that they were enthralled with the personal computer.

In the highly competitive atmosphere hanging over the high-tech world, one of the key metrics, John Chambers believed, was customer satisfaction. The way to get customer satisfaction was to listen to customers. He knew that he understood that simple notion. He also understood that many of his colleagues in the high-tech community had trouble getting their arms around the idea.

Companies within the high-tech industry simply evinced little interest in customer satisfaction. Chambers explained: "They understood conceptually that there was a one-to-one correlation between customer satisfaction and profit. But the industry didn't focus on customer satisfaction, because it takes 12 to 24 months to show up. And we are remarkably short-term in the computer industry."

It was not simply that John Chambers felt customer satisfaction should be stressed; Cisco has a long history of paying attention to customers. Sandy Lerner is recalled admiringly by many at the company, not only as one of its two cofounders, but also as the originator of customer advocacy within the company. But customer advocacy remained unsystematic for some time. When they had complaints, customers would write e-mails to Cisco's engineers, and whichever engineer knew the answer would respond. No tracking system existed for those complaints. Far from ideal, these arrangements took up too much of the engineers' time—but they at least bound the company's product-development teams to customers. As Cisco grew, it could not afford to "waste" engineers' time answering e-mail from customers.

In February 1990, at the time of Cisco's IPO, 40 percent of its business came from the universities or the infrastructure of the Internet. The other 60 percent came from such customers as Boeing, Motorola, Salomon Brothers, Citibank, and the federal government; the government represented 15 percent of all Cisco business. As Cisco grew, more of its customers were manufacturers, financial and brokerage clients, and the federal and state governments. The university business stayed the same in absolute terms but declined as a percentage of overall Cisco business. (Cisco acquired more business from the telephone companies and Internet service providers, many of whom became Cisco resellers.)

By the early 1990s, Cisco was emerging as an important player in networking, but enterprise customers had not yet become convinced that the company was formidable enough for them. With customers demanding better and better service, it became crucial for Cisco to pay special attention to them. Cisco's rivals were larger and appeared more powerful than the Silicon Valley start-up. Wellfleet was the main rival to Cisco. IBM was only dabbling in Internetworking, linking locations with diverse networks together into a single network. It had taken a stab at the simpler networking, and as long as Big Blue was in the field, customers would have a hard time choosing Cisco over the computer giant.

By 1992, Cisco began offering a way to directly attach its networks to IBM mainframes, setting the stage for Cisco to get its foot in the door and eventually replace the IBM network. Coincidentally, this shift began to trivialize the role of the mainframe and set the stage for IBM's eventual demise as a major network equipment supplier. The strategic buyers—the chief information officers, the chief technology officers, the top communications officers—eventually began purchasing Cisco products, betting their jobs on Cisco.

When John Chambers arrived at Cisco in January 1991, the term *customer advocacy* had already been embedded in the company's culture. But with Sandy Lerner's departure in 1990, a gap in customer advocacy at the senior executive level required filling. In August 1991, Chambers hired Doug Allred as a new vice president to promote that cause.

TELLING THE CUSTOMERS FROM THE CISCO PEOPLE

When Allred arrived on the scene, he was amazed at how cozy customers were with Cisco's engineers, even to the extent that customers would visit Cisco's technical advisory group meetings: "They had this personal relationship," recalled Allred. "You couldn't tell the Cisco people from the customers." The group would listen to what the customers had to say and then would offer comments to try to satisfy customer requests. It was a perfectly workable system as long as Cisco had only a few hundred customers. But it could not scale.

Meanwhile, John Morgridge was pushing customer advocacy aggressively from the top. He initiated a program called Networkers, inviting major customers to San Jose to meet with Cisco's management and engineers. Customers themselves directed and otherwise participated in panels at conferences, usually with four customers and one Cisco employee on a panel. Questions came from the audience, providing a kind of intelligence system. (The Networkers program still exists, with John Chambers and other senior executives attending conferences.)

Morgridge was adamant about pleasing the customer. In the fall of 1990, Cisco executive James Richardson arrived for the company's first customer satisfaction conference accompanied by a half dozen customers. Morgridge approached him.

"So, young man, what are you doing here?" the president of Cisco asked.

"I have customers here," Richardson replied, pointing to the group, assuming that Morgridge would be pleased.

"But," Morgridge said, "you have one customer in British Columbia in trouble. Why don't you go travel there? I'll take care of your customers. Go bleed with those customers in British Columbia." And Richardson went. That, to Morgridge, was customer advocacy at it its finest.

By the time Doug Allred attended his first board meeting in the summer of 1991, he discovered that three-fourths of the board's discussion was taken up with customer experiences. The trouble was that no one was seeking answers to how the company would handle customers once Cisco grew larger. To Doug Allred, the answer lay in utilizing the new information technology (IT), and he planned to deliver that message to the Cisco board, hoping to win it over.

Nearly a decade later, Doug Allred recalled that first board meeting and the frustration that engulfed him. He had been in the job only a week, and in that short time he had to prepare a presentation to the board on Cisco's service and support strategy. The first two-thirds of the presentation went exceptionally well, he thought. He had felt quite comfortable explaining the company's service and support strategy. He was also pleased to find no one challenging him; they simply assumed that he would know how to get the job done. But the truth was that he had no idea how much technology would be needed to handle the inevitably heavier burden in customer service; nor could he be sure that the board would back the heightened use of information technology that he knew he would need.

Still, he decided to bring up the whole IT matter, noting that Cisco had a very small IT team: 123 people. (The customer advocacy group was less than half that size: 50 people.) He then made the casual observation that Cisco was spending a mere 0.75 percent of annual revenue on IT. Other high-tech firms were spending much more, 3.5 to 4 percent. As a result, he suggested, Cisco's senior managers were not getting anywhere near the benefits from IT that they should be getting. The company, he concluded, must spend more on IT. He thought the paucity of IT resources had created a crisis at Cisco, and he hoped a remedy would be forthcoming quickly. That was his message to the board.

A FRUGAL BOARD

In the job only a week, Doug Allred had not had time to get acquainted with the main elements of the Cisco culture, especially frugality.

"Doug," began one senior board member, "do you realize that 0.75 percent is a lot of money? And what *you* are saying is that we should spend more?"

That *was* exactly what he was saying, but he adopted a more reserved tone now, realizing that he had probably made a huge mistake at this early stage of his career at Cisco. Still, he carried on, noting that other high-tech companies that had spent too little on IT had experienced hits on their market caps: "I think we're exposed too. But I'm too new. I can't tell you how exposed we are or how much we should spend. But I think we're in trouble here. It's our Achilles' heel."

The board failed to get Allred's point, and assumed that Cisco, because it was a technical company, an engineering company, should not have to earmark large sums for IT. Allred knew that he had a challenge on his hands.

Cisco's revenues stood at $183,184,000 in 1991, and it was clear that the company was going to grow rapidly over the next few years. New steps would have to be taken to accommodate that growth. "The challenge," Allred recalled, "was how do we sustain the notion of customer advocacy, in Sandy's vernacular, and how do we extend it to Morgridge's vernacular of measuring customer satisfaction in everything. We wanted to involve the customer in all processes, including services, support channel, and financial management process, not just products."

Walking out of the meeting together, Doug Allred and John Chambers decided on the spot that Allred would have to create a scalable model for customer satisfaction. The new model would place accountability for customer satisfaction and financial performance in the hands of the managers. All managers would be rated on these two criteria. Rating these two criteria would require the creative use of technology. To aid the managers, Allred and Chambers decided that IT would no longer be centralized in its own department; rather, each manager would decide how IT resources were allocated in order to strengthen customer relationships. The search for a top-notch chief information officer became a priority.

The new model took 18 months to implement. When it was in place, the effect was remarkable. All of the cash spent on IT was earmarked for increasing customer satisfaction by making employees more efficient and effective. IT staff members could consult on how much IT was required, but they were no longer the decision makers; the managers were. By the fall of 2000, Cisco was spending 3.75 percent of its annual revenues on IT. By June 2002, it was up to a bit over 5 percent.

John Chambers grew obsessed with customer issues. He had paid close attention to what had happened at DEC and at Apple Computer, noticing that when their customer satisfaction ratings dropped, it took only another year or two for their revenues to drop. He became convinced that a one-to-one correlation existed between customer satisfaction and revenues.

Teaching the need for customer satisfaction to the whole company was difficult for Chambers at first. Most Cisco employees had a hard time understanding why it was so important to worry about customer satisfaction. Chambers said, "I knew why it was so important. Twelve to 24 months later, after IBM and Wang lost customer satisfaction, they were dead."

Chambers developed a systematic approach at Cisco toward customers. He ranked each vice president and each senior vice president on how many customer visits they made, and he took notice of their customer evaluations. The Cisco executive saw or phoned numerous customers every day he was in the office.

Chambers made a large portion of Cisco executives' bonuses dependent upon customer satisfaction. Customer surveys studied 70 aspects of the customer relationship. Among them: How was product quality? How easily did the product fit into the customer's existing networks? How effective was the sales representative? How easy was it to find information about Cisco? To bother customers with such evaluations might create some awkwardness, but Chambers felt it was necessary to make sure that customers were indeed satisfied.

Throughout the second half of the nineties Chambers was spending half of his time as president and CEO talking with customers. ("Too much," he observes, remembering the multitude of plane rides.) He was visiting with five to 10 customers a day when on the road, traveling hundreds of thousands of miles a year in that mission. (Back in the office, he would see or talk on the phone with one to five customers a day.) He believes that contact with customers is crucial: "If I really believe getting too far away from the customer and employee is what could trip Cisco, then I shall spend the majority of my time making sure we don't get tripped."

AUTOMATED WATCHING

Cisco's philosophy toward customers is rooted in the belief that the most important time to be available to them is at their worst moments of stress. When a customer has a problem, says Chambers, "that's when we're there for them. You don't build relationships when things are going well. You build a relationship in times of stress. It's for customers to know that we'll move heaven and earth to make the relationship successful. We have a fanatical approach to that. Walking the talk, if you will."

A good deal of the customer relationship has been automated.

Relying upon Web-based programs, Chambers can take a look at a summary of customer satisfaction on a continuing basis. He can look at an automatic roll-up of every router around the world and drill down into the four large geographical theaters by country, by city, even by individual sales representative.

When he is at home, he monitors customer complaints on his computer. Chambers keeps tabs on the most worrisome accounts. He looks at every critical account in the world each night. If someone's network is unstable, Cisco describes that situation as "critical A." If the network has the potential to become unstable, that's a "critical B." The account needs to be watched. Chambers receives reports on all critical A accounts in the world—as many as 15 per evening. All too aware that he is getting to only 15 accounts out of thousands, Chambers still feels the monitoring is vitally important as an early-warning signal. Even if only two or three customers have a certain problem, that is enough for him to raise the issue with colleagues.

He also spends some 90 minutes a day on voice mail, one-third of which deals with customer comments.

Listening to customers is part of his DNA. He is sometimes amazed when visiting other companies that the word *customer* never enters into the conversation. He cannot understand it.

Chambers says you have to make sure you listen to the right customer at the right time: "If you listen to the right customer, you will hear a repeating theme. You will be able to pick up that theme much quicker than your counterparts. Getting those inflection points is the key, and that is what Cisco is so great about."

He notes that by the time the majority of customers spot a trend, it's too late: "So recognizing the early leaders and understanding when the transitions are happening is so key." That, he explains, is precisely what Cisco was able to do in listening to corporate leaders and, most lately, university presidents, who were saying that they wanted to learn how to use the Internet for their own business processes. Once it became clear to Chambers that these business leaders would be eager to learn how Cisco was using Internet technology for its own business processes, he was able to create a whole new core competency for

Cisco, promoting the company as a model E-company: "It's been shocking to me," said Chambers, "that none of our peers are making that transition."

GOING END-TO-END

He also listened to customers in January 1996, when two of them from large financial institutions urged him to adopt an end-to-end approach in the kind of networking equipment Cisco sold. Though Chambers admits that he had no idea what they were talking about at first, he subsequently learned—and put into practice—the notion: developing all kinds of networking equipment that provided a kind of one-stop shopping approach.

"Don't you want best in class in each category?" Chambers asked one of the customers.

"Well, you've already got us in probably eight or nine out of our top 10 or 11 categories," the customer replied. "If you'd either build or buy one of the others, then we would like to go with you."

To Wall Street, the end-to-end concept sounded arrogant. It sounded a lot like an IBM trying to own the entire computing infrastructure, in a proprietary manner. But Cisco's customers understood that was not the case.

Finally, listening to customers—specifically, the service providers—on other occasions led Cisco to converge video, data, and voice in its products.

Gary Daichendt worked at IBM and Wang before coming to Cisco Systems, and in November 2000 he was executive vice president for worldwide operations. (He left Cisco the following month.) In his view, what separates Cisco from his first two employers is the company's passion for the customer: "Most companies look out for customers out of pragmatism. It's incorporated into our culture that it's fun to help a customer with a business solution. When a customer has a problem, it's in the culture here that we're going to solve the problem. Nobody asks, 'Can I have a plane ticket to solve the problem? Can I substitute the equipment?'"

Earlier, when Daichendt was Cisco's vice present for intercontinental operations, a Korean customer required repair on a product that had cost $500,000. Daichendt required no higher approval. He simply went ahead and spent the money on the repair. Other companies would have returned the customer's money. It would have been easier. Not Cisco. Daichendt says: "What I admire about Cisco is that it is ingrained in the culture that we're going to fix your problem. We're in this together and we're going to solve your problem."

Underpinning this aggressive approach to customer support is the confidence that Cisco has in its engineering team, in its ability to turn out great products; for as Gary Daichendt notes: "I can't afford to give $500,000 in repairs to every million-dollar customer. I couldn't afford to pay out in repairs 50 percent of the cost of the product." Customers don't complain that Cisco isn't throwing enough resources at their problem. Some customers do, however, want to make sure that their problem has the attention of John Chambers or another senior executive.

Yet it is the way that Cisco reacts to customer complaints that has shaped its reputation within the industry. Carl Redfield, the senior vice president for manufacturing and worldwide logistics, enjoys telling the story of a customer—one of the large financial institutions in New York—who had a network problem in 1999. A large router seemed to be in need of replacement, and the customer placed a call to Cisco's service staff on a Saturday, eager to get the replacement right away. The skeleton staff prepared the piece of equipment to the customer's specifications, had it packaged, and then chartered a jet for delivery! One employee had to enlist the help of a colleague because the first one did not have enough credit to hire the plane. Redfield says matter-of-factly, "Of course, the employees were reimbursed." The two employees received congratulations from superiors for using initiative and creativity. "In any other company, solving the problem," says Redfield, with a look of satisfaction, "would have waited until Monday." Other companies would have looked at that issue as a transaction, Redfield notes, while to Cisco it was purely a matter of customer satisfaction.

At the time of the economic downturn of 2000–2001, according to company executives, the "listening to the customers" strategy helped Cisco respond to the sudden drop-off in sales orders faster than many of its rivals. Certainly that was the case. Cisco moved into recovery mode very quickly once it became apparent in early January 2001 that the economy had gone into a deep sleep. At the time, Cisco officials were not prepared to acknowledge that the company had taken its eye off of the customer throughout the previous year or two, and that that neglect might have been a contributing factor to how difficult it was for Cisco to recover from the economic slump. That would take some time. Eventually, by the spring of 2002, John Chambers was telling employees privately that indeed Cisco had performed less than ideally when it came to listening to customers. He especially noted Cisco's underperforming when it came to dealing with service-provider customers. A new market for Cisco, there had been many players to get to know and not enough time to meet and cultivate them.

9 Silicon Valley Is Our Lab

Hell-bent for hypergrowth, John Chambers pursued an acquisition strategy more aggressively and, for a time at least, more successfully than any other leader in Silicon Valley. He was, however, swimming against the tide. Acquisitions were not a Silicon Valley custom.

But Chambers believed that the Cisco strategy that placed a sharp focus on customers was inextricably linked with an acquisitions strategy: because customer expectations changed so rapidly in the high-tech world, and because customers were more and more looking for end-to-end solutions in networking, a horizontal business model reflecting that end-to-end approach would always trump a vertical solution.

The choice for Chambers was to provide that horizontal capability in the product line either through the company's internal research and development program or through acquisitions. Chambers felt that it simply would not do to rely upon Cisco's own engineers. The company had to search for the best talent wherever it was. He believed that the markets he was in were growing at huge rates, and he equally believed that Cisco should acquire a large share of those markets. Speed, though, was of the essence. It would not do to simply wait patiently for his engineers to come up with the required products. He decided to go after tiny Silicon Valley start-ups that were on the verge of the next product breakthrough. Against that background, the strategy of acquisitions was born.

As Rick Justice, Cisco's senior vice president for worldwide field operations, observed, "The point was to sell the full potential of the network, not just components. The idea was that people would want a computer network in the same way that they wanted a phone network that worked. But we had to be one or two in every point of that network" because customers would want the value of the whole, without compromising on the pieces.

None of Cisco's acquisition strategy would have been possible without the wherewithal to purchase companies. Cisco's rarefied stock value throughout the 1990s provided the necessary support. In the decade after the company had gone public at $18 a share in February 1990, the stock had climbed 8,000 percent. That stock price permitted Cisco to make offers to other firms—paying for the firms with Cisco stock—that other companies could not possibly match.

Embarking on a strategy that was as controversial as it was creative, Chambers pursued a stream of acquisitions as a way of keeping up with the lightning-fast market transitions that were a trademark of the high-tech industry. Seven years after embarking on the strategy in 1993, Chambers understood the connection between acquisitions and hypergrowth: "What we did that was so unique was instead of thinking we could do it ourselves, we went out and acquired, and that was what started the whole change. The companies that were successful in our industry in the last decade learned how to acquire. That was the breakaway strategy."

FILLING IN THE HOLES

If the SynOptics gambit had created a fault line through Cisco, the unhappy experience, interestingly enough, did not sour Cisco executives on acquiring other companies. "We were a public company," recalled Don Valentine, who at the time was chairman of the Cisco board, "and we had an incredibly valuable currency. I remember having this conversation with a number of people in [Cisco] management about the idea of using the currency to have effectively two research and development operations. We didn't have to buy a company that was almost as big as we were [an obvious reference to Syn-Optics]. We could buy lots of start-ups that were developing point products that were progressively stronger to take to market."

Valentine did not have a particular start-up in mind when he held those conversations during 1993. He urged John Morgridge and the others simply to take a hard look at the "mosaic of their product plan" to see where there might be holes. "My suggestion was to use this currency in part to fill in the holes."

Starting in the summer of 1993, it was becoming clear to Chambers that Cisco's customers were finding it increasingly expensive to purchase routers from Cisco and other networking products from non-Cisco vendors. For every $1 spent on networking hardware and software, it was costing customers an additional $3 to $4 to integrate those products and administer them. Even worse, when problems arose with one of the products, the customer would get different answers from different vendors.

Cisco's "problem" was that it supplied only routers. To become a full-service provider, the company could not rely upon its own engineers. Nor could it purchase one of the other large networking enterprises, such as 3Com, which was too costly and would put Cisco in only a few new markets. Networking start-ups appeared the best bet. The plan was to help these start-ups complete their products, then use Cisco's muscle in sales and distribution (through its partners) to build new businesses rapidly.

John Chambers, John Morgridge, Don Valentine, and Ed Kozel pored over a list of potential purchases. They were eager to find companies that could help them offer increased bandwidth. This would improve a network's ability to move traffic smoothly, without delays. Although routers could expand bandwidth, they were not very fast, they were expensive, and they were hard to manage when many were in use. Nor did intelligent hubs (devices that make it easier to detect network crashes or faults) increase bandwidth. Network companies like Cisco required a new device that combined the intelligence of the router and the simplicity of the intelligent-hub architecture.

The answer came from networking hardware vendors that began selling local area network switches (so called because they "switched" traffic from point to point). Vendors such as Kalpana, Synernetics, ALANTEC, Network Peripherals, Grand Junction Networks, and Crescendo Communications were getting into the new LAN switch business. These switches would eventually displace intelligent hubs because they offered huge increases in bandwidth. (By early 1994, the LAN switch market had grown to just above $100 million, part of the overall $3 billion networking market.)

In the early summer of 1993, Mario Mazzola was presiding over Sunnyvale-based Crescendo's 52 employees. Born in Italy, Mario had come to the United States in 1977 to work for Olivetti. He left Olivetti and started a company in 1982, which became David Systems, an early integrator of voice/video and data. For eight years, he was David Systems' vice president for engineering. In 1990, David was sold to Chipcom.

In June 1993, Mazzola learned from a networking magazine that the planned merger between Cisco Systems and SynOptics was not going to happen. Aware that SynOptics and Crescendo had similar technologies, Mazzola picked up the phone to John Chambers. "I thought our switches could be of interest to them," he said later. Mazzola was thinking of a joint marketing scheme with Cisco, not an acquisition.

Chambers and others at Cisco had known of Crescendo for some time, because Don Valentine's Sequoia Capital was a major investor in Mazzola's firm. Earlier in 1993, Valentine had proposed that Terry Eger, who had retired from Cisco the previous year, take over the presidency of Crescendo, but nothing came of the suggestion.

That summer Chambers and Terry Eger had talked of Cisco's buying the start-up, not for its switching technology, but for its copper data distribution interface (CDDI) technology. Cisco was the largest seller of fiber data distribution interface (FDDI).

Terry Eger convinced Chambers that Crescendo would be a great purchase for Cisco because it could then sell a lot of CDDI. Chambers asked Eger what other products Crescendo had. Chambers faced a dilemma: Morgridge was still cool to the idea of buying Crescendo, though Don Valentine favored the idea. Terry Eger, telling him that Crescendo had this "half-built LAN switch in the back room," had no idea what the product did. He had not seen it. He had only heard about it. He had no idea it was meant to replace intelligent hubs.

LISTENING TO BOEING

A few weeks earlier, according to Terry Eger, Chambers had been at Boeing, one of Cisco's largest customers, and had heard the manager of networking for routers and switches tell him, "We're going to go to LAN switches." The networking manager told Chambers that he believed LAN switches were the replacement product for hubs, and that the future of networking would be in a combination of routers and switches. Cisco had struggled to build a switching product, but had not succeeded. Cisco's engineers thought they could fill the hole by improving the performance of routers in switching, but that never proved to be the case.

So when Terry Eger told Chambers that Crescendo was involved in switching, Chambers's ears perked up. According to John Chambers, Boeing pushed Cisco over the edge in switching: "It was Boeing telling us, 'Not only should you be in switching, you should be in fast Ethernet, and, by the way, here's a $10 million order that you're not going to get unless you buy Crescendo.'"

Chambers likes to tell the story, giving Boeing credit for alerting Cisco to the new switching product, for it allows him to provide one more example of how Cisco was able to forge ahead by listening to its customers.

A few moments after starting a meeting with John Chambers, Mario Mazzola realized that Chambers wanted to acquire Crescendo. "We consider the technology you are developing as core technology for Cisco," Chambers told him.

Chambers's first offer was for $65 million. "The Crescendo board was on the greedy side," Mazzola recalled, and insisted that he seek at least $200 million. "I was more concrete and reasonable." To Mazzola, his Crescendo colleagues were overlooking a few important details. Crescendo was only two years old and had revenues of $40 million a year. It was doing well and had some excellent customers (Sun Microsystems, Goldman Sachs, Microsoft, Boeing). But $200 million seemed excessive. He explained all of this to Chambers and told him candidly, "If you offer me $100 million, this deal can be done."

Mazzola liked Cisco's "straightforwardness" and he liked the company's leaders. Other larger companies wanted Crescendo's technology for free. Cisco was willing to pay. Still, some Cisco board members worried that Cisco was taking too big a risk in buying Crescendo. High-tech acquisitions were rare and therefore uncertain. Though he would later join the bandwagon, Don Valentine was a strong cynic at the time: "The majority of acquisitions fail," he told Chambers. "Just don't let it be your first one or two." Chambers took the warning seriously: "It was a nice way of saying, 'If it is one of your first one or two, you may not be back in the company after that.'" The board backed the Crescendo deal, however grudgingly. On September 23, 1990, Cisco agreed to pay $95 million for the company.

Slow to understand that switching would become a new force in networking, Wall Street analysts fretted at the seemingly exorbitant price that Cisco had forked over for Crescendo. Why pay $95 million for a small firm that had yet to make its first switch? What had happened to the vaunted Cisco frugality? Paul Johnson, the analyst at Robertson Stephens, told the New York Times that it was a dumb idea, paying nearly $100 million for a company that had been forecast to sell only $10 million of equipment over the next year.

Seven years later, Cisco's switching business, thanks first and foremost to the Crescendo purchase, had become a $10 billion a year business, almost half of Cisco's annual revenues that year.

Amused at how wrong he had been ("a slight misanalysis," Johnson acknowledged), the analyst suggested that the Crescendo deal could be called "absolutely one of the greatest technology acquisitions in history." The Crescendo switching product was resulting in nearly half of Cisco's revenues in 2000. Calculating what 40 percent of Cisco's market cap was in the summer of 2000, Cisco's switching business was worth $200 billion, and to reach that stratospheric height, Cisco had spent only $95 million.

It was the start of the John Chambers strategy of going after acquisitions aggressively, paying what seemed like a huge amount of money for companies that thus far had shown little revenue promise, relying on Cisco's stock to underwrite the deals. Because the Crescendo acquisition enriched Cisco beyond anyone's wildest imaginations (Mazzola's included), the acquisition strategy, from the very start, had the ring of success. John Chambers had found the keys to the kingdom of hypergrowth.

Mike Volpi graduated from Stanford University's business school in June 1994 with an MBA and began working for Cisco Systems on August 1, 1994. He remembered the early weeks as painful: "Every day I came to Cisco seemed like the last day of our lives." Competition was fierce. On the day that he graduated from business school, the Cisco stock was at $40 a share. By his first day on the job, it had fallen to $20. He remembered the gloom that had fastened on to the place: "People thought growth was over. The game was over. They thought ATM [asynchronous transfer mode] would replace IP technology. People were worried that we wouldn't make the transition to LAN switching." Mergers appeared to be strengthening Cisco's rivals: SynOptics and Wellfleet, Chipcom and 3Com. The purchase of Crescendo seemed like an ill-founded decision: "People said, 'Why don't you buy big companies and get bigger faster?'" But Volpi sensed that Cisco was on the right track: "Generally, innovation in our industry happens from small companies."

It took some time, but eventually the Crescendo purchase looked like a gem of a deal. Cisco's new switching product was highly suitable for enterprise customers, and hence played to the company's strength. The Cisco product proved scalable, so it was highly attractive to large customers such as Boeing and Merrill Lynch.

Cisco's revenues moved up steadily: from $649 million in 1993, to $1.2 billion in 1994, to $2.23 billion in 1995.

The Crescendo purchase eventually gave Cisco the ability to compete with Cabletron and SynOptics as hubs gave way to LAN switches. Indeed, the purchase of Crescendo set off a chain of events that eventually transformed Cisco into the leading force in networking.

The Crescendo purchase validated Cisco's theory that it could introduce "cores" of technology into the company by absorbing start-ups into Cisco's culture; it could multiply the start-ups' revenues by using its own much larger and powerful sales and distribution teams without slowing down the rest of Cisco. The purchase also reinforced the notion held by Cisco's leading executives that a merger of equals (such as SynOptics or 3Com) would have resulted in a collision of cultures and a slowing down of Cisco. Finally, the Cisco acquisition did *not* dilute Cisco shareholders' stock, as a merger between Cisco and SynOptics would have.

It was no wonder that Cisco liked the Crescendo acquisition so much more than the proposed merger with SynOptics. In the case of SynOptics, as Ed Kozel recalled, "They weren't even a LAN switch company yet. They were pure hub. We just didn't like the culture. And we were very afraid of these mergers of equals."

Crescendo looked much, much better. "We liked their leader, their technology, and they were very small, so we could blend them." Indeed, Crescendo taught Cisco how to do acquisitions. "We learned," Ed Kozel added, "that if you take an excellent team and give them a lot of fertilizer, the plant grows very quickly."

Listening to John Chambers seven years after the Crescendo purchase, one senses that its success was hardly considered a sure thing:

"Understandably, a lot of people thought we should combine with SynOptics, an equal peer. Or Cabletron. And a lot of people thought we should go toward ATM technology, and it was really Ed Kozel and I who both felt that this would be our enterprise product and be key to the future. We didn't share this with anyone. And we deliberately protected Crescendo over to the side and let it just grow and added a lot of resources to it and then let the market determine whether we were right or wrong. Today the heart of our current product strategy is this LAN switch [which Cisco gained from Crescendo] with router and other technology built into it. The LAN switch is now the core of our enterprise business."

LET'S DO ROUTING AND SWITCHING

What prompted that decision?

For Chambers, the simple answer was not to get overly wedded to one technology. "Our company thought of ourselves as routers. And we thought the competition was not only other router business but that the switch competitors were our competitors. And so we didn't fall in love with technology. Most companies that were router companies would have stayed a router company. We moved into LAN switching. We didn't view LAN switching as competitive. We viewed it as complementary. I learned the hard way at IBM with mainframes and at Wang with minicomputers that you don't argue about technology trends; they are undeniable. Either you participate in them or you get left behind. So I said we should do both, we should do routing and switching. Nobody had done that move before."

Cisco's success with the Crescendo purchase opened the way for other acquisitions. Mario Mazzola knew just where Cisco should turn to next. The switching product line that he had developed — the Crescendo Catalyst 5000 — was high-end. It focused on 100-megabit Ethernet technology. Designed as a very modular system, it was more expensive and more scalable than lower-end products. But Mazzola believed that the switching market would grow as well at the middle and low ends. The low end centered on 10-megabit Ethernet technology.

He suggested to his Cisco colleagues that they search out possible acquisitions in the middle- and low-end segments of the switching market. Cheaper products were required for Cisco's reseller channel under any circumstances. Crescendo's products, because they were high-end, were more suitable for Cisco's selling directly to customers.

At the time of the Crescendo purchase, Kalpana, a company located in Sunnyvale, California, with 150 employees, owned 100 percent of the Ethernet switching market. That was the good news. Less exciting was the fact that the Ethernet switching market was very nascent, with an overall value of only $90 million. Kalpana discovered early in 1994 that one of its partners, IBM, wanted to secure a deal with it. When Mario Mazzola learned from the newspapers that IBM was pursuing Kalpana, Mario arranged for John Chambers to meet with the Kalpana team: Jim Jordan, the CEO, and Charlie Giancarlo, the vice president of product marketing.

Cisco wanted to make the Kalpana purchase because Crescendo did not have a low-end, inexpensive Ethernet switch. Crescendo was planning to come out with a high-end, expensive Ethernet switch. Cisco offered to buy Kalpana for $200 million in Cisco shares ($20 million higher than the IBM offer). Three days later, Cisco and Kalpana agreed to the deal at a price of $220 million.

To its chagrin, Cisco eventually learned that Kalpana's products were not cheap enough. Cisco wanted a product that was truly at the low end of the switching market. The answer came with a company called Grand Junction Networks. Howard Charney, the man behind Grand Junction, was one of Silicon Valley's wizards. He had already cofounded 3Com, a leading networking company in the Valley. Back in September 1991, Charney and some friends decided they would try to make the Ethernet run 10 times faster. Grand Junction was born in February 1992. Sales came to $4.5 million the first year, and $7 million the second. Sales were so good in 1995 that Charney planned to take the company public. The market for Grand Junction's products was skyrocketing.

Eager to find low-end, fast Ethernet switching products, Cisco cast its eye on Grand Junction, which was estimating that it would do as much as $65 million in revenues for 1996. Unbeknownst to Howard Charney, Cisco executives were predicting that if they acquired Grand Junction, the start-up's revenues would in fact be $119 million in 1996.

Meanwhile, Howard Charney and his colleagues at Grand Junction filed to go public on July 31, 1995. It was then that Mario Mazzola called Charney. The two men had known each other since the early 1980s. Charney, quite aware that Cisco had bought Mario's company, Crescendo, was fond of Mazzola and trusted him. Mario said he wanted to talk. Charney agreed, though he wondered why Mario wanted the meeting.

Sure, Cisco had acquired Crescendo, then Kalpana, but why would they want to talk to him? Grand Junction was growing, but it baffled Charney that a networking giant like Cisco would want to do business with a relatively tiny start-up: "They must know everything in the world," he told himself. "They must have all the technology in the world."

FINDING A LOW-END PRODUCT

Certainly conscious that the switching market was mushrooming, Charney nonetheless had no clue that Cisco lacked low-end switching products. He knew that Cisco had come out with the Catalyst 5000 the previous May, but he didn't know it was a high-end product. Nor did he know much about the Kalpana switching product. It was, in fact, selling at a price of $1,300 a port, and there was no way to reduce that price—something else Charney could not have known. Grand Junction's products were as cheap as $250 a port. Charney simply assumed that to develop a low-end product, Cisco would figure out how to reduce costs on the Kalpana switch: "I didn't appreciate how hard that would be for them."

Cisco's dream was to sell products to customers through distribution via resellers. From its founding in 1984, it had relied on direct sales. In its early days, it made more sense to sell a complicated product directly to the customer rather than to rely upon resellers to provide advice and support. But now Cisco wanted to get hold of a low-end product for that distribution channel, targeting medium and small businesses. The Kalpana product, because it was too expensive, was just not doing the trick. The Grand Junction product seemed just right for Cisco to expand its reach with customers.

Quite aware that Grand Junction was about to go public, John Chambers, by now seven months into the job of CEO, asked Howard Charney if he would want to go public even if Cisco would offer him $200 million in Cisco stock.

Charney took the Cisco offer to his board, which at first was reluctant to drop plans for the IPO. Board members grew concerned, however, that Cisco might buy a Grand Junction rival, causing Grand Junction trouble.

Chambers raised the ante, offering $225 million, then $275 million. Just what would it take to win over the Grand Junction board? he asked Charney.

Chambers heard the answer and didn't blink. He closed the deal to acquire Grand Junction for $325 million in Cisco stock. Then, while Chambers was on a business trip overseas, Cisco's stock climbed by $5 a share; in November 1995, Charney and Chambers agreed to a standstill agreement that amounted to $345 million.

And what about the $119 million in revenues that Cisco had projected for Grand Junction in its first year after the deal? Cisco exceeded the figure, as Grand Junction revenues produced under the Cisco umbrella came to $124 million in 1996.

"It meant," said Charney, "that Cisco was really smart. They knew what they were doing. There's a progeny business that Cisco doesn't break out—that's a multibillion-dollar business in revenues—it's called low-end switch. It's evolved into desktop connectivity or desktop switching. That's the essence of the home run. You pay $345 million in funny money [shares] and take an entity that would do $65 million, and in the first year you own it, you double what it planned to do, and then over the next several years, you do billions. This was really a good deal for Grand Junction." And it was a good deal for Cisco.

Now Cisco owned Crescendo, Kalpana, and Grand Junction. With these purchases carried out from 1993 to 1995, Cisco had acquired the talent that would give it the switching product it required. The results were spectacular. By 1999, fully 39 percent of Cisco's $12.1 billion in revenues came from switching (41 percent came from routers, 13 percent from access products, and 7 percent from other products). As of spring 2002, routing represented 30 percent of Cisco's business, with switching at 40 percent; access products amounted to 5 percent; others, like optical and software, came to 8 percent; services, 17 percent.

The acquisition strategy was in place. Cisco executives were confident that they could build a product line that would meet the needs of customers who liked dealing with only one vendor.

Early in 1996, Chambers heard customers for the first time encourage him to build an end-to-end business, as customers saw an advantage in having one strategic provider for all of their networking purchases. Once-skeptical customers, who had doubted that any networking company could deliver across the whole spectrum of networking, now began putting their trust in Cisco Systems.

Cisco began a buying spree that brought the company into every aspect of the networking industry.

Cisco's acquisition strategy got a further boost as more data, graphics, and video were put on the Internet, requiring companies to sell more routers and switches to direct the overwhelming traffic.

To make sure that it had all the products that were required for an end-to-end strategy, Cisco needed to keep purchasing companies. In April 1996, it made its largest purchase yet, paying $4 billion in cash and stock for StrataCom, a frame-relay and switch maker with 1,200 employees and $400 million in annual sales. The purchase price was 12 times larger than StrataCom's 1995 revenues and marked Cisco's first billion-dollar acquisition. Cisco's plan was to develop a high-density ATM core switch, thanks to the integration of StrataCom's engineers, but it never did. Defending the acquisition, Chambers notes that in the same way that Crescendo got Cisco into switching, StrataCom got it into the carrier market. Until the start of 1996, Cisco's strategy had focused on enterprise or corporations. It was selling a great deal of LAN switching product.

Cisco was selling the StrataCom products—data switches used in large networks—to Internet service providers as well as emerging phone carriers. Yet the traditional phone carriers continued to purchase those products from Nortel, Newbridge Networks, and Ascend Communications (which by 1999 was part of Lucent).

By September 1996, Cisco had a market cap larger than $30 billion. By embarking on its acquisition strategy—scooping up 13 companies at a total cost of $5.5 billion—it had the broadest technology lineup of any networking supplier; its products ranged from access servers to routers and switches. Some predicted that Cisco's luck would run out and that one or more of its acquisitions would fail. But John Chambers vowed to push on to pursue six to 10 more acquisitions over the next year.

Cisco had achieved a dominant position in most of the markets in which it was engaged. It had a 72 percent market share in high-end routing. It was number one in LAN switching, with 35 percent of the market; in the enterprise market, it was nearing 50 percent market share with its Fast Ethernet Catalyst 5000 product. It was also number one in the IBM SNA/Internetwork marketplace, with 73 percent of the market share.

WHY THE RUSH?

Why the rush to buy all these companies? Chambers was asked.

The Cisco CEO explained that customers had been adopting a new end-to-end strategy, using a single vendor for their network purchases. Accordingly, Cisco was trying to acquire the best-in-class products in each segment.

In 1997, Cisco's executives began to sense that a market transition was occurring and that it would be prudent to take on the data/voice/video market aggressively. As a result, Chambers planned to step up acquisitions in this field. Cisco's main competitors were Lucent and Nortel. Lucent had revenue of $38 billion in 1999; Nortel, $17.6 billion.

The battle began to heat up early in 1999, when Lucent acquired Ascend Communications, a manufacturer of data-networking equipment, for $20 billion. Lucent's aim was to keep its telephone customers, who were adding data to their networks in response to the emergence of the Internet. Cisco now found that it was competing against Lucent over who would control the next generation of telephone service in the United States. Cisco, the leading manufacturer of data-based equipment, was receiving one-third of its $8.4 billion in revenues from phone companies. It hoped to double those sales over the next year. Chambers suggested that phone service could become free for subscribers to the Internet and video services, since a phone call required only 1 percent of the bandwidth available to homes utilizing advanced cable systems.

From 1993 to 1999, Cisco had acquired 40 start-ups for a total of nearly $20 billion.

It was becoming clear to Chambers that Cisco had a vast market opportunity with the convergence of data/voice/video. The great advantage of entering this field aggressively was its $140 billion market.

The Internet has spurred the telecommunications companies to build fiber-optic networks in order to carry more information by converting it into pulses of light. Optical networking has become the hot market for Internet equipment. Fiber-optic cables transmit data, voice, and video across both phone and data networks.

In 1998, Cisco had still not penetrated fiber optics, and was in danger of being excluded from that market. The one bright spot was the 9 percent stake it had taken that year in Cerent Corporation, a telecom-equipment start-up company whose product made it cheaper to move phone calls and computer traffic on and off fiber-optic lines.

In May 1999, John Chambers was attending a technology conference near Laguna Beach, California. There he met Carl Russo, CEO of Cerent whose equipment was deemed superefficient at moving voice and Internet traffic onto high-speed optical fibers. Founded in 1997 and employing 287 people, Cerent had one product—the Cerent 15454, a box the size of a microwave oven, which used sophisticated software to organize and compress data. The 15454 substantially increased the size of the pipe through which information was sent. Letting Internet service providers change the effective size of the data pipe—the bandwidth—virtually on the fly, the Cerent product enabled service providers to allocate bandwidth in a matter of minutes rather than several days.

HOW MUCH WOULD IT COST?

John Chambers quickly realized that by making Cerent part of Cisco, he could help Cisco become a major supplier for the core of phone networks. "How much would it cost me to buy you?" Chambers asked after some brief chitchat.

"How much would it cost for you to leave us alone?" Russo fired back with a smile. He was hoping to take his company public in the fall of 1999.

By midsummer of that year, Chambers was ready to move. He liked the 100-member sales team, unusually large for a start-up, since it resembled his own sales staff; and he liked Cerent's crowded offices in Petaluma, California. Russo presided from an eight-by-eight cubicle, a John Chambers kind of office. Cerent's growing list of customers was especially appealing to Cisco.

The deal was finalized quickly after Mike Volpi, who was handling Cisco's acquisitions, met Russo at San Francisco Airport, in the United Airlines Red Carpet Club, on August 11. Volpi offered to buy Cerent for over $4 billion. Although Cerent was losing money—it lost $29.3 million on sales of $9.92 million for the six months that ended June 30, 1999—its annual sales when the two men spoke had a run rate of $100 million.

Russo boldly countered with his own demand: $6.9 billion. Chambers offered him $6.3 billion for the 91 percent that Cisco did not own. Chambers was persuaded that Cerent's technology was essential for linking the Internet and telephone-system worlds, and so he agreed to match Cerent's expected high IPO value. It was Cisco's largest acquisition.

At noon on August 25, Cerent employees gathered in a hotel ballroom, thinking they were to hear an update on the company's planned IPO. Instead, Carl Russo announced the news of the acquisition. But the workers at Cerent's loading dock had learned the news even earlier that morning, when they opened a box of coffee mugs carrying Cisco's logo and the inscription "Welcome to the team."

Cerent at first appeared to be a winner for Cisco. Over the next year it had an estimated $1 billion in revenue run-rate. Forecasting the optical transport market for equipment that Cerent made at $10 billion by 2002, Chambers was hoping to grab a significant chunk of this sizable market.

The Cerent purchase marked Cisco's entry into the optical transport market and was part of the company's new strategy to target companies that were developing ways to help service providers transport voice, data, and video over a single network using ATM and IP technology.

Cisco became very active, acquiring companies in the convergence field. The competition for this market has been fierce, with Cisco, Lucent, and Nortel Networks, as well as smaller data networking and telephone equipment companies, competing to sell the equipment that allows service providers, such as cable and phone companies, to run voice, data, and video across one network.

In October 1999, John Chambers passed the word that Cisco planned to step up its dizzying pace of acquisitions and would probably buy more than 20 companies in the year, spending $10 billion in cash and stock. Cisco had already bought 40 companies. It had purchased 10 in 1999, including Cerent. It would be going after companies in areas that dealt with voice as well as data, and video integration. As it had predicted, by May 2000, Cisco had added another 15 companies—making 55 in all since it began its acquisition strategy—paying out $20.4 billion. That number had grown to 69 by December 2000.

Then came the economic downturn, and strong obstacles appeared that stood in the way of Cisco's aggressive acquisition policy. With the plummeting of the Cisco stock, no longer was there the readily available currency to use for those purchases. Equally important, as the company downsized in the spring of 2001 for the first time, it no longer seemed logical to add large numbers of employees. Essentially, the strategy was put on hold as Cisco began its recovery program, declaring that it would continue to purchase companies but that it would take its time and go after only those that truly made sense. Over the next 18 months—through the spring of 2002—it added only another six purchases. During that 18-month period, Chambers developed a new secret weapon that could put Cisco back in the acquisitions game: he was now sitting on $21 billion in cash. Not that he would use most or all of that money to purchase new companies. But when the stock was no longer available in such large quantities as before, he now had a new financial source to go after certain companies that could help Cisco.

The acquisitions policy played an important role in the creation of Cisco's hypergrowth. Some acquisitions proved successful, but there were disappointments as well. John Chambers likes to say that 90 percent of his acquisitions were successful; but others, both inside and outside the company, find that percentage far too high. "Almost all of our competitors' acquisitions have failed," Chambers said. Speaking in 2000, he noted: "Probably 80 to 95 percent of our acquisitions have worked. It's off the charts."

The biggest success by far was Crescendo (indeed, some argue that it paid in large measure for all the other purchases). Other notable successes were Grand Junction and Cerent. All three purchases had product when Cisco bought them.

There were a few other marginal winners, such as Granite Systems; but according to some Cisco watchers, most of the acquisitions were losers. The losers included LightStream, Kalpana, StrataCom, Combinet, Newport Networks, ArrowNet, Fat Pipes, a bunch of software companies, NewSpeed, Nexis, and Monterey Networks. By one estimate, Cisco spent $35 billion in stock for these acquisitions.

The key to success was how well Cisco was able to integrate the newly acquired companies into the Cisco Systems world. The integration process proved to be highly sophisticated, and we will discuss that process in some detail in this chapter; but what counted most in determining the success or failure of an acquisition were only a few critical factors.

Did the newly acquired company have a product that Cisco could nurture and distribute? As it turned out, many of the companies Cisco acquired did not have a full product when they were acquired. What Cisco was acquiring was their engineering talent and technology. Upon being acquired, the new collective team developed a product, or tried to.

While Cisco would have liked to acquire a company's products immediately, that prospect was small if only because almost all of the companies Cisco looked to purchase were start-ups.

The trouble with acquiring companies for their talent (and not their products) was this: the engineers and management, who when they were part of a start-up had an incentive to work 20 hours a day, suddenly no longer had that incentive. Once they got stock in a public company, they had little reason to work 20 hours a day for the next 12 to 18 months to finish the product. When the stock was vested, many of them left.

One of the variables John Chambers uses in determining whether a company is a suitable acquisition for Cisco is the need to understand what is being acquired and to protect it at all costs: "When I buy a company, I pay $500,000 to $20 million per acquired employee. All I'm acquiring is people and next-generation products. If I paid that price for what they were selling today, I made a terrible investment for my shareholders." When he and his Cisco colleagues studied most of their competitors, they found that they lost 40 to 80 percent of the acquired engineers and top management within two years. "Our attrition rate is 6.5 percent. Understand what you're acquiring and protect it."

Cisco executives believe they have learned how to retain employees, since their attrition rate is only 6.5 percent. But retaining employees is not the only measure in determining successful acquisitions. Some Cisco watchers prefer looking at the profit-and-loss statements of the individual companies. They argue that if a simple profit-and-loss criterion were assigned to each Cisco acquisition, we would see that a certain number have succeeded spectacularly whereas others have hardly gotten off the ground. Cisco executives counter that using the profit-and-loss criterion alone misses the point, which is that it becomes impossible to say what the profits and losses of any acquired company are *after* it joins the parent company.

Cisco officials say they do not track the precise amount of revenue that is generated as a result of acquisitions "because," said one official, "it is very difficult to determine when a product is considered acquired and when it is considered a Cisco product. So many of the companies we've acquired didn't even have a full product when they were acquired; we were acquiring their engineering talent and technology. Then, after they were acquired, the new collective team develops a product. But it is fair to say that a significant part of our revenue over the past has been related to past acquisitions."

By November 1999, Cisco had spent $18.8 billion on 42 acquisitions. As long as its currency—Cisco's stock—remained strong, the company could carry on with its acquisitions indefinitely. In 1999, Cisco's stock had risen 162 percent, trading at $72 a share. It was a year in which Cisco absorbed 10 companies. Its sales grew 44 percent, and its profits, 55 percent. If these statistics were at all relevant, it appeared that Cisco's acquisitions worked!

Cisco's first attempt at integration—bringing in Mario Mazzola and his team from Crescendo—got off to a rocky start. In the fall of 1993, no systematic integration scheme existed within Cisco. Everything was ad hoc. The initial confrontation between Crescendo and Cisco personnel occurred over the question of selling switches, Crescendo's new product. Prior to the Crescendo acquisition, as Mario Mazzola noted, Cisco's sales force had treated other firms that sold switches "if not as the enemy, then as an alternative to switching." Cisco's employees had been groomed to believe passionately in routers. "So the initial change was not easy," explained Mazzola, "convincing Cisco's sales force that there was real business blending routers and switches."

With no integration team in place to make them feel welcome and to explain to them how Crescendo would fit into the Cisco culture, Mario Mazzola and his team displayed no great enthusiasm in the early weeks after the acquisition. Nor did Mario feel anything but a sense of obligation to his new owners. "When Cisco acquired Crescendo," he recalled, "I was compelled to work for Cisco for two to three years. It was my duty and the duty of my team to do our best. That is different from feeling a real sense of ownership and passion."

THE MARIO RULE

Prior to signing the acquisition deal, Mario suspected that Cisco executives would fire some Crescendo personnel. Again, with no clear-cut integration program in existence at Cisco, the whole issue of which employees from the acquisition target would be offered jobs remained a thorn in Mario's side. Crescendo's executives were only vested two years out of a four-year program for their stock. Mario sympathized with his Crescendo executives, who were concerned that Cisco would fire them, keeping the last two years of their stock. Mario worried that his manufacturing and finance staffs were especially vulnerable: "I didn't like it." He told John Chambers that he could not allow himself to sign a deal that would put his employees on the job market in a matter of weeks. Mario demanded that Chambers agree not to fire anyone at Crescendo without Mario's consent for the first two years after the acquisition.

This became known as the Mario rule.

Chambers, deciding to apply the Mario rule to other Cisco acquisitions as well, noted, "Mario and I learned how to do acquisitions together, and thank goodness, because neither one of us could have anticipated all of the challenges. Mario was very concerned about his people, and I said I will not change anyone without him and me being in agreement. And only with your permission will I let anyone go. And that's the Mario rule that we used with each acquisition after that. It allowed the president of an acquired company to feel a sense of confidence that he or she could protect their employees."

With the Crescendo, Kalpana, and Grand Junction deals under their belts, Cisco executives began to sense that integrating future acquisitions must become a top priority. John Chambers undertook a search to find the right person to take on the integration program.

It was early February 1995 and Charlie Giancarlo had just come over to Cisco as part of the Kalpana deal. He was trying to figure out where he fit into the new company, and Chambers had just taken over as president and CEO of Cisco. Chambers knew that he wanted to make a big push in acquisitions, and he asked Giancarlo to head up the operation.

Giancarlo was at first reluctant, quite pessimistic about the prospects of an acquisition working, and equally disenchanted with the way acquired companies were being integrated into parent companies. He was, he told Chambers, no "deal junkie," and he had little interest in going into a project that seemed doomed to failure. For the next two months, he and Chambers continued to discuss the job offer. Finally in April, Giancarlo agreed to take the job (a prime example of the great salesman that John Chambers is!).

The prevailing attitude among Cisco engineers was to sneer at acquisitions. Becoming a convert himself, Giancarlo worked hard in his early days to change that mentality: "I started equating an acquisition with a marriage, where everyone knows that in a marriage both sides have to work hard to make it work. But you don't marry for strategy. You can't just marry anyone and make it work. The selection of the mate is critical to making the marriage work."

Giancarlo injected a new idea into the integration process. It had always been clear that both the acquired firm and the parent company had to find long-term benefits from the acquisition. But he said that both companies had to experience short-term wins as well. That wasn't apparent at first to those involved in Cisco's integration efforts.

The new Cisco employees had to be convinced that their products were going to be produced and marketed quickly. A way had to be found not to annoy resellers. Because Kalpana's products were being sold through resellers, those resellers became nervous the moment that Cisco announced the Kalpana acquisition; they feared that Cisco's direct-sales force would compete against them. Had Cisco's integration team been in place at that stage, it presumably would have calmed frayed nerves.

Almost by default—because no one else was acquiring the expertise required for that integration—Mimi Gigoux became Cisco's chief integration officer. In October 1994, she had come to Cisco when it had acquired its third company, Kalpana, where she had been its human resources manager. Because she had been one of the two people handling Kalpana's due diligence of Cisco on the eve of the acquisition, Mimi Gigoux was in an ideal position to smooth out the wrinkles in the deal.

She ran into obstacle after obstacle at Cisco. She lacked such vital information about Cisco as people's names and phone extensions. For nine months, former Kalpana employees remained in the dark about what they were supposed to do at Cisco.

It eventually dawned on Mimi Gigoux that Cisco would benefit in its next acquisition if someone were given authority over the integration process; ideally, it should be somebody who had survived an integration at Cisco.

She began making presentations. She put together documents. "I did it that way as this sporting event for about three years." The workload kept increasing, from one or two acquisitions a year when she began, to nine in 1996. The deals had a similar thrust: going after essentially small research and development houses with a sprinkle of administrators who tried to make it look like a grown-up company.

Though Cisco took some flack at first from critics who believed that it was better off trying to acquire larger companies, it stuck with the policy of seeking out smaller enterprises. It seemed far more practical. "At the time," noted Mike Volpi, at one stage Cisco's chief strategy officer, "our strategy was completely unproven. People thought it was more important to get critical mass more rapidly than to build a strong technology base. The popular belief was to get big fast. But when you buy a smaller company, you can transform it into Cisco more readily." He likened the process to adopting a smart, capable young child: "You can weave him or her into your family a lot easier than a teenager." In time, Mimi Gigoux was given full-time responsibility for handling integration.

RETENTION MATTERS

"We acquire people," reminds Mimi Gigoux. "We're not interested in the products they have on the manufacturing floor. We're interested in the products we will do jointly."

Conversations at Cisco are peppered with references to the numerous executives who have come over from acquisition targets and been successfully integrated into Cisco's management. Among them are Crescendo's Mario Mazzola, Kalpana's Charlie Giancarlo, Grand Junction's Howard Charney, and Granite's Andreas Bechtolsheim. A cofounder of Sun Microsystems, Bechtolsheim left the $7-billion-a-year firm in 1995 to start Granite Systems, a high-performance-networking company. He sold Granite a year later to Cisco for $220 million.

The greatest challenge Cisco had in bringing employees from the newly acquired companies was keeping them.

One day after the announcement that Cisco had acquired Cerent in August 1999, Cisco's integration team began working on the largest acquisition ever—and the integration team's greatest challenge. The Cisco integration team took over a second-floor conference room at Cerent and started to "map" each one of Cerent's 266 employees into a Cisco job. The team spent hours performing that task. A few days later, the Cisco computer squad showed up to work on the conversion of Cerent's computer systems.

Everyone on the integration team recalled the mishaps during the 1996 StrataCom integration, when one-third of StrataCom's sales force resigned within a few months of the acquisition; they were miffed after losing accounts to Cisco salespeople and after they learned that the commission plan had been altered. The integration team dealt with that flaw in the process and allowed Cerent's sales force to remain independent, keeping their accounts even if Cisco people already had called on the same company.

The employee mapping process for Cerent staff ended in late September. Most employees retained their jobs and their bosses. The sales force got pay boosts of 15 to 20 percent in order to put their pay packages on a par with Cisco's. Thirty Cerent employees chose to resign after learning that Cisco had people doing their jobs already.

On November 1, 1999, Cisco officially took over Cerent, and the acquired firm's employees lined up for photos for their new ID cards that morning. By midweek, most of them had new business cards. During the next weekend, Cisco's technical crew worked 24 hours a day to make Cerent's computers look like those at Cisco, installing software, upgrading Cerent's connections to the Internet, redirecting them through Cisco's Internet network. Voice mail was also connected to Cisco's system.

By the time Cisco took control of Cerent, every employee had a title, a boss, a bonus plan, a health plan, and a direct line to Cisco's internal Web site.

Some of Cisco's rivals are not keen to press too hard to make acquisitions. They prefer the more popular Silicon Valley way, getting their engineers to come up with new products. Scott Kriens is the CEO of a Cisco competitor in high-end routers, Juniper Networks. He gives Cisco credit for doing a better job of acquiring and integrating companies and people than most others: "It's become an effective tool for them to use in place of their own innovation. At Juniper Networks, we are asked: 'Why don't you do more acquisitions?,' but when we look at the companies like Intel, Sun, and most other companies that we would model this to be like, most of those companies were built by innovation, and we think innovating is how we will succeed in our market. We've made acquisitions and we'll make more of them. But fundamentally our default behavior is to innovate and to hire people one at a time to do that. There's a danger in being overly acquisitive if you become dependent on it. So we're going to be quite certain that we have control of our own destiny and don't depend on others to build what we need for our future. Cisco has succeeded in building its own products internally. They're not without the ability to innovate, but they've also done a great deal through acquisitions."

It is of course hard to come up with a formula for Cisco's acquisitions success. John Chambers thinks he knows the broad outlines: "In terms of acquisitions, some would say it's the integration strategy that is key to the success. I believe it's the selection process. If you choose a partner for life, your probability for success is probably not going to be very good. But if you knew your decision criteria and really got to know your partner well ahead of time, your probability for success is going to be much higher."

Cisco's selection criteria focus on five key elements:

1. Commonality of vision
2. Short-term win-win
3. Long-term win-win
4. Chemistry
5. Geographic proximity

Chambers talks about the commonality of vision as vital: "When you combine two companies that have different visions, you are constantly at war within your organizations. If your visions aren't very similar, in terms of product direction and industry direction, you never really get it right."

Chambers advised against putting companies together that have different visions: "I can tell by walking into a company whether we're going to get along or not. I look at the size of the president's office. My office looks like any other office. I look at an office that the president can play basketball in and the employees are stuck over in grungy areas. It isn't going to work. You look at how the stock options are spread between leadership teams and employees. If all the stock is at the top, we're not going to get along. If we're talking to the acquisition target and they don't talk about customers, we can tell it won't be a culture match and we may as well go home. You can tell if they're creating a win-win or a win-lose in negotiation. If they don't think win-win, it's not going to match. Is it a culture of empowerment? It doesn't mean one culture's right or wrong, because there are many cultures here in the Silicon Valley. You just don't combine two dramatically different cultures."

Using these approaches, Chambers believes he has come up with a formula that has succeeded most of the time.

While Chambers would have us believe that he has a magic formula for acquisition success, he has one way of judging the performance of his acquisitions; and some Cisco watchers have other ways.

THE THREE BUCKETS

Ed Kozel, a former member of the Cisco board and onetime CTO, breaks down Cisco's acquisitions successes and failures into three "buckets":

1. Painful failures: "Here money was not the issue, but the company spent a great deal of time and energy—which you don't have—and it was painful. There was diversion and we got absolutely nothing out of these. We don't dwell on these publicly other than learning the lessons internally. We don't look back. There have been about five of these."

2. Neutral acquisitions: "Those which sort of worked but didn't hurt a lot; but Cisco didn't get a lot of gain from them. This is a large bucket."

3. Stunning successes: Whether in terms of revenue technology or people. Cisco does acquisitions, Kozel suggests, for many reasons: sometimes to buy a team of really good people and other times to get a billion-dollar revenue stream. "So the success criteria differ from one acquisition to another. I'd put the success ratio at 60 to 65 percent."

To Kozel, Cisco has always inherently known the right way to approach acquisitions. "Where we have really screwed up, it is when we violated one of the rules that we set for ourselves: partnering only when there's a personality match; when the culture is similar; when there's a vision match; if we both think the market is going in a certain way; not making a religion out of technology; no merger of equals. These are really simple rules."

The most visible violation, he suggests, came in the StrataCom acquisition, because it was the first billion-dollar acquisition that Cisco did. "We knew we were violating one of those four rules. We thought we could compensate for it. The rule that was broken was that their culture wasn't our culture. They were slower to move. Their CEO had a personality that was not like ours at all. He was very English. He was aggressive, but in a different way. He had religion. He thought ATM was perfect and didn't like the other technologies, meaning routing or frame relay. He was very good for StrataCom, but not for Cisco. So we spent a horrible amount of time and energy. We made lots of money. It didn't fail. I would put it in the middle bucket."

Cisco's big acquisition successes occurred, Kozel observed, "when the leader and the team were like us, high-tech, go-fast people, listening to customers, responsive to the marketplace. The big examples are Crescendo and Cerent. We magnified each other. We didn't have to learn about each other. We were like brothers who never met. We got together and we said, 'Let's go rock and roll.' The leverage was immediate. They had a great product, and we had a great sales and support and marketing end."

One only has to spend time walking the corridors of Cisco's head-quarters to appreciate how far the integration process has gone. There is no Cerent division, no Crescendo division, no Grand Junction division.

Ammar Hanafi, Cisco's vice president for business development, the person in charge of its acquisitions, noted: "We're creating one company here, not different divisions with different cultures: a single manufacturing organization, a single sales organization, a single finance organization. In that model you have to have very good integration."

WE COULD NOT HAVE DONE THAT

Andy Grove of Intel once visited Cisco and asked a group of employees how many of them were from acquisitions. Fully 30 percent of the group raised their hands. "We could not have done that at Intel," he acknowledged.

By the fall of 2000, Cisco had become the modern-day role model for integrating acquired companies. Historians go back to the early part of the 20th century to find someone who handled acquisitions as well: Theodore Vail, the AT&T CEO who purchased hundreds of small phone companies and put together the first nationwide network. Cisco gained its reputation for doing acquisitions well thanks in large measure to a whole series of magazine and newspaper articles. John Chambers attributed the positive news coverage that accrued to Cisco to the dramatic contrast between Cisco's successes in acquisitions and the failures of its rivals. He suggested that journalists became interested in Cisco's acquisition strategy when they discovered that most of Cisco's rivals failed at acquisitions and only one company (Cisco) got it right: "Ascend was a great company. It was combining with Cascade [Networks, an Internet access and data services company] and combining with Lucent that killed them. Wellfleet and SynOptics were great companies, but then they combined the two, and then sold it as combined to Nortel. It was those combinations that caused the largest part of our competitors to fail, so that's what got everybody excited. You have one company that does it [well] and everybody else in the industry messes it up. That's why everybody wrote about that."

PART FIVE

Adjusting to a New Reality

10 Preparing for Adversity

What can business executives learn from the experience of Cisco Systems as it went from being the most successful high-tech company of the nineties to one that, at least temporarily, had little about which to boast?

We can learn a great deal.

There would be little to learn if we were to regard Cisco as nothing more than the victim of a "100-year flood," helpless in the face of the sudden, surprising unraveling of the American economy.

We do not want to suggest that adhering to the lessons we will mention would have kept any company, Cisco included, from escaping damage from the economic downturn of 2000–2001. However, paying attention to these lessons can cushion the blow and enable a company to ride out a 100-year flood far more smoothly than Cisco did.

It does seem reasonable to ask whether CEOs should be expected to take into account the ups and downs of the economy and to prepare for both in the best possible way.

And indeed, Cisco felt that it had prepared itself for a possible "down" in the economy. The only trouble was that Cisco defined a "down" in a way far different from what actually occurred in the winter of 2000. Cisco believed that any downturn would be gradual—that is, there would be plenty of warning, as much as six months—and that it would have only a slight effect on Cisco's balance sheet. It seemed highly unlikely that Cisco could have any worse than a 5 percent loss a quarter in revenue or earnings.

It had not occurred to Cisco's leadership that a downturn could come suddenly and be so devastating that it would affect everyone, Cisco included.

Cisco believed that it was exempt, that it was in the right markets at the right time, and this bred a feeling of invulnerability. Though no one would admit it at the time, that feeling of infallibility bred a complacency that made it even harder for Cisco to deal with any sudden setback. As Cisco's vice chairman Don Valentine noted: "Even in 2000 and 2001 Cisco was the poster child of Silicon Valley. It was the company that had never stumbled, couldn't make any mistakes, significant ones. Nobody was prepared for the fact that Cisco management could be wrong. Cisco sales could go down; earnings could go down; people had been so accustomed to the fact that this is an unusual company and its stock price never goes down. So John [Chambers] has never been criticized since he had been at Wang and that was ancient history."

Add to this the not irrelevant fact that Cisco's employees reaped huge rewards for their labors, thanks to the skyrocketing stock price, rewards that many could never have imagined in their wildest dreams. And the more the rewards came in, the more routine they seemed.

OUR STRATEGIES WORKED

For all of these reasons, Cisco's leaders believed strongly that they had done nothing wrong in the months leading up to the setback of 2001. They genuinely believed that their strategies were what had got the company to the peak of success before disaster occurred, and that those same strategies would help it recover from the disaster far more quickly than most other companies.

Indeed, John Chambers confidently advanced the notion that had

Cisco abandoned any of its growth-promotion policies in the months preceding the "100-year flood," it would have endangered its chances to be a major player in its industry. So many high-tech markets were blossoming, so many opportunities were presenting themselves, that Cisco had no choice—so the argument goes—but to make large bets in these markets. To play in these markets, Cisco had to take risks.

It has always been Chambers's policy to pursue growth even in the down times, and it has been his strong belief that it is in those down times that a go-go company like Cisco can take advantage of the greater travail affecting its rivals, and push ahead to gain greater market share.

In short, no one at Cisco with whom I talked in the wake of the setback thought the company should have adopted a rainy-day strategy, one that would have been far more conservative toward growth, with less hiring, less building of company infrastructure, etc. Rather, company officials insisted that if Cisco had adopted such a rainy-day policy, it would never have become the company it did, that is, it would not have climbed to the top of the field.

Some Cisco leaders expressed sympathy for adopting a rainy-day policy, but one senior figure thought the problem was what kind of rain you planned for. "You can plan for a gradual slowdown," argues Don Valentine, "but if indeed a 100-year flood occurs, there's not much you can do about it. Let's talk about rain. Is it a drizzle, or is it the climate of Ireland where it rains all the time, or is it a 100-year flood? It's very difficult to plan for a 100-year flood. Do you plan for a recession or a slowdown? We certainly went through a 100-year flood, and the company was clearly not prepared for it."

It took John Chambers some time to adjust to the new reality. At first, he genuinely believed that Cisco had done nothing wrong.

Chambers offered a spirited defense of the company, arguing that there was very little that Cisco could have done or should have done to avoid the disaster. Events as huge and shocking as a major flood, earthquake, or tornado cannot be avoided, and companies should not devise their strategies as if the only thing that mattered was avoiding a sudden, surprising economic reversal.

He took the view that, along with Cisco, everyone else was caught off guard: "Everybody was surprised. Let's not kid ourselves. And we were as well, and that included everybody from the political leaders to the CEOs to the economists."

The board backed Chambers sympathetically. It shocked him therefore that the media and investors took him to task for allowing Cisco to falter so sharply. He listened carefully to Don Valentine, whom he respected more than most, tell him that he should not let the media or the investors get to him. Cisco was not the only company that had stumbled.

Chambers was still upset with the media attacks.

Valentine pushed on: "John, it's nothing personal. You just have to be the president of the *Titanic*. No one ever thought the *Titanic* would sink. No one ever thought that Cisco could stumble."

Buoyed by Valentine's soothing remarks, Chambers kept suggesting that Cisco had simply had the bad luck of being in the wrong place at the wrong time. If a flood or an earthquake had struck the town in which Chambers lived, no one would have blamed him for living in the wrong place. It would have been just bad luck.

Chambers made a big point that it was the sum total of Cisco's strategies that explained the company's success. But when the company ran into trouble, the CEO insisted that the strategies had not been at fault—that the flood had simply washed over the company—just so much bad luck.

I had a chance to talk with Chambers in September 2001. It was nine months since the downturn had taken hold at Cisco, nine months of hell for the company: layoffs, taking charges on excessive inventory, markets drying up. Chambers had had time to think the downturn through, and nine months later he still felt Cisco had done no wrong. When I asked him what, if anything, he would have done differently, he told me, "The first thing is: You've got to deal with the world the way it is, not the way you wish it was. So the first thing you decide is: What caused this? If the cause is something you did in your strategy, you've got to fix it. . . . Once we decided it was macroeconomic, we said we're not going to change our strategy."

But as time passed and a healing process occurred at Cisco, Chambers began to do more soul-searching. He knew that he had the solid backing of his board. No one on the board was out to punish Chambers. So he felt he could be a little candid about what had actually been going on within Cisco's inner sanctums.

On rare public occasions, though he continued to put a good face on things, suggesting that it was the economy and not Cisco that was to blame for the company's woes, he acknowledged that all that success had been intoxicating, perhaps even diverting. "When you grow so rapidly, you take success at times for granted. You can't do that. When you have growth, you don't focus on profits or on the bottom 5 percent [of employees] as crisply as you should."

Privately, he was more direct. He began to confide to Cisco colleagues that steps could have been taken to ease the pain when the economy sputtered. Yes, Chambers suggested confidentially, still unwilling to offer such thoughts publicly, some of his strategies had not been executed properly. The company had at times taken its collective eye off the ball.

Though he was unprepared to point a finger publicly at Cisco— and thus at himself—he clearly understood that the company needed substantial reforms, and he set out to undertake them.

The announcement of the six-point plan on January 15, 2001, was the strongest evidence that Cisco's leadership understood the need for major reform. The six points were:

1. Slowing of head-count growth and discretionary spending

2. Aligning the company's resources with major growth opportunities

3. A new focus on profit contribution

4. Leveraging E-applications to gain productivity

5. Assuring that all Cisco employees focused on their own areas of improvement

6. Remaining focused on Cisco's breakaway strategy of trying to capture more and more market share once it spotted new market transitions.

In other words, without saying so, Cisco obliquely acknowledged that it had too many employees; it was spending too much money; it was spreading its resources too thinly over a vast array of market opportunities; it was going after revenue at the expense of profits; it was not doing enough to foster productivity; and it was not exhibiting enough teamwork.

In short, if one wanted to discover what Cisco could have done — and indeed should have done — to ease the pain caused by the economic downslide of early 2001, all that was required was to look at the details of this six-point plan.

At first blush, it might seem odd to suggest that business executives could learn valuable lessons from Cisco's experience. After all, Cisco seems unique. No major company has risen so fast and then fallen so hard as Cisco Systems. No major corporation has enjoyed the continuing hypergrowth that Cisco has. Most companies, however — seduced as they have been by Wall Street, the media, venture capitalists, and the like to believe that growth is good — do adopt growth strategies. Accordingly, the lessons of the Cisco experience can easily apply to a good many business executives who dream of Cisco-like hypergrowth.

What then are the lessons to be learned from the Cisco experience?

The first is that companies would do well to adopt a rainy-day strategy in order to avoid the stinging effects of a sudden major stoppage in the economy. A corollary of this lesson is that even when you are a successful CEO, be prepared at all times for a sudden deterioration in the economy. Chambers had no such plans in place. If he had, Cisco would not have felt the full effects of the economic difficulties. Cisco's leaders acknowledge that the only way to behave in an economy that throws off tornado markets as rapidly as this one did is to try to exploit as many market opportunities as possible. That means building, hiring, and acquiring. Others who wish to learn from the Cisco experience would do well to ponder, however, whether growth policies should be allowed to run unchecked, or whether it is wiser to apply the brakes on hypergrowth, and go for a little less growth, as a means of protecting against the pain of a sudden downturn.

MATHEMATICALLY IMPOSSIBLE

Chambers could not contemplate applying the brakes if only because he could not imagine a downturn that would cause Cisco serious damage.

With all that growth, all that euphoria, and all of those fail-safe protections that the company had built for itself, why should John Chambers build some "rainy-day scenarios" into Cisco's game plans?

In fact, Cisco executives genuinely believed that they were applying the brakes on an even more aggressive growth strategy. Larry Carter, the Cisco CFO, noted that "we could have grown faster possibly; we were trying to grow as fast as we could in a controlled way; there wasn't open hiring across the board; we were very rigorous. We could have built a few more campuses; we had the cash; we were growing about as fast as we wanted to from a control perspective."

A second lesson is to avoid being too optimistic. Optimism can be an important business tool in trying to persuade Wall Street that you know what you are doing and are going in the right direction; but it can trap you into adopting a mind-set that does not allow for sudden downturns in the economy.

The Chambers optimism encouraged others to believe that he

could do no wrong, that he knew how to get Cisco out of trouble. After all, as part of his optimistic stance, Chambers liked to boast that Cisco thrived during downturns; it was a great time to pick up market share. Wall Street did not see the boast as mere bravado. Chambers was simply offering the analysts fresh guidance. He was almost always right, so it paid to listen to him. He was Mr. Immunity: The economy could fall apart; John would know how to fix things.

And one did not need to be swept away by Chambers's optimism. Cisco really appeared to know what it was doing. It encouraged—though later it would suggest that it had not—a rosy belief in the infallibility of its forecasting systems. As it turned out, the company's forecasting capabilities, which it boasted about, looked very fallible indeed. Cisco tried to put a good face on things by suggesting that the systems were never intended to provide accurate forecasting of trends, which in retrospect seems to have been true.

A third lesson is for a company to take a hard look at its forecasting capabilities and check whether its systems are comprehensive enough to enable a fast, accurate read on sudden changes in the economy. Having said that, companies need to look as much at how well their own staff can read the data as at how reliable the data are.

Chambers had promoted the strategy of turning Cisco into an E-company, putting most of its business processes and functions on the Internet, as a key reason the company would always be on top of situations. He had ascribed great capabilities to its electronic systems, as the company was able to keep an eye on all kinds of data from margins to sales orders.

Throughout the fall of 2000, I met with executive after executive at Cisco who boasted that its E-company Internet systems were the shield that would protect the company from any disaster. It sounded very convincing. Not only did CFO Larry Carter have a few good examples of how those systems had kept Cisco out of trouble in the past, but also important segments of the business community were buying into what Cisco was saying. How else to explain the senior executives from major companies who were knocking on Cisco's door to learn how the company had put together its E-company strategy?

Whatever was happening at Cisco Systems, plainly its forecasting capabilities did not render the company foolproof when it was most vulnerable. By promoting itself as a model E-company, one with systems that could keep it from getting into trouble, Cisco left itself open to challenge on just how effective those systems were. One former Cisco executive was brutally blunt: "If all these tools existed, how do you run the son of a bitch off the cliff? Either the tools don't work or they were not listening to what the tools were saying."

I asked Chambers, "If the systems were so good, how did you miss a quarter?"

"As for the January [2001] quarter, that we missed by a penny. We were within the range, but it was the first time we didn't hit the number or go above. And we knew exactly where we were every moment including the capability 20 minutes ahead of the close on Saturday night here. I was spending Sunday morning in Davos and was able to know exactly where we were overall. So the issue was not that the systems didn't work. They worked remarkably well in terms of telling us where we were. The systems are not a crystal ball. They are not an indication of the future."

Should the systems not be able to tell you when a downturn is. going to start?

A BRILLIANT MAN

Chambers defends the systems, noting that they "are no more accurate than the data that you put in. I would argue that some of the most effective organizations in the world and some of the most brilliant people I have ever met missed this by a long way. Mr. Greenspan is a brilliant man, but make no mistake, he clearly missed this one and, like all of us, wished we had moved earlier. And so I know no one who signaled anywhere near how rapid this downturn would be. Now, we realize that without the systems we would really have been in real trouble. We would not have known [what was occurring]. We would not have been able to adjust the [February 2001] quarter. Without the systems we would not have made our quarter. We would have been off by several cents. And we would not have been able to adjust quickly on how you handle the inventory issues and adjust one time to them."

When the downturn hit so suddenly in early 2001, Cisco's leaders took a new look at the company's forecasting systems and argued defensively that they were never meant to be predictive. They were never meant to detect trends. They could only tell what was occurring on a particular day. The trouble was, listening to Cisco officials, everyone got the impression that they were indeed supposed to forecast trends.

When Cisco began to analyze what it could do to improve things after the downturn, it concluded that it had not been inputting data on its component suppliers. The downturn had shown that what Cisco was lacking was an advance warning that one vital part of its outsourcing process—its component suppliers—was not doing well.

Chambers said: "We have to take our systems all the way down to the component level whether we own inventory or our partners own inventory, and be able to know exactly where you are not just at the subcontractor level—contract manufacturers—but at their component level. Because we got into trouble both ways. We got whipsawed. For almost a year the contractors didn't know exactly what the component manufacturers just had for them, and we constantly got surprised. In other words, we weren't able to deliver the products at the pace that we were committed to. And then when [the economy] turned down, sometimes the contract manufacturer shared that with the component manufacturer, sometimes they did not. And so we got whipsawed both ways, as did our partners, so all of us have an interest in improving this."

A fourth lesson: Face reality and act on that reality as quickly as possible.

John Chambers had his own view of reality. He was an eternal optimist. He believed he had good reason to be optimistic, that reality would bear out his optimism. He believed in the myth of unstoppable growth. He believed that he had a grasp on his customers. He believed that he had an unparalleled intuitive grasp of the markets and market shifts. He genuinely believed that he had learned the mistakes that IBM and Wang had made, and that he would not allow Cisco to be arrogant, to miss market transitions, to fail to listen to customers. He also believed, falsely, that Cisco had erected a set of disciplines that would keep the company from slipping: the vaunted Larry Carter–initiated early-warning system that would prevent surprises.

That was Chambers's reality.

Sure, he made noises that suggested he would always act conservatively.

He talked of the need to be paranoid, and the need to face reality. But when the economy turned sour late in 2000 Chambers blamed all of Cisco's problems on the sudden implosion of the American economy, arguing that the economic downturn was the equivalent of a "100-year flood," surprising everyone, devastating even Cisco by its speed and intensity. That remained his reality for some time. He would modify it in time. He would admit that Cisco's team had taken its eye off the ball on occasion. He had trouble making those admissions. But he did make them—eventually.

One reality that Chambers took for granted—and in fact promoted aggressively—was the growing importance of the Internet. He quite correctly argued that businesspeople would benefit enormously from the efficiencies and speed created by the Internet. Indeed, his strategy of evangelizing the Internet worked marvelously well for a number of years.

It worked exceedingly well for Cisco Systems, which appeared to have an unstoppable, unbeatable method for attracting business. The method: convince business and political leaders to fall in love with the Internet, and they would flock to buy Cisco products. It was simply assumed that the Internet would attract millions upon millions of people over the next decade, and that nothing could stand in its way. Unfortunately for Cisco, that was not the case. The reality was that many of the businesses that had attached themselves to the Internet would fast disappear, crushed by their own failure to grasp reality: they had no viable business models!

Chambers remained unstoppable, unflappable. He could not travel enough. He could not speak publicly enough. He could not talk up the Internet enough. He could not forecast high enough figures for Cisco and for the Internet. It sounded fine. It sounded plausible—at the time. But in retrospect, the strategy contained the danger of linking Cisco inextricably with the fate of the Internet. That seemed a wise and prudent policy as long as the Internet sailed along smoothly. But then came the collapse of the dot-coms; and later, much of American business decided it could no longer afford to invest in Internet infrastructure. When the Internet collapse occurred, Cisco had little choice but to absorb some mighty body blows.

Lesson number five: Get the metrics right.

By getting the metrics right, business leaders will get early warning signals when things go awry. Using the wrong metrics can put a company in the dark about the economy.

To be sure, the warning signs that were given off to Cisco were at times faint and easy to miss. Given the euphoria prevailing at Cisco, combined with the complacency, it was all too easy for Cisco's leaders to skip over the warnings. By not paying careful attention to the increasing debt loads of certain customers, Cisco ignored one vital metric that could have tipped it off to coming trouble. As one Wall Street analyst observed: "Cisco, like others, ignored the stress that some of the carriers and carrier customers felt. Cisco really underestimated the chain of events and how like a house of cards all this spending could evaporate so quickly.

"No one realized how much spending was being done, not to maintain the current network infrastructure, but for competitive reasons. Qwest was spending more because Sprint was. Enterprise customers had to be E-commerce-enabled, so they spent money; you had to have an on-line trading infrastructure.

"One of the things we all underestimated was how much of the spending was frivolous. It was based on these really optimistic scenarios that everyone was going to download videos from the Web, and everyone would want a wireless device, and there would be more and more demand. Napster [the music Web site] was a big driving force. At one time it was 13 percent of Internet traffic. All that expectation over Napster made things frantic. But then it shut down just before the downturn."

NO REASON TO SLOW DOWN

Believing that the Internet was the growth tool of the era, Cisco saw no reason to slow down. As long as the orders kept piling in, there was little reason to measure anything but customer-order run rates and customer satisfaction. But the order rate remained deceptively high even as a volcano in the U.S. economy was slowly erupting late in 2000. And customer satisfaction told Cisco officials too little about the precise state of the economy.

The one big metric that Cisco should have heeded was the gradual slowdown of the Internet growth rate and the easing up on the purchase of wireless devices. Said one former Cisco executive: "If John had been looking he would have seen the signs of the slowdown. He just believed everything was going along fine. He wasn't looking for signs of trouble. He assumed that the forecasts were right; he kept hiring; he demanded that people work to meet those forecasts and gave them tons of stock to make it happen."

We come to the sixth lesson: Avoid complacency.

Companies must make sure that when things are going well, rather than just pay lip service to being paranoid, they keep employees on their toes and not let them slip into complacency.

It was hard for Cisco not to become complacent when the orders kept coming in, when the growth rates were skyrocketing off the charts. It was this runaway go-go growth culture that had encouraged

Cisco to hire 1,000 employees a month ("obscene," a former Cisco executive told me) and build campus after campus to house them ("our own edifice complex," said the same ex-executive). Ron Ricci, the senior vice president for marketing positioning, recalled what Cisco was like when he joined the company in the summer of 2000: "The news was so good. I couldn't believe it. My first quarter here we grew 70 percent. It was not hard working here. The fax machines were rolling in with orders. The magazines wanted to do cover stories on us. They asked us what stories they should tell. But the place grew complacent. I would choose that word because we didn't have to work hard. It happened because we were on this ride up."

To impose discipline on a runaway growth engine would have required a mind-set that was alien to Cisco executives. Managing growth was fun and exciting. Imposing discipline meant establishing a rigor that would have been unpleasant. To be sure, John Chambers encouraged a work-hard culture, and many employees worked hard. But working many hours is not the same thing as being managed carefully. And in times of hypergrowth, it was hard for managers to question the methods of their inferiors too much; after all, the company was on a roll. How badly could people be performing? It seemed safe to assume that with all the success it was enjoying, Cisco would have plenty of time and opportunity to deal with problem areas that had crept into its operations.

Finally, there was the compensation.

With Cisco employees getting wealthier and wealthier, it seemed to make little sense to question the company's methods. "It's hard to be paranoid when you're blowing the doors off the top line," said Ron Ricci.

John Chambers had explained Cisco's remarkable success by pointing to the business strategies that he and other executives had employed. These strategies were supposed to guide Cisco to prosperity and see the company through the down periods.

It is Chambers's contention that Cisco became prosperous by following these strategies.

And when, at least at first, he argued that Cisco did no wrong on the eve of the economic downturn, he implied that Cisco's strategies contained no flaws.

As time went on, Chambers continued to insist that the strategies had been correct and remained so; but he did find it easier to acknowledge that here and there Cisco executives had taken their eyes off the ball, had in fact not followed the strategies carefully enough.

We begin with "listening to customers," undoubtedly the most important strategy to Chambers and Cisco. Chambers liked to say that by listening to customers as closely as he did, he could detect earlier than most when markets were going through transitions. For quite some time, Cisco's customers kept Chambers well informed, especially when it came to their growing interest in investing in the Internet.

But when the crunch came early in 2001, when customers began telling Chambers that their businesses were drying up, Cisco was caught off guard, with too little warning to recover.

The reason?

Though Chambers did not want to admit it at first, Cisco had not sensed the seriousness of what was happening to a number of its customers, especially the new telecommunication start-ups, who were encountering increasing financial difficulty. The very fact that Cisco had to provide vendor financing to a number of these firms should have served as a precautionary signal, but it did not. One former Cisco executive suggested that "there's listening to customers, and there's asking and investigating. The questions you ask are important."

By staying in touch with customers throughout the early phases of the downturn, Cisco was able to recover far faster than its rivals. By the time orders stopped in mid-January 2001, the company had already curtailed spending, imposed a hiring freeze, and engaged in other cost-saving measures.

. . .

Though not listed as one of John Chambers's 12 crucial cultural elements, building Cisco into an E-company was supposed to give the company the necessary protection to ward off trouble.

Cisco had become a model company for the entire high-tech industry in its use of technology. No one used the Internet as a business tool better than Cisco's executives.

When the economic downturn hit in early 2001, the question arose: What had happened to Cisco's vaunted E-systems? What had happened to their predictive capabilities? Chambers defended those systems, insisting that the systems had not failed him even in the not-so-good times. "The systems are not a crystal ball for the future," he said later. "But they are very accurate for where you are. Without our systems, we would not have been able to adjust as we did." He was pleased that, thanks to listening to customers and to the systems he had in place, "we saw it quicker than most of our counterparts did and publicly said it." He felt good that the technology that he had boasted about in the past had not let him down. When the crunch came, he noted that Cisco's systems poured out data on a real-time basis, alerting him and his colleagues to the slowing of the economy and thus allowing him to take cost-cutting measures rapidly, and earlier than many other businesses.

NOT PREDICTIVE

The problem was not that the E-systems were flawed. They were not. They did not forecast the sudden economic downturn, but they were not supposed to predict macro trends. They were simply supposed to take a snapshot of the company and the industry on any given day, hour, minute. The problem was that Cisco had promoted the E-systems as the business tool of the future, and if the company had not boasted of the systems' forecasting capabilities, it had implied that their true value lay in providing sufficient early intelligence to ward off any dangers. If that's not forecasting, what is?

What Cisco did learn from the experience was that even though the E-systems were not predictive, they could be beefed up to provide data on parts of the manufacturing process that had not been monitored before but should have been. By monitoring those parts of the system in the future, Cisco would have a much sharper picture of what was truly going on in the company and in the industry at large.

Cisco's strategy of buying one start-up after another had been one of John Chambers's proudest achievements. Revolutionary for a Silicon Valley enterprise, the Cisco acquisition program became one of the key engines of the company's growth. Most analysts, taking their cue from John Chambers, were convinced that most of Cisco's acquisitions were worthwhile. The strategy seemed to have very few flaws. Some did argue that while the old Cisco knew how to get into markets successfully, the current one (on the eve of the 2000 downturn) was having a hard time producing the right kind of products and buying the right kind of companies that would accelerate growth.

For evidence, they argued that engineers were leaving the company at a much higher rate than most would admit to; that Juniper Networks and Redback, two important Silicon Valley start-ups, had almost 500 former Cisco engineers between them. In the past, even if engineers left, Cisco always had the chance to acquire new engineers when it bought start-ups. But, said these cynics, watching Cisco's stock tumble in 2001 and 2002, it had become less likely that the company could purchase quality companies.

In the first few months after the economic downturn, Cisco officials insisted that the acquisition policy remained in full force despite the company's travails, but privately senior managers acknowledged that acquisition efforts were on hold. Cisco could not, in the view of these same senior managers, lay off thousands of employees, as it announced it would do, but scoop up new companies, effectively adding new employees to its payrolls. With a weakened stock, it also no longer had substantial amounts of cheap currency available for acquisitions.

The strategy of buying start-ups had appeared a great success, as

Cisco became a high-tech titan. During the heady growth years, the media promoted the company as a model for how to acquire companies, an almost alien concept within Silicon Valley. As it turned out, quite a number of the companies that Cisco bought, using its golden currency, the stock, proved very costly, while the company gained little in return. The acquired firms delivered relatively few products or markets.

Cisco's pursuit of a high rate of growth through this strategy had set the company apart from most other high-tech enterprises. Not a true son of Silicon Valley, Chambers found it much less complicated to pursue a strategy that ran counter to the conventional wisdom in his midst. Fueling Cisco's growth policies, the acquisition strategy encouraged a kind of euphoria, fed by the huge success of the company's very first purchase (Crescendo).

John Chambers found it easy to do those things that led to hyper-growth, despite their going against the grain of Silicon Valley, despite their irritating his own employees (engineers), and despite the fact that integrating acquisitions was very, very hard to do.

To justify the many acquisitions, he argued forcefully that Cisco knew how to *do* acquisitions; he knew what to look for and what not to look for. He justified what he did by saying that as many as 95 percent of his acquisitions were successful, but he was referring to the integration of intellectual talent (skipping over the question of whether the company gained in products and markets from these purchases).

For as long as the economy and Cisco's stock held up, the acquisition strategy appeared wise. Prior to the downturn few questioned whether Cisco was truly benefiting from the strategy. Cisco offered few facts and figures on the individual acquisitions, so it became nearly impossible to judge which ones had been successful and which had not. But in the wake of the downturn, as the acquisition strategy ground to a virtual standstill, the questions began to surface: How valuable were all those acquisitions? Was Cisco getting a sufficient number of products from the engineers of these companies, after acquired, to justify the expense? Should the acquisition strategy carry on even when Cisco's stock was so low? These were questions that Cisco officials were asking of themselves internally. In the early days after the downturn it was clear that the company had opted for a far more cautious approach to acquisitions. As it accumulated more and more cash (it had $21 billion in June 2002), Cisco's leaders passed the word that the company would look favorably in the future upon buying more companies. It had no desire to purchase them as long as the economy had not fully recovered. But it would wait and see and look for opportunities. It was sure those opportunities would present themselves.

In this chapter, we have talked about the lessons to be learned from Cisco's experience of running into trouble at the end of the year 2000. We have also talked about how some of the vaunted Cisco strategies held up or did not hold up in the weeks and months leading up to the downturn. With time proving a good healer, John Chambers eventually gained enough self-confidence to suggest that it was not *only* the 100-year flood that had affected Cisco Systems; the inner workings at Cisco had also contributed to the events that befell the company in the winter of 2000 and 2001. He genuinely believed that none of his strategies were flawed; but he did come to appreciate that they were not being executed 100 percent correctly.

That is why, as we will see in the next chapter, the great lesson he gleaned from the experience in trying to get the company back on track was to give far more emphasis to "focus and execution," a phrase that was quickly becoming a mantra along the corridors of Cisco Systems.

11 The Recovery

In the wake of the economic downturn, Cisco Systems was a different company. The pace of work slowed. Conversations were muted. The smiles that had seemed permanent appeared only some of the time. Everything seemed to move in slow motion. The company had taken a punch to the gut and needed time to recover.

The shock was indeed deep and wide. Chambers likened the pre-downturn Cisco to a racing car that is driving 200 miles an hour when suddenly the rules of the race course change: "Anybody who has ever raced, you go around that turn at 200 miles per hour, and they turn on you, I don't care how good a driver you are, I don't care how well prepared you are that things might change, you weren't expecting that."

Later, much later, Chambers would take great comfort from some advice from former GE chairman and CEO Jack Welch, namely that "until we got knocked on our tail, we'd never have a great company." Chambers knew the advice was well intentioned, but all he could think was, But we've done that. Previous Cisco crises in 1991, 1994, and 1997, said Welch, were not really hard knocks. Nor had Chambers been through them with many current Cisco employees. Your team has to go through the adversity, and so does your employee base, Welch told him, adding: You have to go through the troubles as a team. It's going to be painful and it's going to be longer than anyone would have wished, but in the end a good company can become great. It was advice that Chambers had wanted to hear, for he knew that the recovery would not be easy.

For one thing, the media would be there every step of the way. In past crises, the media had hardly paid attention nor had the shareholders for that matter. But this crisis had come when Cisco was at the top of its game. This was Cisco's most public crisis.

Once, the media had fawned over Cisco. "On the way up to a stock market value of half a trillion dollars, everything about Cisco seemed perfect," wrote *Fortune* magazine in its May 14, 2000, issue. With the economic downturn, some in the media turned against Cisco, blaming it for promoting itself as capable of doing things that in the end it could not. The brunt of the criticism was aimed at Chambers directly.

But he vowed that he would not quit. This was not his first crisis, though it was by far the most serious. He genuinely felt a responsibility to Cisco employees and customers. Quitting would be letting them down, in his eyes. "This is when the leader has to be strongest of all. And you can't flinch. I was pretty sure what needed to be done. And I had reasonable experience versus almost anybody in our industry—unfortunately, I had gone through this kind of thing, but not as severe as it was." He was comforted to learn quickly that he had the full support of the board.

Mindful of the 10,000 percent increase in Cisco's stock since Chambers took over, and agreeing with the CEO that a 100-year flood had indeed swept over the company, the board backed its leader, though leading board members did take Chambers aside for some friendly advice. John Morgridge told Chambers that he should cease at once making pronouncements that Cisco would likely achieve 30 to 50 percent revenue growth rates once the downturn abated. There would be a recovery, Morgridge told him, but Chambers would have to button up and let the numbers speak for themselves.

In a mighty reversal of his previous management style, Chambers chose to spend more time in his office, to stay close to the business over the next year or so, to skip most meetings with political leaders, and to avoid most Internet forums—in short, to adopt a very low profile: "That was not a time to be driving the industry. That was a time to say let's understand what's going on and how do we navigate through these unchartered waters at a speed that no one's seen before, and be realistic at what we need to be better at. It was a time when we did not talk about the Internet revolution and show how you could improve your company."

Hoping to avoid giving the impression that the company was rudderless, Chambers declared that he would not alter Cisco's basic strategies. That might have spelled disaster in the minds of customers and shareholders. When other companies shifted strategies too often, they got pummeled. But he *did* in fact shift certain strategies: the whole emphasis on growth was shifted to a new stress on profits. That meant fewer people being hired, fewer acquisitions, and a freeze on building. It meant adopting a more cautious attitude toward entering new markets. Still, Chambers did stick to the basic strategies that he felt had always worked for Cisco: listening to customers, not being wedded to any specific technology, seeking to catch market transitions early, etc.

While he could not admit it openly even to himself, Chambers did acknowledge that Cisco had been pursuing growth too zealously. The admission came in the form of Cisco's recovery program.

When Chambers planned Cisco's recovery, though he continued to absolve himself of guilt for the downturn, he undertook a series of internal reforms that were so far-reaching, so revolutionary for Cisco, that there was only one conclusion to draw: Chambers finally understood that the company had been pursuing hypergrowth without sufficient regard for what might happen if the economy suddenly turned sour, as it had.

The reforms were designed to make sure that Cisco would not get itself into a similar position. In the event of another 100-year flood, this time Cisco would be prepared to withstand the harsh blows with far less harm done to the company.

What were these reforms all about?

They were about paying attention to the basics, paying attention to all those things that had been neglected in order to keep the company running at 200 miles an hour around that race course. "When you're growing rapidly," Chambers acknowledged, "sometimes you don't pay as much attention to that as you should."

The reforms were about cutting back on expenses; about limiting head count; about giving priority to profits over revenues; and about getting employees to adopt teamwork more.

Cisco took off over $1 billion in its expense run rate in less than two months largely from a combination of discretionary spending and head count. It used its technology to hold more worldwide conference calls. It used IPTV more. It sent presentations to customers rather than have them show up in San Jose headquarters.

FOCUSING ON CERTAIN MARKETS

The company put a sharper focus on certain markets, not going after every imaginable market opportunity. It shifted the fewer resources it now had to those markets that seemed most promising. It continued to take risks on what markets would prosper, but those risks were more calculated.

The reforms were also about improving teamwork. Chambers would not admit to such disarray, but he did hint that too many people were off doing their individual things, working to make their own numbers, not worrying about what was good for the overall company.

He declared unambiguously that anyone not playing on the team would be fired. He would also not tolerate any backbiting. The company could no longer afford it. In its early days, the company had suffered from such backbiting, but at least the employees had performed solidly. This time around, any internecine warfare could only damage the company's performance. Chambers warned his colleagues: "Don't let the finger-pointing begin so that each group points out another group's problems." That was his job, not theirs. "The whole team understands: We're flying in formation. This is the time when there isn't any room for wild ducks. You cut down the wind resistance by flying in formation. If they can't fly in formation, they won't be part of a team."

Teamwork under the Chambers reforms also meant instilling in sales and marketing people a greater appreciation for all of Cisco's products, not just the ones for which they were responsible.

His own personal priorities in the reform program were "a focus on profit contribution and teamwork more aggressively, and changing people who could not get it right."

I caught up with John Chambers on April 14, 2001. The January–March period had been the worst in the company's history. Just eight days earlier, on April 6, Cisco's stock had reached a 52-week low of $18.68. Investors seemed to think that Cisco would be the next high-tech giant to cut revenue and earnings targets. Yet, John Chambers remained upbeat, firmly believing that the economy would right itself soon. "We don't think the economy will be negative over the next three to five years." He also believed that Cisco, the most powerful equipment maker for the Internet, remained in the right market, supplying Internet infrastructure, and that with or without Cisco the market was going to grow 30 to 50 percent over the next three to five years in good economies. Since then, he has avoided such forecasts.

The only question for Cisco was whether it would execute well, and thereby capture much or all of that growth for itself. He was buoyed by the fact that Cisco was still towering over its rivals, its market cap ($131 billion on that April day) higher than those of its next eight competitors combined ($120 billion). Chambers believed that Cisco would return to its days of glory sooner rather than later. Indeed, he was planning on it: "We will break away in the next decade more than we did in the last. I think that over the next ten years, Cisco has the chance, if we execute well—we will view this as just one more bump, and people will say, 'Wasn't it a buying opportunity?'"

Just two days after we talked, Cisco announced restructuring costs and other special charges of $1.2 billion and an additional excess inventory charge of $2.2 billion. Cisco officials predicted that third-quarter sales would fall by 30 percent. The company formally announced the 7,900-person layoff.

. . .

The damage that the economic downturn had caused was felt most directly in the financial report Cisco gave that summer. Cisco's sales for the fourth quarter of 2001, which ended in July, were $4.298 billion, compared to $5.7 billion the year before. In terms of income, the company ended with a $7 profit. For the same period the year before, it enjoyed a profit of $796 million. Cisco posted a $1.014 billion net loss for the fiscal 2001 year ending on July 28. A year earlier it had yearly income of $2.668 billion.

Chambers clearly hoped that this would be the last of the bad news coming from Cisco. While he would not say it publicly, he felt that the company had reached a bottom and that the only news from now on would be good. In his conference call, Chambers continued to predict that Cisco might return to 30 to 50 percent sales-growth levels. Confidence in Cisco remained high, especially since it was sitting on $12 billion in cash, a figure that would grow steadily (by June 2002 it had reached $21 billion).

Believing that the worst of the bad news was behind it, Cisco was ready to shift into high gear to get the company ready for the inevitable economic upturn. In August 2001, Cisco undertook the largest part of its reform, the revamping of all of its businesses.

Until then Cisco had been organized according to what it called Lines of Business (LOBs): service providers, enterprise, and commercial. Each LOB contained numerous business units.

ELIMINATING BOUNDARIES

The purpose of the "reorg" (Cisco parlance) was to eliminate the boundaries that existed among the LOBs. Under the reorganization, engineering efforts would be aligned around 11 large technologies, for example, high-end LAN switching, core routing, access, or aggregation.

A major dividend of the reform was to provide Cisco with greater flexibility in shifting resources from one product line to another, because now the resources would be assigned inside the same unit. In the past, it had been difficult to shift an engineering team that was expert in access router technology from the service providers to the enterprise segment of the business. Now it would be easier to shift these resources when necessary.

Mario Mazzola was given responsibility for the 11 new technology groups, making him one of the strongest figures in the company. He went from running the enterprise line of business to a new post, chief development officer in charge of engineers. That put him in charge of Cisco's engineering and product efforts.

His first priority was to push greater cooperation among the various Cisco segments, "to instill in people the importance of sharing more; sharing in terms of information, in terms of technology." In the past, he said, many routers had been built, but he was now cautioning Cisco engineers "before we develop the next one, let's be sure there are good reasons why we wouldn't use one that already exists."

Conscious that young engineers often hoped to produce "the next great thing," he asked them to sacrifice such innovation in order to "take a current platform to the next level in a way that provides continuity for our customers." In the fast-growth days of the past, it was "easier and more appealing to do a lot of my own thing instead of under-standing how to evolve the platform into something more powerful."

Mazzola's mandate included resolving the issue of product over-laps: "In moments of huge growth, you feel that you can afford more levels of redundancy. One way to react to this is to add more resources in Internet service providers, to enterprises, whereas when there's a downturn, you feel that it's more appropriate to try to leverage with the highest possible level of resources that you have."

By the end of the summer Cisco was clearly on the path to recovery. No one imagined that Cisco would be able to return to the strato-spheric growth levels it had achieved just before the downturn; recov-ery, in this case, meant leaving losses behind and aiming for more moderate growth levels of 15 to 20 percent a year. The Cisco reforms gave a bounce to its stock, which shot up 8.9 percent on news of the reorganization. It stood at $18.25 on August 24, with a market cap of $133 billion. The media showed increasing support for Cisco's internal changes, suggesting that by making tough decisions, showing strong leadership, keeping his team focused, and retaining only the best executives, Chambers was pulling off a turnaround that very few other beleaguered CEOs had managed to do.

With leaner times, productivity was due to become a major Cisco focus. One measure of productivity Cisco used was annualized revenue per head count. Before the downturn, Cisco was running at $700,000 per employee. Afterward, the figure dropped to a low of $442,000. By June 2002, it was back up to $530,000. Chambers hoped to return to a $700,000 level in the near future, and eventually to achieve his stretch goal of $1 million. Cisco rivals meanwhile had fallen to the $300,000 level.

Clearly unintentionally, Cisco benefited from the September 11 terror attacks on the United States. It installed switches and routers to direct data traffic and connect people to the Internet and re-create its customers' networks at different locations. Some estimated that Cisco would get a decent portion of the $300 million that was likely to be spent on the replacement of networks lost in the attacks.

Chambers was increasingly optimistic. He did not believe that the Internet had been stigmatized by the downturn. He was grateful that the downturn had come when it had, and not three years earlier, when CEOs and business leaders had still not fully appreciated the value of high tech, viewing it more as a mere expense item than a tool that would change their businesses.

"Today," he told me in September 2001, "I'm talking to the same business leaders as before, I talked with the prime minister of Japan a week and a half ago, I've talked with more CEOs in the last week and a half than I ever have. The CEOs get it. The government leaders get it. They understand the correlation between this [the Internet] being the key productivity tool for the future and the way to generate profit." However, he was uncertain how quickly these CEOs would reinvest in Internet infrastructure.

Still, Cisco was quietly gaining market share more rapidly than at any time in its history. It had gained against almost every single rival in the previous quarter. He took heart from having $17 billion in cash (more than all his competitors combined), and a market cap that exceeded his next eight competitors'. He was again buoyant: "The market has already voted about one company breaking away." It gave Chambers great joy to remind people that only a few years earlier his main competitors were far larger than Cisco.

By October 2001, the media were confidently predicting that Cisco would get back on its feet again, although it seemed unlikely that it, or anyone else for that matter, would be enjoying growth rates as high as in the past. When Chambers asserted on October 3 that Cisco would meet earnings expectations of 2 cents per share for the first quarter of 2002, Wall Street gratefully spiked Cisco's shares up 21 percent on that news, to $17. It had reached a low of $11 only a few days earlier.

In November 2001, Cisco weighed in with first-quarter results that indeed seemed to indicate that it had reached a kind of bottom.

The analysts were kind to Cisco, playing down the fact that Cisco had posted a net loss of $268 million and that sales had dropped to $4.48 billion. Cisco noted that it had earned $290 million by selling excess inventory, written off as worthless just seven months earlier, and excluded that portion of the earnings from the pro forma results on which analysts base their assessments of the company's operations.

There was reasonable optimism because Cisco had been able to sell $4.4 billion of equipment in that quarter, when the economy was slipping into recession. Its cash had risen to $19 billion. But the stock continued to languish at $18 a share.

It was crucial to Cisco that it be portrayed as getting over its woes. It was vital that the media regard Cisco as recuperating, getting back its energy, its morale on the rise. And so the company was stung when a *Business Week* reporter attended an internal Cisco meeting in November and subsequently reported that the questions put to John Chambers at that meeting betrayed a "sagging morale and unease that until recently were unknown inside this high-tech stalwart."

BACK TO BASICS

As the year 2001 wound to a close, Cisco was still pleased with the continuing pattern of sales dating back to June, though it could not tell beyond the next month how it might do. The recession was still at its peak. Throughout its 2001 analysts conference on December 4 and 5, Cisco officials went heavy on the theme of "back to basics." The company's focus would be on increasing market share, on profit, and on increasing productivity (via E-business applications especially).

Another bright spot: Gone were the days when Cisco was suffering huge inventories, as they had dropped from $2.5 billion to $1.3 billion.

Second-quarter results for 2002 showed quite a bit of improvement, as revenue reached $4.816 billion and net income was $660 million.

The acquisition binge had slowed to a snail's pace. Cisco had been doing 20 a year; then, after the downturn, Chambers predicted that it would do only eight to 12 annually. But by the end of 2001 it had truly taken a pause in this strategy. By the spring of 2002, Cisco officials made clear that only when the economy recovered would Cisco go back to the acquisitions business.

Dan Scheinman, senior vice president for corporate development, was put in charge of business development and strategic alliances in 2001. He was understandably in a wait-and-see mode: "There are a lot of venture-backed companies doing interesting things. But given the market, we can afford to let them mature. We can reduce our risk and increase our certainty that we've got the right company. During the boom we were forced to move a lot earlier and in some cases before companies had a robust, fleshed-out product. Now we can see more of the product and really understand what the product's strengths and weaknesses are." He could not say how large Cisco's acquisitions program would become: "I don't have a crystal ball; but I know the strategy is right."

With the stock still quite low, Cisco no longer wanted to use market cap as a measure of its success. The stock continued to trade at a remarkable 95 times estimated 2002 earnings. So Cisco preferred to use the amount of cash it was holding ($19.1 billion in January 2002) as a key new metric. To indicate how it was breaking away from its rivals, Cisco made sure to let others know that the figure represented more than double that of competitors Alcatel, Lucent Technologies, and Nortel combined.

The market-share metric was critical to Cisco as well, and there it was doing better and better, dominating the $15 billion market for corporate network equipment, increasing market share in certain product segments such as routers. But as long as the corporations and telecom carriers kept their capital expenditures on Internet infrastructure low or nonexistent, Cisco stood no chance of returning to the 70 percent growth rates it had enjoyed just before the economy fell apart. In its best days Cisco was receiving 40 percent of its business by selling to these telecoms, many of them upstarts who were challenging major players such as Verizon Communications and Sprint Corporation. When the upstarts collapsed, Cisco was forced to rely on the established corporations, but they were keeping their capital expenditures low or nonexistent during the recession.

By the spring of 2002, Chambers was coming out of his shell, spending a good deal of time with customers, meeting with political leaders, again brimming over with self-confidence. He had devoted more than a year to running the company on a hands-on basis, behind his desk, very much a personal presence at San Jose headquarters. Now he felt the company was on the upswing, and he could move out into the field again.

In mid-April, Chambers reported these promising aspects of the Cisco recovery: it was growing 40 percent faster than its top 10 competitors in North America; it was generating $1 billion a quarter; expenses had fallen by $2.5 billion per year; gross margins, which had been in the low 50s, were nearly at the 60 percent target (and would rise to 63 in the spring of 2002); and inventory turns, which had dropped to 4.2 during the worst moments of the downturn, were at the 7 to 8 level.

The most concrete sign of the recovery was not so much Cisco's posting of third-quarter sales of $4.822 billion, just a slight bit up from the previous quarter, but the company's profits of $838 million, a 10 percent quarter-over-quarter growth. Those results were the best evidence thus far that Cisco had made important strides toward recovery.

That news drove Cisco's stock up 24 percent on May 8, 2002, to $16.27, adding more than $20 billion to Cisco's market cap. The good news from Cisco gave NASDAQ its eighth largest percentage gain ever, 7.8 percent.

The recession, though easing in 2002, still kept Cisco's customers in a conservative spending mood. In the past, those customers had been quite willing to consider regular upgrades of their networks, given the rosy forecasts of Internet growth; now they had adopted what John Chambers called a "show me" pose, unwilling to upgrade until assured that they were getting the greatest possible use from their current network.

It was tough going for Cisco if only because nearly all of the markets it had once identified as breakaway possibilities had either shrunk or disappeared in the wake of the economic downturn. The optical market had slowed, as had mobile wireless. Voice over Internet Protocol (VOIP) had witnessed a significant slowdown. It remained, however, a promising growth industry: with Internet-based phones, or so-called IP phones, a company could use VOIP to avoid investing in the building and servicing of a separate voice network.

Some markets looked promising.

The $15 billion security market had suddenly come to the forefront in the wake of the September 11 attacks on the United States. The security business was looking better, and Cisco, with 20 percent of that market, was hoping to expand its share significantly.

In the heyday of hypergrowth, Cisco could afford to take a spray-shot approach to all potentially good markets. "Now," says Mike Volpi, one of Cisco's key strategists, "you take the resources you have and apply them to the market segments in which you want to be successful."

Cisco was also investing considerable sums in the $4 billion storage-networking market in the spring of 2002. Storage networking allows companies to easily secure and retrieve data. This market was growing in excess of 30 percent a year, and Cisco had no market share whatsoever. Some were suggesting that the service-provider portion alone of the storage-networking market could reach $15 billion by 2005, an increase from $273 million in 2001.

Cisco was also investing in IP telephony and wireless LANs for the enterprise market. Every year enterprise customers purchased $8 billion of IP telephony, and since Cisco had only a 10 percent market share, it saw a very good growth opportunity.

NICE GROWTH

With respect to the wireless LAN market, Cisco had a 30 percent share of that $2 billion market. Since that market was growing at a 50 percent annual clip (it should hit $3 billion in 2003), that kind of increase would give the company "nice growth" (Mike Volpi's phrase) in the coming period.

Cisco market strategists acknowledged that given the kind of business environment that now existed, it was unimaginable that Cisco would return to the 50 to 70 percent annual growth increases it had once enjoyed. A more reasonable goal for the company would be 30 percent annual growth.

The company retained its focus on routers and switches. In the third quarter of 2002, routing was 30 percent of the business, and switching, 40 percent. Access products were 5 percent; services, 17 percent; and others, such as optical, software, and IP telephone, came to 8 percent.

In many ways, Cisco was doing things differently because of the downturn. In earlier days, it had simply geared up for the growth by turning on the growth machine full-steam without worrying too much about the consequences. But now it was taking its time, being more careful about how it did things. "We had such a high demand for people," says Kate DCamp, the senior vice president for human resources, "that we had to create a high-volume efficient recruiting machine." Yet, integrating all those people into Cisco was tricky. "There was a certain amount of sink and swim."

With less resources for recruiting, Cisco began focusing on searching for the few recruits that it truly wanted. It took a close look at the people it had already hired, searching for "buried treasure" (Kate DCamp's phrase), people who were so eager to work at Cisco that they took jobs that were "small for them"; from this pool could come future company leaders.

In June 2002, CFO Larry Carter was working on accelerating Cisco's reporting of its financials to the authorities. Current rules called for companies to file 45 days from their quarter, and the time period was likely to be shortened to 30 days. Cisco was already reporting within 30 days.

Carter had set himself the challenge of reporting within 48 hours of earnings. By the spring of 2002, Cisco had became one of the first companies to include with its press release a full cash-flow statement. Cash flow had become one of the key financials that people wanted to see.

He was also busy closing loops on the forecasting side. In the past, the sales organization had provided a high-level forecast by theater (as Cisco calls its geographical regions) 180 days in advance. Product groups provided a product-by-product forecast that the manufacturing segment needed to load the factory. But the components supplier, looking only at run rates, did not have a clear enough picture. Cisco's forecasting systems now allow the product groups to forecast a more detailed product mix—mentioning, for example, not just the product, but the various configurations of that product. Now component manufacturers have a better way of telling what demand is for various products. Carter says that Cisco has still not developed a crystal ball. Its systems still produce only a forecast. But a loop has been closed between the field products group, manufacturing, and contract suppliers.

What pleased Carter more than anything was the $21 billion in cash that Cisco was sitting on. During turbulent times, cash becomes the greatest comfort factor for shareholders and analysts. The timing was working out well, as more and more analysts were looking at a company's cash as a key metric. "At the end of the day," says CFO Carter, "cash flow is really the best thing you can measure, because it's real. Earnings can be based on a lot of accounting rules that are complex; every company is a little different; how do you do depreciation, revenue recognition, what's your inventory? The quality of the reporting on earnings is not as tangible as cash."

How does Cisco use the cash?

It has used $1 billion of its cash to begin a $3 billion stock buyback program; it has made investments of 5 to 10 percent in a number of small emerging technology enterprises, to gain access to new technology. Some may become acquisition targets. It also does a good deal of equipment leasing, using cash.

What about John Chambers's future? In the fall of 1999, John Chambers told the Cisco board that he would stay through 2004; he also said that he might stay on for 10 years if everyone would have him.

For all the attention Chambers has gotten in the United States and around the world, he remains the company's president and CEO, but not its chairman of the board. John Morgridge has kept that title ever since turning over the company to Chambers in January 1995. Chambers insists that his relationship with Morgridge has never been better. "He's a neat person. I trust him with my life. He's the ideal chairman. He is my complete confidant in everything. We've developed a great friendship." Chambers also points out that Morgridge has told him that he [Chambers] could have the chairmanship "when I wanted it." But Chambers quickly adds, "I don't want it. I'm very comfortable with my role and what I'm bringing. I think the two of us together are more effective than I would be in total."

Despite Chambers's constant assertions that he plans to stay at Cisco into the indefinite future, there is a belief among some Cisco watchers that Chambers is eager to launch a political career. He has a lot going for him, including the kind of friendly and warm personality that could garner lots of votes. He has a stellar reputation within the business community, giving him a natural built-in constituency to launch his candidacy for any electoral job. He is also superwealthy and could spend his own millions on his candidacy.

Those who have been close to Chambers speculate that his dream is to become president of the United States. They add that he would like to launch his career by becoming the next governor of California. Some speculated that George W. Bush had his eye on Chambers for a cabinet seat, with secretary of commerce appearing the most obvious. But Chambers passed word that he had no desire to leave Cisco. When it was announced, the Bush cabinet did not include John Chambers.

While he denies any interest in a political career, insisting that he plans to teach business and/or business ethics after he retires from Cisco, John Chambers certainly enjoys being on the receiving end of the public's attention. His face has been splashed on the cover of every business magazine, and just about every list of high-tech leaders has had Chambers at or near the top. He does not boast about such things in public. But he is clearly proud that in headier days the media and the business community anointed him the King of the Internet, its chief evangelist, and its most important promoter. He is proud that major corporations send their management teams to visit Cisco and that world leaders are eager to meet with him. He is most proud of Cisco's accomplishments during his time in power, and he makes no secret of his desire to rule one day over the most powerful and influential company of all time.

What will the Cisco of the future look like? It will remain a network company. It will be inextricably linked to the Internet. It will move—or attempt to move—into a whole variety of segments of the communications industry.

Beyond this, it is difficult to say. Too much is in flux. It is possible, however, to say what are the areas of business in which Cisco will not participate. John Chambers promises, "We will never be a service provider, a systems integrator, or have a large role in consulting. We will not be in a market where we don't bring an expertise or an advantage, and a minimum of 25 percent market share, with 40 percent plus being our goal."

The Internet remains an integral part of Cisco's future: "What we outlined in our mission," says Chambers, "was to change the way the world works, learns, lives, and plays. And our purpose within that mission is to shape the future of the Internet by creating unprecedented opportunities for our customers, employees, shareholders, and partners. That is a pretty broad net we cast seven years ago. The Internet will be synonymous with all types of networks, data, voice, and video. And the productivity looks like it will change work even more than we originally thought. I do believe the network virtual organization will be the most fundamental change in business in the last half century."

How specifically might Cisco change, if at all? I asked.

"I think companies get into real trouble when they get away from their core competencies. That doesn't mean we make networking hardware only. We're in software. We do middleware applications. There are multiple ways from here. But I don't think this market will be confined by growth opportunities in the next 10 years. There might be related fields that we might have to get into to get the growth."

12 Getting Ready for the Upturn

May 29, 2002. It had been 20 months since I had first met John Chambers. Then, Cisco had been at its peak. Since then it had slid into the valley, and now it was working hard to climb back up to the peak. Standing at the peak makes one feel mighty and strong. Climbing to the peak is bound to inject some humility into a person. And so it was a different John Chambers I encountered on that late May morning when he gathered Cisco's leaders for a summing-up of where the company was at that moment. There were a thousand people in the audience, directors and above, all from Cisco Systems. The very first words out of Chambers's mouth were that this meeting with the team was one of his most important. It was important for me as well: it provided the chance to see Chambers in full recovery mode talking to Cisco managers.

As I listened to him intently, I realized what was different about him: he seemed more cautious, more sober. He was still exuberant and charming; he still spoke as if his lips were in a 100-yard dash. But the events of the last 18 months had made him sound less super-charged. He exuded a certain calmness, a serenity. He recounted what Jack Welch had told him, how companies could only become great by going through a serious test, and he relished the fact that

Cisco now seemed to have passed that test remarkably quickly and successfully.

Chambers, as usual, raced up to the stage and peered over the audience. It was very much a Cisco audience. Fully 283 of those in the audience had been hired in the past year.

If the CEO had a theme for the day, it was getting the company to employ teamwork more than ever. "The key to our future is that we move with one team, one destiny," Chambers said at first. If there was a word that he used more than any other during the session, it was *productivity*. "What will drive the industry?" he asked. "It's all about productivity. That's why I'm optimistic about the industry."

Another phrase that cropped up over and over during the meeting was *focus and execution*. "Our destiny is clearly within reach if we execute properly," Chambers promised.

Chambers was feeling pretty good about Cisco. He believed that things were finally going well for the company again. It was improbable that Cisco would reach the heights it had attained just two years earlier, at least in the short term. But Chambers took heart that the company was moving in the right direction: "This is the year that Cisco will break away, and very possibly quicker than I anticipated."

Still, it was going to take some time for the economy to truly turn around, and Chambers was taking that into account along with realizing that Cisco was not immune from anemic capital spending. Unlike in the past, when he believed that Europe would lead the world out of the slump, he now was convinced that this would be a U.S.-led recovery.

A FOCUS ON PRODUCTIVITY

For much of the rest of the meeting he dwelled on productivity. "What will drive the industry? I'd like to say it is technology. It's not. It's productivity. Cisco was very early in terms of understanding the potential productivity increases for major countries around the world. People realize that networking increases productivity. Five years ago we viewed a 3 to 5 percent productivity increase to be a realistic stretch goal for the United States. Today, we realize that 3 percent is attainable and 4 to 5 percent is not out of the question. The implications in terms of productivity and standard of living are huge for countries that do this. Half of the productivity increase is due to the Internet and Web-based applications. The network equals productivity. Cisco equals the network. Cisco equals productivity. That is the challenge. We have to make Cisco equal to productivity. Cisco is right in the sweet spot for making this happen."

He added, "The way to judge whether companies become great companies is how they handle their successes and how they handle the setbacks. In going through the data with my leadership team and reflecting how we've done versus our peers, the results of the last year really stood out. While nobody in the industry was pleased with the events of the last year, Cisco probably executed the best against the available market. In the most recent quarter Cisco's $838 million in profits represented 100 percent of the industry's profits. Its $130 billion in market cap represented 75 percent of the industry's market cap. Its $21 billion in cash represented 100 percent of the industry's cash."

Noting how disastrously all of Cisco's rivals had collapsed in the past year, Chambers remarked: "This is probably the most fundamental breakaway that has ever occurred across any major industry in one year. We're proud of what we've accomplished this year."

Chambers said that he had been trying to listen to customers intently and he was hearing that they wanted Cisco to make their networking products transparent. "Unlike many major high-tech companies, Cisco believes it is possible to be 100 percent driven by the needs of your customers. They will give you enough runway to adjust to their needs. And, candidly, we got into trouble when we were not listening as well to our customers. Whether it is in the service-provider or enterprise accounts, what gets us into trouble is saying 'this is what you need to do' instead of listening, sharing, and delivering.

"We must build this into our DNA to avoid this. For over a decade we've said that what would always trip Cisco would be getting too far away from our customers. Whether with our customers, employees, or shareholders, Cisco's credibility and ability to keep its word are extremely important. While we might make mistakes, which happens when you're growing quickly and taking risks, it's important to be candid about our opportunities and challenges both internally and externally.

"If you look at the track record of the last four quarters, it has shown improvement in each quarter with higher gross margins, inventory turns, and after-tax profits. In short, we've managed through the downturn and positioned for the upturn with unusual focus. As we begin to see our way through this turnaround—now that we are more than one quarter into it—we have made organizational changes to segments such as engineering.

"While most companies would have been pleased with our market share position, we looked at the missed market opportunities and how we could do better. So we moved from a focus on lines of business to a focus on product segments. Part of that was to prevent product overlap; another reason was to make sure that our competition was external, not internal, and part was to move resources toward areas of productivity."

The very next day I had a chance to sit down with Chambers to follow up on some of the points he had made in his talk to Cisco's leaders. We talked first about just how difficult the period after the downturn had been for him.

"I can say it now because we're through it, but during the time it was extremely challenging and honestly not fun. All the experience that I've achieved over 20 years of business and the quality of the leadership team made me very confident in our strategy, our ability to adjust to the slowdown and to position ourselves for the upturn. But until you see the result of the strategy, you can't be sure. Now looking at the results it looks like we were right on the money. An element of this was maintaining the strategy, adjusting for the breadth and depth of the downturn, and getting ready for the upturn. For example, we took action with employees very quickly, we were decisive and eliminated uncertainty as quickly as possible—eliminating expenses and adjusting head count once as opposed to numerous times."

What had made him so miserable, I asked? The layoffs? The media attacks? Or knowing that he might have done things differently? The answer was slow in coming: "The real issue for me was disappointing people—customers, shareholders, and employees. There was never an issue about integrity or our long-term survivability. But, you always wish you had been smarter and been able to avoid some of the pain that everyone felt. There is always a tendency to second-guess."

Pointing to what he would have done differently to lessen the damage caused by Cisco's downturn, he said that once the lead times had built up during the year 2000, he should have kept his foot on the brake longer. Instead, to try to reduce lead times, he built up inventories, so when the crunch came, Cisco was stuck with having to take $2.2 billion in charges for the built-up inventory and commitment to suppliers.

He admitted, "This is a race being run at a tremendous speed, one that has been modulated by applying more or less pressure to the gas pedal rather than by applying the brakes. Companies that had their foot on the brakes were long since history. After chasing lead times for almost 18 months and not meeting customer expectations, we took the inventory levels up and took lead times down. While that served us well for two quarters, when the business dropped off quickly we had to take the $2.2 billion write-down."

ONE TEAM

Chambers suggested that in today's marketplace the ability of the entire company as one team to move toward opportunities and to address exposures is key. One thing he would have done differently was to insist on teamwork. "I'm learning how really important teamwork was. You're got to have a team that plays well together, in good times and in bad." Chambers favors changing 10 percent of his leadership team every year to 18 months.

I mentioned that I thought he was especially candid in admitting to his leaders that Cisco had taken its eye off the ball when it came to customers. How did that happen? I asked.

"Well, we moved into a new major market [service providers]. We weren't as familiar with that market. Without realizing it we slowly got our eye off the ball. I don't think we realized until afterward how far off it was. Until we went out and talked to a segment of these large service providers, we didn't realize that we had become overconfident. We weren't listening well enough, and worse, we were telling them what to do. We're now rapidly repairing that and we have a very good chance of being the number one player in the service-provider marketplace. Having said that, our typical Cisco luck and the service-provider downturn, as painful as it was for us, allowed us to correct our mistakes and maybe to become the number one player."

I asked Chambers how, after listening to customers in 2000, he had not picked up the warning signals that his customers were getting into trouble.

"As late as December 2000, our number one issue for customers was that our lead times were way too long. Our customers said the growth was going to be there; they were financially sound, they could buy the equipment, etc. And, in certain segments of the market, the situation was even amplified by customers' confidence and their industry segment—this was particularly true of new service providers. Without challenging how many competitors were going to come into the market or their business plans, we went along with that plan. Now when we go to our partners, even the large ones, the most successful ones, we try to ask politely, 'How do you make money on this? How are you going to get the productivity out?' Customers are much more receptive to that as well. Whereas before, they might have said: 'That's none of your business. That's our business.' Now we [at Cisco] are making it our business."

I then asked how he responded to those who contended that while Cisco had promoted itself as a company that could forecast itself out of trouble, it had not done so on the eve of the downturn.

Historically, Chambers replied, Cisco had picked up industry trends and done very well because of advance warnings.

"It was scary how accurate we were in terms of data, voice, video consolidating, and of voice commoditizing over time. We said voice would be free. Not only the consolidating in data communication companies, but later the consolidation of data and voice manufacturing companies, service providers consolidating; almost all things being connected. When we gave that speech, nobody believed us, and that was a 10-year scenario. It was five years. So we got a lot of the trends right in many areas. And that's because of listening to customers and also because we have a lot of experience on seeing the industries involved. Occasionally we miss, and when we miss we try to adjust."

But what about Cisco's vaunted systems? I asked. Weren't they supposed to dig Cisco out of any downturn in the economy, sudden or gradual?

"Our systems are very good at telling you where we are at a given point in time. But we've always been very up front that our sales teams never forecast the turns up or down. We always shared our concern, but not everyone listened. We always said our growth rate was dependent upon strong economies. And it would not surprise us that if the economy went down, our business would go down."

But Cisco simply didn't believe that the capital spending would collapse almost overnight.

"We had never had a down quarter in our history, and modeling down 5 percent or perhaps down 10 percent seemed like a doomsday model. Our industry had never experienced that type of free fall, much less something in the 50 percent plus range. What can sometimes be overlooked is that over the last decade there have been numerous IT and networking slowdowns and industry consolidations. If we had our foot on the brakes each time those concerns occurred, we probably would not have survived, let alone won the race. And so we've been able to negotiate the quick turns better than anybody. When you've had 300 competitors and you're the clear leader, how can you argue with the strategy that's been employed over time?"

Chambers believes that competition is important and helps a company move faster. "Competition is a major positive force for a company. It forces those companies that survive to be more realistic in meeting customer needs. What got IBM and Wang into trouble was not competition, it was the lack of competition. What got us into trouble in high-end routing was that we didn't have a competitor for a long period of time. And when we finally did, we were too slow to react. Now we've corrected that. It was very painful, very humbling; it was very good for us. You want competition. It's healthy. It makes us better. It forces you to move faster, it pushes us to stay close to our customer. I love competition. I try to beat the competition every time that we can. But the way we compete is different from most companies. Most competitors would like to be acquired by us and most have a lot of respect for us. Without competition we'll get ourselves into trouble."

Could Cisco go back to the incredibly high growth rates it had sustained before the downturn?

Cisco's growth rate, Chambers said, would be determined by the growth rate of the industry as Cisco is becoming a larger and larger part of the industry. "A very good job is growing 10 percent faster than the industry, and only time will tell if we can achieve that goal consistently. I do not think it is possible for us to continue to grow 45 percent faster than our peers, as we have over the last 12 months. The market, unfortunately, is just not that big."

How can Cisco decide what markets to enter when there have been so many rosy projections about markets that eventually weakened or disappeared?

First, says Chambers, there was a combination of factors that led to the slowdown that are unlikely to repeat themselves—nearly unlimited capital and too many competitors in segments of our customers' markets. "Traditionally you often have five to seven competitors in an emerging industry segment. However, during the bubble as many as 30 competitors in the U.S. service-provider segment were created and almost none survived. And too much competition without differentiation causes companies to compete only on price, which takes the profits out of the entire industry and, therefore, reduces the long-term survivability of a company. And it's always easy to see in hindsight that many people got their eye off the ball in terms of productivity and cash. We tried never to take our eye off that ball. Until the downturn very few people ever gave us credit for our cash accumulation or our focus on cash and on profits more than on market share. Now we all understand how important all three are."

What will happen to Cisco's acquisition policy?

It will return in full force when the economy comes back, says Chambers. "I believe you acquire when you begin to see the potential for a market upturn. To acquire someone else's problems in a market that is in a downturn requires a company that thrives on turnarounds—and that's just not Cisco's core strength. We have to understand that we're a company that scores 200 points a game. We don't think anybody else can score 100. We're really good at that. We're not good at going in and turning around a company and then making them capable of scoring 200. We're good at getting another company with a similar culture and probably a similar geography, and together we score 200 points a game."

Why the new emphasis on profit?

"Our focus had always been on both revenue and profit growth and we had driven it through our culture better than most of our competitors. One of the first things that we addressed during the downturn was a profit-contribution mentality and a back-to-basics approach with ownership in each functional area from engineering to manufacturing to sales. It is really the entire company's focus that resulted in our profit contribution today."

The John Chambers I encountered that week in the spring of 2002 was pretty upbeat. He kept seeing Cisco's uniqueness. He kept seeing Cisco's successes. He could not help being cheerfully optimistic. "No company has changed as radically or as quickly. GE, which I admire greatly, evolved over multiple decades. Our industry went through more dramatic change in 10 years than other industries have gone through in 100. Think about it: four generations of competitors who have come and maybe gone in a decade. That's unheard of. I do not think there's been an industry of this importance that's gone from pretty much lots of competitors to being an industry that's breaking away in a period of 12 months—ever: 100 percent of profits; 100 percent of cash; and 75 percent of market cap. I'm not aware of it ever happening in an industry in this century that quickly.

"If you look at what the financial markets have said, Cisco's out-executed its competitors to where 75 percent of the future of the industry is probably going to go Cisco's way. We came back with remarkable speed versus even the most optimistic projections. At the same time it's important to realize that this industry will continue to evolve at a rapid pace and that if we don't execute properly on the basics we can be left behind. It's this unique balance of optimism and healthy paranoia that we hope to maintain at Cisco."

Cisco remained unique for having such incredible growth in such a short time frame. It was unique for other reasons: it had produced the stock of the decade; also, no company has gone from a start-up to the levels that it had hit.

Chambers said little about the stock's performance. He always liked to say that if Cisco performed well, the stock would take care of itself. With the stock sinking in 2001 and 2002, Chambers tried to put some historical perspective on things: "People forget that while we are obviously disappointed with the performance of the stock in the last years, since 1995 the stock is still up more than 500 percent. This is a tremendous accomplishment given how rough the market has been for the last two years. I don't know that any company has grown this fast in this time period and survived. Microsoft is the only one that might come close."

Again he hearkened back to what made Cisco unique: "I'm not aware of any company that has gone through the four generations of competitors, that has reinvented itself eight different times in terms of delivering a primary value to the customers. It is also very humbling to have what many people view as such a major role in a company's or a country's productivity and standard of living."

He was clearly glad that the worst of Cisco's woes stemming from the downturn appeared to be over: "The last 18 months was miserable. I hated it. I'm glad that it's over. But you can't show that at that time.

You just have to share with people the strategy, what you're going to do, and you have to realize you're going to get a lot of constructive criticism. You live with that. Some will be fair. Some will not. It's like a family. When a family is in trouble, that's when it needs you the most. That's not when the parent should show any lack of direction or decisiveness. We exit this challenging time a much stronger company, and I think we have the opportunity to be one of the top companies of all time. However, it is important to remember that no company has ever moved at this speed or this rate of execution."

Finally, I made the point to Chambers that capturing a company that changed so frequently and at such speed was challenging for an author. When did one see the real Cisco? When it was heading off the charts in hypergrowth mode? When it was struggling through economic downturns?

For Chambers, the answer was easy. Cisco had one consistent theme. It knew how to adapt. "We can adapt to whatever environment we find ourselves in. If we continue to do that, that really is the mark of a great company. In a league where batting .300 is almost unheard of, we're batting way over .500. Nobody's perfect. We sure aren't.

"But when we have a bad game, when we make a mistake, we recover. We learn from it very rapidly. We adjust appropriately. We come back. While most people thought we could not come back this quickly, we are pleased that we have. That said, we are very focused and don't want to take our eye off the ball. Time will tell if we've accomplished our goals. I sure hope we can and, if not, it would not be from lack of effort or commitment. It's very important to always listen to our critics. We've proven almost every critic wrong. Dozens. [He whispers.] Dozens. Nobody thought we could come back this quick. Nobody thought we could come back to the level that we have."

A little over two months later (August 6, 2002), Cisco produced fresh numbers, revenues and earnings for its fourth quarter for fiscal 2002. More often than not, the numbers were heartening. Net sales for that final quarter were $4.8 billion, up 12 percent over the fourth quarter of a year earlier ($4.3 billion). Net profit was even more remarkable: $772 million for the final quarter compared to $7 for the final quarter the year before.

The fiscal 2002 tally for revenues was $18.9 billion, down 15 percent from the fiscal 2001 figure of $22.3 billion. It was on the earnings side that Cisco showed the spark of recovery that Chambers had alluded to in our interview two months earlier: fiscal 2002 earnings were $1.9 billion compared to a net loss of $1 billion for the year before.

Cisco had $21.5 billion in cash on hand at the end of the year.

On the day that Cisco reported those final-quarter figures, Chambers noted, "Throughout this challenging time, we have focused on four key areas: profits, cash generation, productivity, and profitable market-share gains. We have consistently improved quarter by quarter in each of these categories, with our fourth quarter bringing in more than $1 billion in pro forma net income, $1.6 billion in cash from operations, a 22 percent productivity increase over last year's fourth quarter, and 12 percent year-over-year revenue growth compared to a 44 percent decline by our top ten competitors."

The numbers were there to show that John Chambers had indeed steered his company through the technology collapse. Always it had dominated its markets and, as it moved through the recovery period, it continued to dominate, holding 81 percent of the $7 billion router market and 62 percent of the $11 billion switch market. Chambers was right that no other company had gone on a such a roller-coaster ride, hitting its peak in March 2000, skidding down the mountain a mere nine months later. All of these dramatic changes had occurred to Cisco in full public glare making it one of the most important bellwethers of the American economy. It had been so during its glory days and it remained so after experiencing its shocking setback. Now Cisco watchers are paying close attention because Cisco's full recovery and its return to even a part of the glory it once knew would signal a happier time for the economy.

 Notes

Introduction

"100-year flood": John Chambers, interview with author, September 17, 2001. When Chambers spoke at a company meeting that I attended or spoke to a reporter, I cite the quotes in the text. All other Chambers quotes in the book are from my interviews with him.

Chapter 1

"I can type 15 words . . .": "Chief Executive of the Year: Cisco Systems' John Chambers," *Chief Executive*, July 2000.

"tends to talk like Mister Rogers on speed": "Computing's Next Superpower," *Fortune*, February 12, 1997.

"It's the only company . . .": Chris Stix, interview with author, July 28, 2000.

"I can only make so many decisions . . .": Thomas L. Friedman, *The Lexus and the Olive Tree* (New York: Farrar, Straus and Giroux, 1999), p. 71.

"We like to say . . .": Michael Ching, interview with author, July 25, 2000.

"Brutal may be not . . .": Robert Peters, interview with author, July 31, 2000. All other Peters quotes in the book are from my interview with him.

"John . . . was this almost . . .": Carly Fiorina, interview with author, December 7, 2000. All other Fiorina quotes in the book are from my interview with her.

Chapter 3

"When you're trying to get . . .": Larry Carter, interview with author, October 15, 2001. All other Carter quotes in the book are from my interviews with him.

"One tool we should have . . .": Ron Ricci, interview with author, October 15, 2001.

Chapter 4

"I just didn't think that . . .": Stephen Segaller, *NERDS 2.01: A Brief History of the Internet* (New York: TV Books, 1998), p. 241.

"domestic politics": Kirk Lougheed interview, September 13, 2000. All other Lougheed quotes in the book are from my interviews with him.

"with tears in our eyes . . .": *NERDS*, p. 244.

"This was a start-up that had . . .": Don Valentine, interview with author, September 28, 2000. All other Valentine quotes in the book are from my interviews with him.

"the steal of the century": Terry Eger, interview with author, July 30, 2000. All other Eger quotes in the book are from my interviews with him.

"Don's opening words to me . . .": *NERDS*, p. 261.

Eger was even instrumental . . . : Terry Eger told that story of Don Valentine's selection as chairman of the board at John Morgridge's retirement party in the mid-1990s, getting a laugh from Morgridge, who said he had always wondered how Valentine had been selected, since there were no records of how and when it happened. Cisco's official records indicate that Valentine became chairman in December 1988 when in fact it occurred six months earlier.

"Cisco developed the reputation . . .": Robert Sweifach, interview with author, August 1, 2000. All other Sweifach quotes in the book are from my interview with him.

"It was a company . . .": Ed Kozel, interview with author, September 12, 2000. All other Kozel quotes in the book are from my interviews with him.

"In his own way . . .": John Morgridge, interview with author, November 17, 2000. All other Morgridge quotes in the book are from my interviews with him.

"had no trouble lighting . . .": Greg Satz, interview with author, August 16, 2000. All other Satz quotes in the book are from my interviews with him.

"We really said that . . .": James Richardson, interview with author, December 6, 2000. All other Richardson quotes in the book are from my interview with him.

"We may have been . . .": John Bolger, interview with author, August 1, 2000. All other Bolger quotes in the book are from my interview with him.

Chapter 5

"Tell me about this guy . . .": Kathryn Gould, interview with author, August 15, 2000.

"smart, very personable . . .": The IBM veteran asked not to be identified.

"young lad with a bit . . .": Lydia Blankenship, e-mail to author, September 18, 2000.

"Oh my gosh . . .": Mark Dickey, interview with author, August 2, 2000.

Chapter 6

"We shouldn't be . . .": Pete Solvik, interview with author, September 15, 2000. All other Solvik quotes in the book are from my interview with him.

"Customer satisfaction went up": Rick Justice, interview with author, September 13, 2000. All other Justice quotes in the book are from my interview with him.

"John came to speak . . .": Jack Welch, interview with author, December 18, 2000.

"Where everything is horizontal . . .": Bill Nuti, interview with author, October 20, 2000. All other Nuti quotes in the book are from my interview with him.

Chapter 7

"So there's more empowerment . . .": Ray Bell, interview with author, August 29, 2000.

"I hadn't asked them . . .": Michelangelo "Mike" Volpi, interview with author, December 6, 2000. All other Volpi quotes in the book are from my interviews with him.

"We always have two numbers . . .": Carl Redfield, interview with author, November 13, 2000. All other Redfield quotes in the book are from my interview with him.

"the desks were made . . .": Barbara Beck, interview with author, September 8, 2000.

Chapter 8

"They had this . . .": Doug Allred, interview with author, September 14, 2000. All other Allred quotes in the book are from my interview with him.

"Most companies look out . . .": Gary Daichendt, interview with author, September 8, 2000.

Chapter 9

"I thought our switches . . .": Mario Mazzola, interview with author, November 14, 2000. All other Mazzola quotes in the book are from my interviews with him.

"a slight misanalysis": Paul Johnson, interview with author, September 25, 2000.

"They must know everything . . .": Howard Charney, interview with author, November 16, 2000. All other Charney quotes in the book are from my interview with him.

"I started equating an acquisition . . .": Charlie Giancarlo, interview with author, November 17, 2000. All other Giancarlo quotes in the book are from my interview with him.

"I did it that way . . .": Mimi Gigoux, interview with author, December 13, 2000. All other Gigoux quotes in the book are from my interview with her.

"It's become an effective . . .": Scott Kriens, interview with author, July 31, 2000. All other Kriens quotes in the book are from my interview with him.

Chapter 11

"We had such a high . . .": Kate DCamp, interview with author, June 6, 2002.

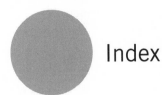

Index